Rebuilding New Orleans

Sarah Fouts

Rebuilding New Orleans

Immigrant Laborers and Street Food Vendors in the Post-Katrina Era

THE UNIVERSITY OF
NORTH CAROLINA PRESS
Chapel Hill

This book was published with the assistance of the Fred W. Morrison Fund of the University of North Carolina Press.

Set in Quadraat and Neue Kabel by codeMantra
Manufactured in the United States of America

Portions of chapters 1 and 3 originally appeared as Sarah Fouts, "Re-regulating *Loncheras*, Food Trucks, and Their Clientele: Navigating Bureaucracy and Enforcement in New Orleans," *Gastronomica: The Journal of Critical Food Studies* 18, no. 3 (Fall 2018): 1–13.

Cover art: city map of New Orleans © Adobe Stock/ink drop; taqueria © Adobe Stock/Oleksandr

LIBRARY OF CONGRESS CATALOGING-IN-PUBLICATION DATA
Names: Fouts, Sarah, author.
Title: Rebuilding New Orleans : immigrant laborers and street food vendors in the post-Katrina era / Sarah Fouts.
Description: Chapel Hill : The University of North Carolina Press, [2025] | Includes bibliographical references and index.
Identifiers: LCCN 2024045141 | ISBN 9781469685014 (cloth) | ISBN 9781469685021 (paperback) | ISBN 9781469685038 (epub) | ISBN 9781469687438 (pdf)
Subjects: LCSH: Central Americans—Louisiana—New Orleans—Social conditions—21st century. | Mexicans—Louisiana—New Orleans—Social conditions—21st century. | Day laborers—Louisiana—New Orleans—Social conditions—21st century. | Street-food vendors (Persons)—Louisiana—New Orleans—Social conditions—21st century. | Immigrants—Louisiana—New Orleans—Social conditions—21st century. | New Orleans (La.)—Race relations—21st century. | New Orleans (La.)—Politics and government—21st century. | BISAC: SOCIAL SCIENCE / Ethnic Studies / American / General | COOKING / History
Classification: LCC F379.N59 C344 2025 |
DDC 305.8680763/350905—dc23/eng/20241204
LC record available at https://lccn.loc.gov/2024045141

For product safety concerns under the European Union's General Product Safety Regulation (EU GPSR), please contact gpsr@mare-nostrum.co.uk or write to the University of North Carolina Press and Mare Nostrum Group B.V., Mauritskade 21D, 1091 GC Amsterdam, The Netherlands.

for El Congreso and Stand with Dignity members

Contents

Illustrations

FIGURES

MAPS

Rebuilding New Orleans

Introduction
Right to the City

In the Latin Quarter, near the French Market, one hears more Spanish than French spoken; and here, too, are the little bodegas and cigar stores kept by Cubans and Hondurans, where the product of the island and the mainland may be bought.

— LAFCADIO HEARN,
"New Orleans: A Cosmopolitan City," 1885

How are we helping our restaurants that are trying to recover by having more food trucks from Texas open up? How do the tacos help gumbo?

— OLIVER THOMAS,
New Orleans City Council member, 2007

Everyone called Denis "El Chaparrito" (the little guy). But what Denis lacked in height, he made up for in leadership, might, and eloquence. His black leather boots and spiky gelled hair didn't hurt in elevating his stature, either. Originally from Honduras, Denis worked with the Central American and Mexican day laborers who arrived in post-Katrina New Orleans to clean up and rebuild across the region. Denis began as a day laborer—a person temporarily and typically employed in construction jobs—working in demolition and cleanup immediately after the 2005 disaster. But while Denis was on a jobsite, a trailer slipped and crushed his right hand, leaving him with minimal function. Grappling with limited resources, high hospital bills, and a negligent employer, Denis sought support from a local organization to help file workers' compensation claims that he needed to cover his medical bills and lost wages. While he recovered, he volunteered for the organization El Congreso de jornaleros (Congress of Day Laborers; El Congreso hereafter). When it became clear that his hand was permanently injured, Denis sought options other than manual labor. Because Denis had demonstrated organizing talent, he was hired at El Congreso full-time in 2008 to organize workers on the *esquinas*, or corners, where day laborers looked for work.

An organizer mobilizes people at the grassroots level to build and leverage power to fight for change. At the esquinas, this work ranged from documenting countless stories of crooked subcontractors who stole workers' wages to developing leaders for El Congreso's weekly meetings. Under the umbrella organization the New Orleans Workers' Center for Racial Justice (Workers' Center, hereafter), immigrant workers and their families formed El Congreso in 2006—alongside the working-class, Black-led organization Stand with Dignity and the Alliance of Guestworkers for Dignity—with the aim to build multiracial worker power to combat civil, labor, and immigrant rights abuses that plagued the devastated city.[1]

El Congreso was one of many organizations established after 2005 to work with the Spanish-speaking immigrant community, a population that after Katrina more than doubled from 4 to 9 percent.[2] What made El Congreso unique was that its members set the agenda, which offered more than just wrap-around services: they fought for and succeeded in procuring systematic change from local to federal levels by working collaboratively across race, nationality, immigration status, sexuality, and gender. And they fought with Black poor and working-class people, building power between two groups often set at odds by employers, politicians, and media.

Members of El Congreso and Stand with Dignity leading a May Day march in 2017. Photo by Fernando López, @sentir.con.ojos.

I met Denis in February 2011 when I began volunteering with El Congreso.[3] Denis didn't drive then, and my car access, Kentucky-twanged Spanish, and flexible schedule were just the right qualifications to make me Denis's chauffeur. At times, my role expanded beyond driving to include other mundane activities like collecting money to cover a portable toilet fee; coordinating schedules for traffic, municipal, or immigration court appointments; and negotiating with the adjacent property owners (and sometimes police) over rights to the public spaces like the esquinas and parking for food trucks. Other times, I just sat in my car and observed, because of rain or because I was heeding Denis, who sometimes cautioned me that my whiteness and gender might not always be welcome or helpful.

Three days a week for almost a year we kept up a routine: I picked Denis up at the Workers' Center office in the Tremé neighborhood at around 9:00 a.m. and took him to the five different esquinas in the area. After we met with the workers, we sought out food. Within blocks of each of these esquinas, Latin American grocery stores, taco trucks, and Central American restaurants had sprung up, offering a range of dishes like gorditas, tacos, burritos, pupusas, and Honduran specialties to the workers who awaited jobs nearby. As we shared countless meals, I learned to anticipate Denis's orders, and we developed our own collegial tiffs (usually over my driving) until Denis abruptly left for Honduras in late 2011 to take over his family's coffee farm after his father became sick.

Over the time we worked together, Denis introduced me to street food vendors and the day laborers they served: Salvadorans who fried pupusas in the backs of corner stores, Mexican cooks who sold tacos from trucks tucked behind gas stations, Honduran street vendors who offered tamales outside corner stores, and even women who clandestinely served hot dishes from hatchback cars at the esquinas. Many of these food sellers began as itinerant food vendors whose services were integral to addressing food security issues in the aftermath of the disaster. When food chain supplies were disrupted, the street food vendors provided a reliable source of sustaining and culturally relevant foods for Central American and Mexican immigrants involved in recovery efforts. The food vendors settled in the metropolitan area, opening brick-and-mortar restaurants or grocery stores or continuing to sell food itinerantly.

New Orleans natives and post-Katrina transplants quickly caught on to the convenient, delicious, and affordable food establishments. Local food writers would take longer to acknowledge these spaces. Politicians remained dubious. In 2007, Oliver Thomas, a Black City Council member, derisively quipped, "How are we helping our restaurants that are trying to recover by having more food trucks from Texas open up? How do the tacos help gumbo?"[4] Thomas's provocative query fed local apprehensions over how tens of thousands of Central American and Mexican day laborers and food service workers fit within the cultural and social fabric of the city. The sudden ubiquity of these immigrants and their food establishments represented an easy scapegoat for lawmakers and an ersatz existential threat for a majority-Black city undergoing trauma, devastation, and whitewashed redevelopment.

Post-Katrina New Orleans saw a massive movement of people to and from the region immediately after the storm, with most people displaced due to the destruction of 70 percent of the city's housing. Almost a year after the disaster, in July 2006, over half of New Orleans's population (254,502 people) had yet to return.[5] Failed policies resulted in housing shortages and increased environmental risks, leading to the displacement of much of New Orleans's Black population, who shape the city's cultural landscape and have long been the backbone of the working class.[6] Subsequently, much of the depleted workforce was replaced by Central American and Mexican immigrants following the suspension of labor laws in the immediate aftermath of the disaster.[7]

Also following the storm, long-standing state-sponsored institutions like public housing and public schools were almost completely dismantled to pave the way for mixed-income housing and charter schools, forcing divestment and displacement of Black people and their communities.[8] In their absence and at their expense, the culture of local people morphed into a whitewashed caricature used to draw in tourists.[9] Understanding how the deep web of these systems interconnects is crucial to dismantling the power of capital that is central to these processes.

Over the next five years, citywide movements directly addressed this displacement through efforts like the Black-led "Right to Return" campaign after Katrina. Other efforts like El Congreso's "Right to Remain" campaign centered on immigrants' right to stay in the city amid rising deportations and constant surveillance facilitated by increased collusions between immigration enforcement and local police. Bureaucracy also added a layer of complexity that directly impacted marginalized communities and hindered mobility while prioritizing the interests of the dominant system rather than the people whom local and state agencies were meant to serve.[10] Grassroots campaigns that emerged in response were embedded in a right-to-the-city lens, in which people operated "beyond the state and beyond capitalism" to forge their own spaces of participation as part of the wider struggle of organizations like the Workers' Center.[11]

Thus, Denis's story is a thread that intertwines these layers of complexity—exploitation, displacement, resistance, bureaucracy, globalization, and multiracial alliances—that took place in the decade that followed Katrina. Top-down decision-making resulted in policies that served the interests of what George Lipsitz calls "white spatial imaginaries"—tourist industries along with a whiter, wealthier demographic that moved to the city.[12] Tracing the journeys that Denis and I made together to each of the five day-laborer corners links narratives of how poor and working-class people of color fought for their right to remain in the city while also unveiling the failed superstructures that emerged in the rebuilding and recovery efforts that hindered these processes.

As Denis showed me shortcuts across the city and connected me with countless people and institutions, he helped surface the interplay of these issues while also illustrating how people have come together across race to build a class-based movement that affects political and cultural change. That work with Denis also shed light on the growth of the informal economy sector—like street food vending and day laboring—in New Orleans.

Informal work can emerge in response to market failures and is often characterized by an unregulated workplace and includes people who have been locked out of formal employment due to a range of challenges (family obligations, felony records, documentation status, inability to apply for formal licensing, language barriers). Understanding the dynamics of these informal economies and why they exist provides insights into the gaps in and limitations of urban governance while also demonstrating how these workers navigate exclusionary policies and build coalitions to reshape the city on their own terms.

Hidden in plain sight, street food vendors and day laborers play an essential part in the city's economy yet are forced into precarious working and living conditions due to discriminatory tactics and predatory practices. Despite being pitted against other working-class communities of color, Central American and Mexican immigrants use their food cultures, political activism, and multiracial solidarities to resist exploitative models of redevelopment that became part of the flood of changes that radically altered the political economy and cultural landscape of the majority-Black city.

The people behind the taco trucks, tamale stands, and pupusa griddles contribute to the cultural panache of New Orleans—a city lionized by its multicultural gumbos and jambalayas—building upon centuries of migration and exchange that link Honduras with Louisiana through what Kirsten Silva Gruesz calls the "Gulf system."[13] This resistance and these individuals introduce a nuanced layer to the city's history, ushering in their own traditions while also reflecting historical patterns.

FROM BULBANCHA TO NEW ORLEANS: THE NORTHERNMOST LATIN AMERICAN CITY

For over 3,000 years, Bulbancha, the Choctaw name for the New Orleans region that means "land of many tongues," thrived as a multi-ethnic center in the Gulf South, serving as a trade route through the Mississippi Valley and network for over forty Native groups.[14] Native Americans in the lower Mississippi Valley long engaged in trade with the European settlers, paving routes from Louisiana across New Spain to present-day Mexico and New Mexico.[15] Yet after the first major colonization of Bulbancha, officially by the French in 1718, the city was branded La Nouvelle-Orléans. By the summer of 1719, the first 500 enslaved Africans were forced to New Orleans, arriving from present-day Guinea.[16]

Given its location at the mouth of the Mississippi River and due to centuries of exchange and migration between the two regions, New Orleans is often considered the northernmost Latin American city. From 1808 to 1810, New Orleans housed the earliest Spanish-language newspaper published in the United States, *El Misisipi*, a semiweekly periodical produced to help galvanize Latin American independence movements from US shores.[17] In the early 1800s, Jean Lafitte, the notorious privateer who operated through the Gulf Coast region, smuggled letters back and forth between New Orleans and Veracruz, Mexico. Working with Father Antonio de Sedella, a Spanish Capuchin friar rumored to have baptized Marie Laveau, Lafitte—more an opportunist than a geopolitical figure—played an integral role in relaying communication during Mexico's movement for independence from Spain during the early nineteenth century.[18]

Revolutionary figures from the Gulf system, like Mexican politician Benito Juárez and Cuban writer José Martí, spent time in exile in New Orleans. Juárez, fleeing Mexico during the Santa Ana dictatorship, lived in the Tremé, Central City, and Marigny neighborhoods from 1853 until 1855. He earned money by rolling cigars in a Cuban factory and from remittances sent from his wife in Oaxaca to New Orleans before he returned to Mexico.[19] After helping execute the overthrow of Santa Anna in 1854, Juárez became Mexico's president in 1858.[20]

Forced to flee Cuba due to his pro-independence and anti-colonial politics, José Martí traveled between Tampa, New York City, and New Orleans from 1880 to 1892. Martí spent those years in exile writing and galvanizing support for the Cuban independence movement while also publishing articles on labor conditions of cigar workers and opinion pieces on cultural events.[21] Revolutionary figures from Latin America took refuge in the Crescent City, sustaining connections with their homelands and beyond.

While New Orleans maintained robust connections with these Latin American regions, its ties with Honduras emerged as the most formidable.[22]

By the early twentieth century, banana companies had already made a major imprint in New Orleans, impacting the city's economy, culture, and urban infrastructure. Banana companies paved the way for the establishment of warehouses along the Mississippi River and the development of railroads to move their product while also garnering a reputation of exploitation, land grabs, and brutal tactics to maintain control across the Gulf region.

While the United Fruit Company began to sow its invasive seeds across the Caribbean region, eventually earning the nickname El Pulpo (The Octopus) for its overreach in the region, two separate banana companies—Vaccaro Brothers and Company and Cuyamel Fruit Company—emerged from New Orleans. Established in 1899, Vaccaro Brothers, which became Standard Fruit (1924) and eventually Dole (1991), occupied the La Ceiba region of northern Honduras and employed unscrupulous strategies that mirrored the exploitation and land grabs of United Fruit.[23]

Meanwhile, in 1905, Samuel Zemurray, a Russian Jewish immigrant, used capital earned from salvaging and selling discarded bananas to purchase the struggling Cuyamel Fruit Company. The acquisition of Cuyamel forged Zemurray's transformation from resourceful vendor to full-on producer, transporter, marketer, and distributor of Honduran bananas.[24] While Zemurray initially enjoyed support from the Honduran government, by 1910 he came up against unfavorable administrations in both Honduras and the United States that increased taxes on exports and denied him concessions.[25]

With his backdoor deals in peril, a desperate Zemurray again flexed his resourcefulness by organizing a ragtag crew of New Orleans–based mercenaries—including former Honduran president Manuel Bonilla, who was exiled in New Orleans, and mercenary Lee Christmas, who was based there—to successfully overthrow the Honduran government. Reinstated as president in 1912, Bonilla appointed Christmas, a US citizen, as the head of the armed forces and rewarded Zemurray with major concessions that included thousands of hectares of land and tariff-free exports. "Those were the days when they said it was cheaper to buy a politician than a mule," wrote Charles Mercer in the *Times-Picayune* in a 1954 reference to Zemurray's rise to power. "Revolutions were inexpensive and lives were cheaper."[26]

While Standard Fruit relished some early fruit-trade successes, United Fruit dominated all facets of the banana trade. From the company's inception, peasants and workers relentlessly protested low wages, land grabs, dangerous working conditions, and lack of benefits.[27] With few exceptions, governments fought for the interests of the fruit companies; United Fruit's repressive tactics coupled with state support during labor disputes at times proved fatal for workers.[28]

At its peak, United Fruit occupied over 3.6 million acres of land and employed over 67,000 people.[29] That peak came when Zemurray sold Cuyamel to United Fruit for 300,000 shares of stock in 1930, initially retiring from the banana trade.[30] But as the company floundered during the Great Depression, Zemurray came out of retirement in 1933 and officially moved the company's headquarters to New Orleans.[31] With Zemurray at the helm, New Orleans became the banana city, reigning as the country's top banana port with headquarters of both United Fruit and Standard Fruit.[32]

New Orleans culinary traditions reflected these trade ties, most notably the flambéed dessert bananas Foster, which was invented in 1951. Legend has it that Ella Brennan of Brennan's Restaurant (and later Commander's Palace) used surplus Standard Fruit bananas pilfered from her brothers' produce business to concoct the confection. Drawing inspiration from the Baked Alaska dessert, she decided to ignite the rum-soaked fruit, caramelize it, and add ice cream.[33]

In 1957, New Orleans mayor Chep Morrison commissioned the "Garden to the Americas," in homage to the city's Honduran connections. Situated along Basin Avenue, parallel to New Orleans's French Quarter in the Tremé neighborhood, the Garden to the Americas features statues of Latin American leaders like Simón Bolívar, "the Great Liberator" of South America; Benito Juárez, the first Indigenous president in Latin America; and Francisco Morazán, the Honduran statesman and second president of the Central American Republic. Each figure towers over the neutral ground, occupying one city block each on the Basin Street stretch.[34]

As ties with Latin America strengthened, the city increasingly attracted Honduran immigrants, ranging from waterfront workers to business executives. Sllim Ydur, a New Orleans–based musician, producer, and community radio host, was born in Tela, Honduras, in 1943 to Jamaican parents who worked in the railroad and banana industry. He arrived in New Orleans in 1958 at the age of fifteen and began working on the docks, moving bananas from steamships. By 1979 his modest music career took off as part of the reggae, funk, disco, and calypso–infused band Muchos Plus.

I met Sllim in 2017 when he invited me to talk about my research on his radio show, *Da Gumbo Tapado*, on WBOK. His show name is a nod to the soups that showcase his (and the city's) hemispheric roots. Gumbo, the complex dish with Indigenous (Choctaw), African, Caribbean, French, and Spanish roots, is ubiquitous on New Orleans menus. The Honduran dish *tapado* is a coconut and seafood blend of soup with African, Indigenous, Caribbean, and Spanish origins. As part of his music and radio career, Sllim, who calls himself the "Black Latino," has helped bring attention to the links across the Caribbean and Gulf system while also working to bridge coalitions between Black and immigrant communities in New Orleans. His New Orleans story began on the banana wharves, and his calypso rhythms and ability to work across race and class paved the way for other working-class Hondurans in shaping the complex and evolving city.

By the latter half of the twentieth century, Honduras represented "the largest national origin of immigrants" in Louisiana, claiming 12.8 percent of the state's "foreign born" population.[35] To house this growing community and its cultural and social traditions, a Honduran neighborhood, "El Barrio Lempira," developed near the banana wharves in New Orleans's Lower Garden District, complete with restaurants, corner stores, and a movie cinema, the Happy Hour Theatre, that featured Spanish-language films.[36]

However, Mayor Morrison's original dreams of strong and sustained trading ties between New Orleans and Latin America faded in the latter half of the twentieth century. The once intertwined regions united by bananas split when United Fruit left New Orleans in 1965, leaving behind top-down vestiges of banana-bred corporatism through modernist buildings, mansions, wharves, and various philanthropy projects like Touro hospital and the Department of Tropical Medicine and the Mayan Language Institute at Tulane University. Still, there is no doubt that bananas fostered ties that connected New Orleans and Honduras through the people and their culture—familial networks, remittances, culinary traditions, and musical influences like Sllim's Muchos Plus.

By the 1980s, the debt-ridden Port of New Orleans lost ground to newer, more modern ports due to insufficient investment. The Ports of Tampa and Miami emerged as more convenient banana entry points. The Port of Houston, even as it faced a similar debt issue as New Orleans, continued to prioritize port infrastructure development and adjusted to modern systems.[37]

This transition spurred New Orleans's shift from manufacturing to a service-based economy. Protected by unions, the once middle-class jobs within the oil and port industries underwent a transformation into low-wage positions within the service industry.[38] Compounded by white flight in the 1970s and the global oil crash in 1983, New Orleans's overall population shrunk, dropping from thirteenth to thirty-fifth in the United States.[39] Many

Honduran immigrants vacated El Barrio Lempira for the newly developed suburbs built on top of a swamp in Jefferson Parish.[40]

In the decade leading up to Hurricane Katrina in 2005, New Orleans's immigration landscape differed from that of other major cities in the South. Driven by employment opportunities, repercussions of the North American Free Trade Agreement (or NAFTA), the deregulation of labor policies, and a lower cost of living, the broader southern US region underwent an unprecedented immigration boom.[41] But until Katrina, New Orleans diverged from this trend, remaining a predominantly Black and white city as the overall population declined and the city transitioned from oil and petroleum sectors to tourism and service industry economies.[42] With decades-long roots in New Orleans, the Honduran population remained small and largely assimilated into the city's middle-class and suburban areas.[43]

Yet a demographic shift occurred after Hurricane Katrina, marking a departure from the established racial-demographic patterns to an increasing number of Mexicans and Central Americans (mostly Hondurans) in the metropolitan area. During the same period, the implementation of the Central America Free Trade Agreement (or CAFTA) contributed to the decline of rural communities in Central America as the growth of multinational corporations created precarious and exploitative labor conditions and further spurred migration.[44]

These economic disruptions combined with Hurricane Katrina recovery prompted individuals from Central America to seek employment opportunities in post-disaster reconstruction efforts across the Gulf South. Their arrival in the city both addressed urgent labor needs and rekindled connections with the city's historical ties to Honduras but shifted from banana company elites and their domestic workers to working-class Central Americans. At the same time, the Port of New Orleans saw a resurgence after Katrina, with palm oil and coffee production in Honduras surpassing the once-dominant banana trade.

Before he left for the United States, Denis's family owned a meager plot of land on which they grew coffee for trade, along with other sustenance foods, in the lush mountains of the Santa Bárbara Department in western Honduras. Honduras has become a major exporter of coffee, ranking sixth in the world in 2018.[45] Approximately 90 percent of Honduras's coffee comes from small-scale farmers like Denis and his family. Much of this coffee enters the United States through the Port of New Orleans, the "premier coffee-handling port" of the country, which received more than 1.29 million tons of coffee between 2011 and 2015.[46]

Denis returned home in 2011 to a seventeen-acre coffee farm, which had been purchased through remittances he sent his family from New Orleans during his eight-year stint in the United States. Denis went from being a day laborer and organizer to becoming a landowner and manager of his small-scale family farm.

"I'm the boss now; I'm not the worker. You see? It's a whole shift for me. I recruit, set the wage, and manage guys to plant, harvest, do all the in-between on my land now," Denis said in 2013, during the first of three fieldwork visits I made to Honduras.[47] "It's not easy for me. It's a change," he lamented as we ambled through a plot of coffee shrubs on his farm. I picked some of the red coffee cherries, sampling the prematurely ripened stone fruits, early bounty for the fall season.

Later that evening I watched as Denis's mother and sisters prepared a sack of ripe coffee cherries for their home consumption. Through a large iron mill, painted red once but now faded and tinged with orange rust, the women processed the coffee cherries through the mill, removing the outer fruit. Using large plastic buckets and water pumped from the well, they rinsed the remaining pulp, preserving the light-brown beans to spread across the concrete porch to dry in the sun. The rest of the coffee cherries would be harvested in November, processed, and sold at the market for export.

The exchange of ideas, commodities, and culture abound across the region with the movement of people and goods in the Americas continuing its influence on New Orleans. Historically characterized through economic ties like coffee beans and bananas, romanticized through stories of revolution and piracy, and influenced by new ingredients and calypso beats, the post-Katrina iteration of these links ignited another version of cultural and political influence, which can be seen through Denis's story. On a global scale he embodies a web of trade networks via his small-scale coffee farm; on a local level, he characterizes the cultural and political developments through his organizing work that brought together everyday people fighting a shared and multiracial struggle to reshape the city.

CHAPTERS

Spanning the metropolitan area of New Orleans, each chapter begins at one of the five day-laborer corners that emerged in the aftermath of Katrina.

Denis introduced me to these important and ephemeral spaces during our work together. Centering on one type of "right" (labor, land, culture, and space), each chapter uses that right as a thread to connect a web of stories of food vendors and resistance movements to demonstrate the power of these people and their everyday struggles that took place at those sites from 2005 until 2017.

Using a right-to-labor framework, chapter 1 begins at the Claiborne Avenue esquina in Central City, focusing on the first five years after Katrina and on the importance of street vendors who fed day laborers as part of disaster recovery efforts. Stories in this chapter show the intersections among disaster recovery, food access, policing, and lack of housing while also exploring how multiracial solidarities formed, like the founding of the Workers' Center, in response to these injustices.

Using a right-to-land (and housing) framework, chapter 2 is set at the Carrollton Avenue esquina in the Mid-City neighborhood. It connects the story of Costa de Tela, a family-owned Honduran restaurant located in a gentrifying neighborhood in New Orleans, to the family patriarch's bar in a small village outside of Tela, Honduras, near a UNESCO-protected Garifuna village.[48] This chapter shows how the palm oil industry and tourism economy use the same land and similar repressive tactics of dispossession and divestment (often working in tandem with the state) to displace residents. It also illustrates how campaigns emerged to fight against exploitative development like gentrification projects in Mid-City New Orleans and land grabs in Honduras. Chapter 2 further argues that land dispossession and displacement must be centered in discussions on forced migration, rather than on essentializing movements of people solely through decontextualized narratives of violence and poverty.

Set at the Elysian Fields Avenue esquina located on the border of the Seventh and Eighth Wards, chapter 3 uses a right-to-culture framework to understand how policies enacted in the pivotal 2010–12 era resulted in layers of bureaucracy and red tape that inhibited mobility and disproportionately criminalized Black and immigrant communities. Policies pandered instead to a white spatial imaginary—simultaneously attracted to and offended by the joie de vivre that makes New Orleans unique—which has purposefully and inadvertently influenced the urban governance of the city. From bans on taco trucks to criminalizing second line street vendors, the policymakers sought to regulate and sanitize culture in an effort to pander to a whitened population as part of an expanded tourist sector. Campaigns like the NOLA

Shakedown and policies like bias-free policing emerged out of the Workers' Center to help people impacted by fines and fees.

Using a right-to-space framework set at the Gretna esquina in Jefferson Parish, chapter 4 examines the growth of flea markets (or *pulgas*) and food halls in New Orleans to investigate how street food vendors and day laborers asserted their right to space through unexpected alliances and coalitions. Predominantly set in Jefferson Parish, the suburbs of New Orleans, this chapter looks at how street food vendors turned to flea markets to create their businesses and community. It also follows the story of Ivan, a street food vendor at the Westbank Flea Market who used unexpected alliances and capital earned from his street food hustle to put on his drag shows in the suburbs and in the city.

The conclusion is set at the Franklin and St. Claude Avenue esquina, located on the edge of the Marigny, St. Roch, St. Claude, and Bywater neighborhoods in the Upper Ninth Ward. The Franklin esquina stands as a microcosm of *Rebuilding New Orleans* and reflects major themes—food security, displacement and gentrification, cultural production, access to space, and political mobilizing—presented throughout the book.

Taken together, these chapters weave the politics of food and labor by exploring ways that immigrants have navigated and resisted exploitative systems by forging multiracial coalitions and creating their own methods of self-reliance.[49] Not only did Central American and Mexican immigrants who made and sold tamales help rebuild New Orleans, but they, too, became backbones of the growing service sector in a rapidly changing city. Denis's story, told alongside the stories of food vendors and day laborers, reveals the politics of labor, food, housing, and migration in the twenty-first century and helps tell an important history of a complex city.

Chapter 1

Right to Labor

Feeding the Recovery

I just don't know about those sweet beans.

— JOSÉ M., referencing the baked beans at a Stand with Dignity and El Congreso potluck, 2015

We did not lose our ability to fish. Don't bring the fish to our door, just bring us some fishing poles and some bait.

— DYAN "MAMA D" FRENCH COLE, at a congressional hearing on Katrina, 2005

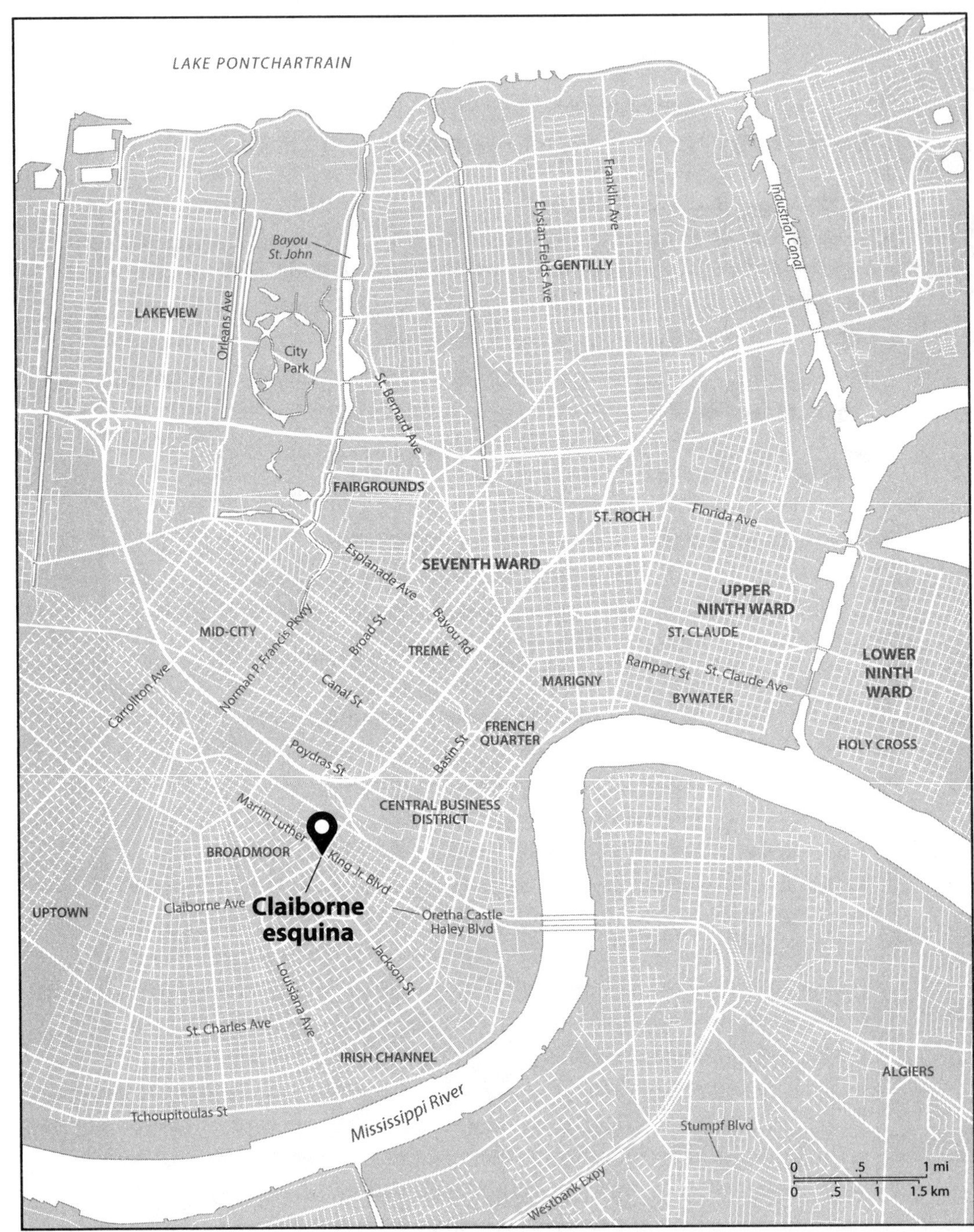

Claiborne esquina in New Orleans.

Denis was privy to the best menu items available at each day-laborer esquina because of his years as a construction worker and organizer with El Congreso. His daily *antojo* (hankering) informed which food vendor we would frequent, and, apart from his "hold the onions," I usually just copied his orders. During our weekly visits in 2011 to the day-laborer corner at New Orleans's Central City neighborhood, the go-to order at the nearby taqueria was the carne asada burrito. For four dollars plus tip, the large burrito—salty pieces of carne asada, rice, charro beans, cheese, and optional *pico de gallo* all generously stuffed into a flour tortilla and encased in aluminum foil—doubled as two meals, a bargain price aimed to appeal to workers.

The intersection of Claiborne Avenue and Martin Luther King Jr. Boulevard initially emerged as a day-laborer corner in the aftermath of Katrina because of its proximity to Home Depot, just a block away. With the Superdome towering just a half mile to the east and live oak–lined residential blocks to the west, the taqueria blended into a fleet of cars parked near the gas station and auto shop.

Like other street food vendors, the *lonchera* (taco truck or trailer) became a fixture at the esquina, offering affordable breakfasts and lunches for day laborers looking for jobs and for people awaiting repairs at the auto shop nearby. In his prime, the Mexican proprietor, Mateo, along with his family, owned three loncheras located across the city. But being a food truck owner was never his intention.[1] Originally from Veracruz, Mexico, Mateo arrived in New Orleans in 2006 to work in construction. "I came here to have a better income, to be able to better provide for my family; that's why I came to this city," he explained.

In the fall of 2005, the devastation of Hurricane Katrina forced the displacement of the vast majority of New Orleanians, and by July 2006 more than half of the city's residents had yet to return.[2] Lack of housing coupled with failed policies and environmental degradation indefinitely forced out much of the city's Black working class. Because of the depleted local workforce, demand for workers grew, along with prospects for exploitation and corruption facilitated by deregulation and privatization.

For example, as an effort to speed up recovery following Katrina, the Bush administration temporarily suspended federal labor laws like the Davis–Bacon Act (prevailing wages for public works jobs), E-Verify (verifying I-9 employee eligibility), and OSHA laws (establishing baseline worksite protections), while also suspending an affirmative action contract-hire policy and allowing for an unparalleled amount of no-bid private subcontracts.[3]

Customers purchase food from a lonchera in 2015.
Photo by Fernando López, @sentir.con.ojos.

When implemented, these policies were the few meager protections against an inherently exploitative capitalist project.

With this exploitative context set in place, tens of thousands of Central American and Mexican immigrants arrived in the region, oftentimes living in tent cities. They made up almost half of the workforce that cleaned up and rebuilt under toxic conditions with few protections.[4] And as day laborers worked relentlessly, they fell victim time and again to an unregulated job market, receiving little to no compensation or protections.[5]

In response, many immigrant workers took it upon themselves to organize to protect their communities from labor abuses and failed housing policies. Facing a dearth of food options and limited resources from FEMA and American Red Cross services, reconstruction workers turned to street food vendors for food sustenance. They also moonlighted as tamale vendors, capitalizing on networks of coworkers. Cleanup crew leaders called in *pedidos* (orders) from vendors who prepared lunches in kitchens in the few parts of New Orleans and the suburbs undamaged by the storm.[6] These itinerant food economies played an integral role in disaster recovery efforts, yet much like the immigrant laborers they fed, their experiences went undervalued and criminalized rather than understood as an integral part of food security measures.[7]

Moving from places like Texas and New York, immigrant vendors set up informal economies, delivering meals to worksites or parking at esquinas to maximize on the demand to feed workers.[8] The informal sector created a complicated paradox for street food vendors and day laborers: at once it was highly unregulated, thus allowing for rampant corruption and exploitation, while, precisely *because of* this deregulation, it provided a pathway for employment for many immigrant workers who were locked out of formal sector jobs due to their documentation status.

Operating in the figurative shadows and blurring the lines between the informal and formal sectors, street food vendors and day laborers existed as an essential part of the disaster recovery yet were forced into precarious work due to the same policies of deregulation that necessitated their jobs. In these contexts, like the post-Katrina milieu, the subcontractors became the purveyor of the informal sector, shirking the state to keep profits high and operating expenses (labor) low. In turn, the day laborer was forced to work long hours with little protections and recourse, due to deregulated systems that prioritized the capitalist boss over the worker.

Engaging this tension, this chapter centers on the right to labor: street food vendors and day laborers who sought out work in public spaces looking for jobs that provided fair wages and worker safety. When faced with exploitation in the post-Katrina milieu, these immigrants used everyday practical acts to forge their own geographies of self-reliance as part of a wider political struggle.[9] From the informal sector and through worker organizing, immigrants navigated the flooded city and formed coalitions to shape policy and culture on a grassroots level.

Networks that linked the esquinas established the foundations of El Congreso as a subset of the Workers' Center for Racial Justice.[10] Worker centers have grown significantly in the twenty-first century and operate as community-based (as opposed to worksite-based) labor movements and as popular education centers.[11] Worker centers also function, to some degree, outside the parameters of the state, beyond federal labor statutes like collective bargaining agreements under the National Labor Relations Board. Yet they can also shape National Labor Relations Board policies and decisions. In New Orleans, through grassroots multiracial organizing, immigrants and Black communities came together to fight for workers' rights and advance racial justice through the Workers' Center context. Overall, as employers sought out a cheap and deportable labor force, immigrant workers used geographies of self-reliance and multiracial solidarities to navigate bureaucratic structures, fight against exploitative systems, and foment political and economic change.

BROKEN LEVEES, POST-KATRINA, AND FORGING GEOGRAPHIES OF SELF-RELIANCE

Peaking with winds at 175 mph, Katrina shifted into a slow-moving Category 3 hurricane, initially bringing massive rains as it tarried across New Orleans. Despite claims that they could withstand a Category 3 hurricane, floodwaters breached over half the levees in the city on August 29, 2005, first in the early morning at the Industrial Canal, inundating the Lower Ninth Ward. Later that day, the levees failed at the London Avenue Canal, leading to floodwaters eventually covering 80 percent of the city.[12] New Orleans became a bowl of toxic, rancid water filled with devastation, debris, and death. Floodwaters, reaching ten to fifteen feet, festered for weeks, leaving in their wake tragedies, trauma, and profound despair that would inspire countless devastating poems, songs, and firsthand accounts.[13] But like Vann R. Newkirk II makes clear in his podcast *Floodlines*, "The disaster wasn't the hurricane. The disaster is what happened after."[14]

Iconic images of New Orleans during the flooding captured the horrific sights: people waving desperately from rooftops and makeshift rafts; 50,000 people sheltered in the unprepared Morial Convention Center and Superdome; and 4,000 people stranded on I-10, exposed to the sweltering August humidity, a climate unbearable in the best of times. Some 1.2 million people (92 percent of the area's population) had evacuated the region before Katrina landed, the largest evacuation in US history.[15] Yet 100,000 people remained, lacking resources like transportation and capital—social and financial—to ensure safety beyond their home.[16]

As atrocities abounded due to blatant state failures, media, politicians, and city officials projected a narrative of hysteria around looting, an embellishment that proliferated as quickly as giardia parasites in noxious floodwaters. Mainstream viewers became more outraged at an image of a young Black man wading through waters carrying a flatscreen television than at the rising death toll, the fifty breached levees, and the complete dereliction of duty by the federal government—a barefaced example of the prioritization of private property over the lives of Black people.[17] Meanwhile, across the state of Louisiana, more than 1,577 people had already died in the aftermath of the storm, with more than 40 percent of them drowning. The storm killed roughly 300 more people elsewhere in the Gulf region.[18]

By September 3, 2005, the people who had remained were evacuated from the city to other shelters. With most of its people forced out, New Orleans was left abandoned, mildewed, and warped. Over 60 million cubic yards of debris littered yards and sidewalks, spilling out of buildings and homes; millions of walls of damaged drywall awaited removal as 250,000 housing units in New Orleans alone were damaged or destroyed; and blue poly tarps blanketed smashed roofs, quasi protection from the merciless rains and scorching subtropical sun.[19]

"Well, there weren't so many houses completely destroyed, but yeah, flooded and uninhabitable," said Alfredo, describing the post-disaster milieu. "Lots of houses still had furniture inside. And those who had already cleared out their houses had taken . . . all of their furniture outside—all the streets were filled with furniture, along with other trash, everything you can imagine, cars, everything." Total cost of damages from the storm amounted to $165 billion, the costliest disaster in US history to date.[20]

But much of the costs were unnecessarily driven up by multitiered subcontracts. A congressional report conducted in 2006 revealed that nineteen contracts costing $8.75 billion were fraught with millions of dollars of waste through layers of unnecessary contracts, double-billing, and extra equipment—like FEMA trailers left unused in other states.[21] These superfluous contracts coupled with the federal government's suspension of key labor policies and the issuance of no-bid contracts precipitated rampant corruption and labor abuses with inadequate oversight. Crooked contractors reaped these benefits off the backs of unpaid workers as billions of taxpayer dollars flowed in unchecked.[22] Risk shifted from developers and contractors onto the poor and working-class people through beefed-up systems of surveillance and control that served the interests of the developers.[23] A growing Immigration and Customs Enforcement (ICE) presence and a "deportation threat dynamic" meant employers could use threats of calling ICE to control workers. Bosses had access to a state apparatus—ICE—to cultivate docility and maximize labor exploitation.

Inventing "Brown Peril" and Exacerbating Worker Precarity

"How do I ensure that New Orleans is not overrun by Mexican workers?" asked Mayor Ray Nagin in October 2005, in an incendiary response to the arrival of immigrant workers who helped clean up his city.[24] Tens of thousands of Central American and Mexican immigrants joined tens of thousands of other workers and volunteers to clear out debris and rebuild after the disaster. Most immigrant workers came from places like Texas and Florida, often recruited by crews located outside the devastated region.[25] Immigrants made up 45 percent of the total workers who came to rebuild, with undocumented workers constituting approximately 25 percent of the entire post-Katrina workforce.[26]

Relaying the mayor's disdain, offensive T-shirts for sale in French Quarter window displays—which usually bore tawdry one-liners like "I Got Bourbon-Faced on Shit Street"—featured the clearly racist phrase "FEMA: Find Every Mexican Available."[27] "Brown Peril" surged in the city, with politicians and businesspeople taking their respective jabs at the immigrant workforce. Meanwhile, evacuees, many of whom were the core of the local workforce, continued to be kept out of the city, away from their homes, livelihoods, and community networks.[28]

In a *Times-Picayune* interview in September 2005, Dyan "Mama D" French Cole, a longtime New Orleans organizer who passed away in 2017, declared, "We want the young, able-bodied men who are still here to stay to help those in need. And the ones that have been evacuated. We want them to come home and help clean up and rebuild this city. How can the city demand that we evacuate our homes but then have thousands of people from across this country volunteering to do the things that we can do ourselves?"[29] As Black workers remained forced out of the city, both volunteers and outside workers arrived. Recruited from poultry factories in Maryland, Native American reservations in Arizona, and recruitment sites as far away as India and Peru, workers were enticed with promises of fair wages and free housing.[30]

Daniel Castellanos was internationally recruited by his employer, Decatur Hotels, through the temporary H-2B visa guest worker program. Castellanos came to New Orleans from Peru in 2005, investing over $4,000 in the initial recruitment program and travel. His employer's guarantee of free meals, housing, and fifteen dollars an hour with a sixty-hour workweek as a construction manager made the investment seem worthwhile. When Castellanos, a trained engineer in Peru, arrived in New Orleans, leaving his wife and two children behind, it was a different story. He was paid between six and seven dollars per hour with only a twenty-five-hour average workweek doing maintenance and housekeeping in a hotel. He and his coworkers walked forty-five minutes to the jobsite and received free food for only the first month, and he slept with eight other people in a rat-infested room with holes in the ceiling. The conditions were far from the standards he was promised, and the funds were insufficient to pay back the debt he owed.[31]

Daniel's case illustrates how recruiters and contractors used false pretenses to attract workers from other continents—great lengths to not have to hire local New Orleanians.

As money flowed into the city through contractors, a small number of workers did get paid adequately for their labor, making as much as $500 a day. But these El Dorado–type legends that lured workers into the city most often provided more lore than return.[32] A report showed that documented workers made $16.50 an hour compared with $10 for undocumented workers, and only 20 percent of undocumented workers received payment for overtime, compared with 74 percent of documented workers.[33] Almost three-quarters of undocumented workers experienced wage theft.[34]

Prior to Katrina, New Orleans did not have active day-laborer recruitment sites like other cities.[35] But Lee Circle (now referred to as Harmony Circle) quickly emerged as the first major day-laborer hub, a site where hundreds of workers congregated early each morning.[36] White, Black, and immigrant day laborers awaited precarious jobs at the base of a towering thirty-foot-tall podium topped by a statue of Confederate general Robert E. Lee.[37] The traffic circle, located on the edge of the Central Business District and a key gathering spot during Mardi Gras parades, provided an opportune spot for recruiters to loop around in their vehicles to pick up workers for that day's toil.[38]

After Denis lost his steady contract work in demolition, he became a day laborer at Harmony Circle, congregating with other workers at a Shell gas station located on the roundabout.[39] Day laborers of all backgrounds competed for jobs in the cutthroat space. Complaints of immigrant workers taking jobs from native New Orleanians echoed across the city and served as a mechanism to divide already vulnerable workers.[40] As workers congregated regularly at Harmony Circle, the area increasingly became a site of surveillance and policing.[41] In March 2006, ICE officials working with local New Orleans Police Department (NOPD) officers took part in a raid at the site, arresting and jailing forty immigrants. "We'll probably keep a dozen of them who turned out to have criminal histories, some of them have violent felonies," said ICE spokesperson Temple Black in an interview with the *Times-Picayune*. Black's quote reveals a clear racial profiling agenda of ICE, an inchoate state apparatus at the time, just having turned three years old that month.[42]

When business owners complained about the day laborers, the surveillance at Harmony Circle grew. As raids continued at the site, workers left

Harmony Circle, moving to other esquinas across the city. Raids soon took place at those sites, too.[43] Denis, still working as a day laborer, moved to the Gretna esquina near a Home Depot located across the Mississippi River in Jefferson Parish. In a raid that took place in February 2007, Denis was arrested for trespassing along with two El Congreso organizers and seventeen other day laborers, only to be bailed out by a Black-led mutual aid organization called the People's Organizing Committee. In return, the day laborers, led by Denis, went to help one of the committee's members rebuild his house. Colette Tippy, a former organizer and Workers' Center founder, said it was one of "many moments" of "intentionally reshaping the narrative in peoples' minds by connecting people to each other." This action demonstrated the growing racial solidarities, an important step to combat Mayor Nagin's anti-immigrant rhetoric and to build a multiracial base.[44]

Precarious Living on Scout Island and Beyond

While Mexican and Central American workers, like Denis, faced hardships at the esquinas due to labor abuses and a growing ICE presence, housing added another layer of precarity to their day-to-day. Rents surged for the limited housing stock available, with leases doubling from $500 to $1,000 a month.[45] Desperate for a place to sleep, some workers camped next to esquinas, like at Harmony Circle, sleeping in flooded-out cars abandoned under the nearby bridge. In other cases, people lived in the same buildings they cleaned out and rebuilt. Workers also rented homes located near esquinas, like Alfredo, who lived in an apartment by the Franklin day-laborer corner in the Upper Ninth Ward. "There were way too many people piled in! Twenty of us, at least, in a half a shotgun—it was too many to even have room to cook if we could," he explained.[46] Approximately 10 percent of immigrant workers reported not having access to a kitchen, running water, or electricity—a brutal reality after a long day's work cleaning muck in a moldy, mosquito-ridden city.[47]

One of several housing campsites emerged in City Park, a massive 1,300-acre urban park and the former location of the former Allard Plantation, owned by enslaver John McDonough.[48] The park became a hub for the American Red Cross and the National Guard to distribute humanitarian aid for people who remained in the city. It also became a brief day-laborer site for worker recruitment and a massive ad hoc living space that turned into a for-profit campground. An estimated 1,000 people lived in the park, with 200 workers living adjacent to lagoons on Scout Island, a landmass encircled by Bayou St. John, located on the northeastern side of the park.[49]

The people in the park included seventy-two members of the White Mountain Apache Tribe, who arrived from White River, Arizona, to help with recovery and resided at the "Apache Camp." Across the bayou, Black, white, and immigrant workers originally from Brazil, Mexico, and Honduras set up tents on plots on Scout Island and throughout the rest of the park.[50] Workers were recruited with promises of reliable jobs, fair wages, and free rent.[51] Many stayed in the park awaiting better living situations. Some remained until the recovery work let up. Meanwhile, others were evicted from the park for "unauthorized camping" after a rental fee was put into place.

The massive campsite, which earned the moniker "Tent City," was managed by Storm Force, an outfit of four men from Mobile, Alabama, who were hired after City Park officials lost the majority of their staff who managed the park.[52] Storm Force contractors showed up with dumpsters, portable toilets, and a newly instated rental fee, charging campers $300 per month for 40 × 30 square feet of swampy land.[53] Workers fit multiple tents and tarps in the small space and relied on coolers, fire pits, and propane tanks for sustenance. In "Shelter 7," one of the few City Park buildings not damaged by Katrina, campers paid $5 to shower in makeshift stalls between 8:00 a.m. and 8:00 p.m.—a contrary time frame for the long workdays that Katrina recovery demanded.[54]

The limited shower and waste disposal efforts did little to assuage the deplorable conditions the workers faced—no electricity, no lighting, no clean running water, no laundry, and no protections. One construction worker who lived at the site for over three months called the situation "pure hell" and complained that the toilets were never cleaned (among other grievances).[55]

In response, members of the People's Hurricane Relief Fund (PHRF)—a powerful grassroots network of individuals, organizations, and institutions dedicated to equity and justice after Hurricanes Katrina and Rita—showed up in solidarity with the people living in "Tent City" on January 27, 2006. They negotiated free showers, lights, electricity, and camp rules (addressing evictions) with the Storm Force contractors.[56] As Storm Force met with the PHRF, campers, and media outlets, the contractors initially blamed the issues on lack of aid from FEMA. One contractor, Justin Briggs, explained, "When you've got just four guys taking money out of their own pockets to do all these things, the government has to step in and help."[57] According to a Congressional Hunger Center report, FEMA had ignored Storm Force's request for $100,000 in aid for basic improvements at the site.[58]

The PHRF and Storm Force agreed to meet the following Wednesday to take further steps, but when PHRF members arrived at "Tent City" on February 1, 2006, they instead found NOPD officers evicting campers accused of not paying rent. The NOPD threatened to arrest the PHRF organizers for trespassing. Over the next few months as evictions continued, the "Tent City" campsite eventually phased out. More permanent housing situations elsewhere opened, and some people just moved to other tent cities across town.

When FEMA officials did attempt to address the housing issues, they put most of their eggs in one formaldehyde-laced basket: FEMA trailers—the notoriously toxic mobile homes that cost a whopping $2.7 billion for 120,000 temporary housing fixes.[59] Formaldehyde exposure is linked to cancer, asthma, respiratory illnesses, and irritation of the nose, throat, and eyes.[60] The FEMA trailers that arrived in the city contained high levels of formaldehyde.[61]

FEMA's other housing solution involved renting out cruise ships for 8,000 people working in recovery. The private cruise ships left taxpayers with a $500 to $1,280 per week per person price tag, one that surpassed some bargain luxury cruises that actually set sail.[62] The massive budget that FEMA committed to either toxic housing or cruise ship cabins suggests that the agency could have supported improvements in ad hoc spaces like "Tent City." Nevertheless, workers were forced to navigate and negotiate with contractors and landlords on their own.

Disaster Foods

Like the informal spaces developed through the esquinas and "Tent City," street food vendors also appeared, functioning as food distributors when options were limited. Reconstruction workers relied initially on foods provided by the American Red Cross, a philanthropic service that supplied a whopping 68 million free meals and snacks in the Gulf region after Katrina.[63] Yet the types of food distributed, while certainly appreciated, were often not culturally relevant for the workers, nor was such food enough sustenance for the long workdays.

"It was like hospital food you get when you're sick," said Alfredo with a laugh, in reference to the foods delivered by the Red Cross to worksites. "First, for breakfast we'd get a sandwich and fruit, with a box of juice or milk. For lunch, we'd get a hunk of bread with ham and a packet of mayonnaise. There'd be a canned vegetable, and a banana or apple."

Alfredo explained that each morning a Red Cross van passed through the neighborhoods, sounding a siren to alert people across the city. People came out to the vans to get food directly from the Red Cross distributors. Then at noon they repeated the route for lunch. In some instances, immigrant workers had issues gaining access to Red Cross services due to their presumed documentation status.[64] The American Red Cross is supposed to serve all relief workers, regardless of factors like race, class, documentation status, and the like; nevertheless, cases of racial profiling fashioned yet another barrier to food security during recovery efforts.

Beyond the American Red Cross, food spaces popped up to feed relief workers. For dinner on the weekends, Alfredo recalled going to City Park for barbecues, which was a refreshing shift from the monotony of the Red Cross fare.

"At City Park," he explained, "lots of people showed up—all the people who lived there and volunteers. Plus, lots of churches that would come and donate food . . . carne asada, grilled chicken, hot dogs—it was much more *sabroso* [flavorful], all homemade."

Alfredo also noted that Black vendors set up grills and smokers in front of gas stations, selling plates of ribs and pork chop sandwiches. Likewise, groups like the "Soul Patrol," managed by "Mama D" French Cole along with a crew of volunteers, delivered foods and other basic needs, pushing carts through the Seventh Ward neighborhood.[65] Other grassroots groups like Food Not Bombs (an all-volunteer international movement that distributes vegetarian meals to participants in protests and disaster scenarios) and Common Ground Relief (a New Orleans–based community-initiated volunteer organization that began in September 2005 and offered assistance and mutual aid) distributed free food to people across the city.[66] But aside from these mutual aid groups and the philanthropic services, food options were hard to come by.

Meanwhile, federal workers were often fed through catering contracts with local businesses. A Brazilian pizzeria chain owner, Rogerio Paiva, was contracted by FEMA to make meals. Rogerio and his crew initially prepared breakfast, lunch, and dinner for 600 workers living in tents at Zephyr Stadium, the minor league baseball field located in Metairie, just outside the city. Converting his business to a catering company, Rogerio and his team trekked three times a day over an hour each way to prepare foods in a functioning kitchen in another chain of the pizzeria in Baton Rouge. Given his efficiency and output, Rogerio was contacted by the US marshals who had set up camps in the Uptown neighborhood and asked him to also prepare foods for the 1,780 soldiers stationed there. Rogerio accepted the challenge and tripled the scale of his operation.[67]

While federal aid workers had funding to feed their cadre of forces, reconstruction workers initially faced much more limited and unpredictable food distribution from grassroots organizations and philanthropic services. With few options available, immigrant workers addressed the demand for food on their own, either calling on family members to sell food or opting to sell on the streets themselves. Soon, minivans and hatchback cars equipped with stainless steel kitchens maneuvered across the city, delivering plates of foods in Styrofoam containers to worksites. Taco trucks and tamale vendors appeared at day-laborer corners.

In some cases, key city stakeholders even recruited food truck owners to New Orleans to sell food to workers. For example, Tulane University relief workers recruited Ruben Leite, a Brazilian American, to bring his fleet of twelve food trucks all the way from New York to New Orleans. When he arrived at the Uptown campus in 2006, Ruben filled a much-needed gap in food distribution.[68]

In many ways, Ruben paved the way for other vendors as well. When his services were no longer needed at Tulane, he took his business to the streets of New Orleans. As the conditions in the city improved and the laissez-faire state of post-Katrina became more restrictive, Ruben used his expertise to help food vendors, like Mateo, navigate policies and get licensing to legitimize their informal businesses.[69] Mateo's own foray into the taco truck business started out by way of renting a truck from Ruben's fleet in 2007. But before the taco truck, Mateo sold tamales on foot at the esquinas.

One afternoon in 2016, Mateo and I met in the back of the Workers' Center office—a nondescript shotgun in the Tremé neighborhood—to discuss the origins of his food truck ventures. When I asked how he started his lonchera business, Mateo, soft-spoken and self-assured, explained that his disillusionment with recovery work forced him to leave that industry. "They want you to work, but they don't want to pay you," he emphasized. "I said, 'No way, it doesn't work like that.'"

After amassing thousands of dollars of wages that went unpaid, he joined his sister and his wife to sell Mexican tamales at esquinas. Maximizing on the connections he made while working in construction, Mateo specialized in tamale delivery at his former jobsites while the women prepared the foods. Making tamales provided them with lucrative work and gave them a flexible schedule to stay home with their young children. The team sold 100–130 tamales each day, making between $300 and $400, which totaled around $7,000 in income generated per month. Their informal street vending economy thrived in 2006 as they sold food at both the Claiborne and Franklin day-laborer esquinas.

The crew realized they needed a space and licensing to maintain their business. A lonchera was the logical next step, but Mateo and his team didn't have quite enough capital to buy a truck of their own. Connected through a mutual customer, Ruben Leite empathized with Mateo's position and the two bartered. Mateo swapped out his old van and $1,000 for the smallest truck on Ruben's fleet—a 1986 yellow trailer with the words "Tacos, Ice Cream" painted on the side. "That's the one we had the money for," Mateo said, laughing. "And I never painted it."[70]

Mateo and his team were among hundreds of street food vendors who sold to reconstruction workers after Katrina. These street foods better fit the tastes of the Central American and Mexican workers and offered more sustenance for the long workdays.

Since Katrina, many of the street vendors have remained in the city. City officials, like Mayor Nagin, who was quick to draw attention to cultural battles, offered little policy solutions or rhetoric condemning issues that directly affected workers: wage theft and lack of housing. Instead, they doubled down on top-down, market-based solutions. Meanwhile, grassroots responses—some of the most effective recovery efforts—were neglected, vilified, and at times criminalized.[71] Given the absence of state support and the levels of labor and human rights abuses, grassroots organizations sprang into action. The Workers' Center, which spawned from the PHRF, the Advancement Project (a national racial justice organization advancing equity), and the People's Organizing Committee, emerged as a key grassroots multiracial organization.

FORMING THE WORKERS' CENTER, MULTIRACIAL SOLIDARITY, AND MOVING TOWARD THE RIGHT TO REMAIN

The New Orleans Workers' Center for Racial Justice formed as a member-led coalition to address labor abuses after Katrina and to advance worker rights. The labor-organizing base members who had been mobilizing prior to Katrina had been forced out of the city indefinitely. Curtis Muhammad, a former Student Nonviolent Coordinating Committee organizer and

Louisiana-based movement leader who passed away in 2022, stated that when first organizing after Katrina, "we tried to put it together in the model that we had been organizing, but now you got to realize, Katrina displaced people. So the same people aren't sitting around the table that we spent ten years with." A somewhat transient community of recovery workers, including workers originally from a range of countries across Latin America, along with residents who remained, made Katrina a particularly challenging situation in which to organize. Still, the wide-ranging labor and human rights abuses made the motive to organize easy.

As the Workers' Center took shape from December 2006 to 2007, members moved from an immigrant model toward more of a multiracial organizing framework with campaigns driven by Black and immigrant members. They also forged a leadership development model to build power "at the intersection of race and the economy."[72] Thus, it is helpful to understand that each of the Workers' Center's three subgroups—El Congreso (mixed-status immigrant workers and their families, which formed in 2006), the Alliance of Guestworkers for Dignity (membership base of guest workers, which formed in early 2007), and Stand with Dignity (Black low-wage worker members originally from New Orleans, which formed in 2007, hereafter called Stand)—had its own genesis, but all included an aim for racial and economic justice. Considering that the scope of this book is focused on immigrant workers, and for the sake of chronology, it makes the most sense to start with the foundation of El Congreso.

Immediately after Katrina, a group of day laborers met up weekly at a small restaurant near the Elysian Fields Avenue esquina to discuss the rampant labor abuses and growing ICE presence.

"Well, six or eight of us would meet. There was a little patio outside and we'd meet for an hour," Santos, an El Congreso founding member, recalled. "And the conversations during that time were about the injustices. A *quienes les habían puesto las esposas* [roughly: Who had been shackled], because it happened to everyone."

At the same time, organizers with the PHRF and members of the National Day Laborer Organizing Network organized workers at the esquinas, galvanizing individuals and groups like Santos's crew at Elysian Fields and Mateo in Central City.

In December 2006, the Elysian Fields esquina workers joined forces with the four other esquinas—Gretna on the Westbank, Carrollton in Mid-City, Franklin in the Upper Ninth, Claiborne and Martin Luther King in Central

El Congreso leaders facilitating a Wednesday night meeting in 2016. Photo by Fernando López, @sentir.con.ojos.

City—to become the Congress of Day Laborers, or El Congreso. The first meeting took place on a Wednesday evening in the Hope House gymnasium in the Irish Channel neighborhood. El Congreso initially began with "Know Your Rights" training, coalition building, and strategies to help day laborers access resources and recover wages.

Soon after, in January 2007, the Alliance of Guestworkers for Dignity formed, joining El Congreso as part of the burgeoning Workers' Center. Daniel Castellanos—who was recruited from Peru as a guest worker and organized his peers to fight against workplace injustices at the Decatur Hotel—became a founding member and organizer. The Alliance of Guestworkers for Dignity's initial campaigns included organizing Indian guest workers who worked for Signal International, an oil rig in Pascagoula, Mississippi, and a campaign supporting Mexican guest workers at Bimbo's Best Produce, a strawberry farm in Amite, Louisiana. This initial mobilization, along with a legal team headed by Jennifer "J. J." Rosenbaum, birthed what would soon be dubbed the New Orleans Workers' Center for Racial Justice (or Workers' Center).

During this first year of development, the PHRF split over strategic differences with the People's Organizing Committee, which was led by Curtis Muhammad. The Workers' Center went with Curtis and the committee, which was also starting to organize Black New Orleanians through a budding group called the New Orleans Survivor Council. But, with the Workers' Center now under the leadership of labor organizer Saket Soni, another schism took place due to strategic differences that (in a simplified description) came down to the Workers' Center following either a 501(c)(3) funding model, which limits the organizing imposed by foundation grants, or a radical, grassroots self-funded model. Much to the chagrin of Curtis, who parted ways with the group, Saket opted for the 501(c)(3) model for the Workers' Center.[73]

Soon after, in December 2007, Stand with Dignity joined forces with El Congreso and the Alliance of Guestworkers for Dignity. Stand consisted of Black New Orleanian workers and their families who initially fought for the "Right to Return," which included campaigns on homelessness, displacement, and destruction of public housing after Katrina. Given the struggles for jobs, they also turned to campaigns aimed at economic justice for Black workers, like fighting for Section 3 policy—which requires employment opportunities for local, low-income residents in federally funded projects—to hire Black New Orleanians who lived in the communities where the jobs took place. While seemingly at odds in a capitalist, cutthroat society, these three subgroups of the Workers' Center joined together in solidarity to fight against the exploitative models of redevelopment taking place in the region.

Mr. Moneybags and Forging Black and Immigrant Solidarities

Mr. Moneybags is the foundational story of the Workers' Center, even though it didn't emerge until four years after the organization's formation. In 2010, during a story circle, members of Stand, El Congreso, and the Alliance of Guestworker for Dignity came together to share their experiences with worker precarity.[74] The ethos of story circles, as articulated by the late John O'Neal, cofounder of the Free Southern Theatre, is "Anybody can learn anything better when the subject matter is based on stories that come from or affirm your own experience and purposes."[75] The Workers' Center members and organizers came together to give their testimonies, listen to each other, and make connections between their respective struggles. Together, they crafted the powerful story of *Mr. Moneybags*, based off a real-life boss, Charles "Bimbo" Relan, of Bimbo's Best Produce in Amite City, Louisiana.

This is an abridged version of *Mr. Moneybags* as told by former Stand organizer Toya Ex Lewis:

> In the first scene of *Mr. Moneybags*, a Black man is at home and his wife tells him he needs to find work to take care of the family. He encounters other unemployed Black men and they go searching for the boss, Mr. Moneybags. When they find Mr. Moneybags, he tells them to come back the next day and he'll hire them. Then it cuts to the next scene. It is early the next day and Mr. Moneybags sent his token man out to hire immigrant day laborers, promising them top wages and breaks. But when the day laborers arrive on the worksite, they are not paid, they are not allowed to take breaks, and they are treated poorly. The Black men arrive to the site looking for the jobs they were promised by Mr. Moneybags, only to find the day laborers working. The Black men ask Mr. Moneybags, "Where did our jobs go?" and Mr. Moneybags responds, "The immigrants work harder, so I'm going with them." The third scene, the immigrant day laborers get off work and the Black workers confront them. One Black worker says, "You're stealing our jobs." The immigrant worker says, "Well ya'll are lazy." The Black workers says, "Well ya'll lower the wages." And it is a back-and-forth exchange until somebody asks, "Who told you that?" And the other side asks, "Who told you that?" And both groups say, "Mr. Moneybags told us this." Then they all go gang up on Mr. Moneybags and take all of his money.[76]

Set at a hypothetical jobsite, *Mr. Moneybags* is about the importance of acknowledging and dismantling racialized stereotypes ubiquitous in capitalist narratives that pit workers against each other to identify that the ultimate beneficiary of their division is the capitalist boss. It's also a reckoning that many of the Workers' Center leaders and members experienced when beginning to organize with multiracial groups of people.[77] Similar stereotypes played out with the Central American and Mexican workers, who through popular education learned to grasp the entrenched histories of racism against and exploitation of Black people.

Moreover, not only did these workers form a multiracial coalition together under the umbrella organization of the Workers' Center, but El Congreso formed as a transnational, multiracial coalition, with membership spanning Central America and Mexico, uniting a diverse group of immigrant workers who drew from traditions of worker organizing in their respective countries of origin.[78] Santos drew inspiration from family members who participated in the General Strike of 1954 in Honduras, when banana workers organized over 100,000 strikers to protest the banana companies. Martincito, one of the founders of El Congreso who passed away in 2016, was a proud Zapatista who fought for land rights and Indigenous sovereignty in the Chiapas region of Mexico. Rito, a longtime leader with El Congreso, successfully organized his coworkers fighting for labor rights in a shrimp factory in Choluteca, located in southern Honduras. Moreover, New Orleans–based Garifuna (Black Indigenous Central Americans) leaders, like Leticia, continue to fight for land and labor rights to protect ancestral lands and livelihoods in Honduras while also fighting for immigrant rights in New Orleans. Thus, *Mr. Moneybags* is a tool used to share experiences and educate members across *both* race and country of origin.

The actual Mr. Moneybags, Charles "Bimbo" Relan, was a strawberry grower in Tangipahoa Parish, located seventy-five miles northwest of New Orleans. Bimbo, described as "cigar-chomping" and "trigger-happy," was sued in 2008 by thirteen Mexican H-2A guest worker plaintiffs whom he employed to work on his strawberry farm. The H-2A guest worker program is a federal program that enlists workers from outside the United States to do seasonal work in agriculture on farms and in the fields. The thirty workers in Amite, many of whom were Indigenous immigrants recruited from San Luis Potosí, Mexico, were forced into "slave-like conditions" on what activist Ted Quant referred to as "the same land where Africans were enslaved and fought slavery and the slave-like peonage system that continued into modern times."[79]

Promised prevailing wages at $8.01 per hour, the workers at Bimbo's Best Produce were paid as little as $2 per hour for the grueling labor, not nearly enough to survive on, let alone make up for the $800 investment they paid to come to the United States as part of the H-2A program. Along with withholding wages, Bimbo threatened workers by shooting his gun over their heads and spraying pesticides in their vicinity in a merciless effort to assert his control. To further crystallize his cruelty, Bimbo shot the neighbor's dog that the workers had befriended in the fields.[80] When the workers complained about their mistreatment, Bimbo confiscated their passports, holding them hostage to prevent their escape.

With help from the Workers' Center, the workers organized by educating themselves on their legal rights, including the Thirteenth Amendment and H-2A laws, and then, together, they fought for their rights. One of their first actions involved clandestinely inviting a coalition of Black leaders—Ted

Quant, Damian Ramos, and Gerald Renoir—to their worksite to share their experiences and to contextualize their exploitation within centuries of racial capitalism on that land.[81]

On February 14, 2008, Valentine's Day, the Mexican guest workers escaped from Bimbo's property. The three Black leaders, Quant, Ramos, and Lenoir, emerged at the worksite and staged a citizen's arrest of Bimbo, charging him with forced labor. Incensed and still in custody of the passports, Bimbo initially refused to return the property to the workers but eventually gave in, petulantly discarding the passports from his truck window. Workers' Center director Saket Soni wrote in the *People's Tribune*, "After we got the passports back, we walked to the police station to file a complaint. Workers returned to their trailers finding handwritten eviction notices scrawled by Bimbo. Bimbo stormed into the trailers later that night, still chewing at the same cigar, to try to illegally evict the workers. But we won—Bimbo was thwarted by police."[82] The citizen's arrest triggered an FBI investigation and initiated a lawsuit against Bimbo for violations of the federal Trafficking Victims Protection Act, the Fair Labor Standards Act, and the H-2A employment contracts of the workers.[83]

The Bimbo case demonstrates solidarities forged in the aftermath of Hurricane Katrina and the interconnectedness of Black and immigrant struggles that expand beyond just urban spaces and take place in rural spaces as well. The Bimbo case also shows the burgeoning power of the Workers' Center and its range of strategies, from direct action and multiracial alliances to whistleblowing and legal defense through lawsuits.

The Workers' Center increasingly became a go-to resource for immigrant workers. When Maria experienced workplace abuses similar to those suffered by the H2-A workers at Bimbo's Best Produce—locked into housing and forced to work under an abusive employer—she was also able to connect with the Workers' Center to fight for her worker and immigrant rights.

The Precarity at the Taqueria: From Wage Theft to the Right to Remain

Maria is explicit about where she is from: "My name is Maria. I am from Guatemala *and* I am also from here, New Orleans."[84] She proudly confirms her roots at the beginning of our interview, right before launching into a detailed explanation on how to make her favorite Guatemalan dish, *pepian de pollo*. Her response is a fair anticipation to my request asking whether I could interview her about food. Just above five feet tall, Maria exudes confidence almost as much as kindness, with large brown eyes framed by steady eyebrows and long black hair. Maria fluently speaks Spanish and K'iche', an Indigenous Mayan language spoken throughout Guatemala.

I first met Maria when I began volunteering with the Workers' Center in 2011. She and I roomed together during a road trip to Alexandria, Virginia, for a National Day Laborer Organizing Network workshop for leadership development with immigrant communities from across the United States. As a member leader with El Congreso, Maria was accustomed to the in-depth training integral to these types of workshops. By day, Maria spoke about her experiences fighting for her own wage theft case, led hard discussions on criminalization of immigrant communities, and sang a Guatemalan ballad a cappella to ovations from her fellow day laborers. By night, she left the hotel to meet up with her brother in Washington, DC, whom she hadn't seen in ten years. Given it was her first time in DC and she was equipped with just a flip phone, Maria navigated the Metro and the DC streets with aplomb, returning just in time the next morning to walk with me over to the conference.

When Maria arrived in New Orleans in 2007, her first steady job was for a Mexican American man, José, who hailed from Texas. Like many others, the Texan understood that cleanup and reconstruction would draw in thousands of Central American and Mexican workers, so he moved to New Orleans and opened his lonchera. José parked his truck, El Chaparral, on Josephine Street, next to the Claiborne day-laborer esquina and just on the other side of the block from Mateo's truck. José converted what was formerly a cashier booth at the gas station there into a taco stand at the same site.[85] The stand, which proved popular beyond the day-laborer community, earned "Best Taco Truck" by food writer Todd Price in the *New Orleans Magazine* "Best in Dining" category in 2006.[86]

New to the city and without a core network, Maria was confined to cooking and living in the Texan's home a few miles away from the taco stand. She prepared meats and salsas from his kitchen, working ten- to twelve-hour days, six days a week.

"I made the beans, rice, red salsa, salsa verde; I prepared it all in the house—the onion, the radishes," she recalled. On the weekend, the work was even more grueling because the *sopa de mondongo* took all night to slow-cook, forcing her to stay awake. After she prepared the foods in the house, José transferred them to his taco stand, where two women sold the food.

The meager allowance she earned was not commensurate with the amount she worked. After a month and a half went by of José not paying her, she had enough. Maria complained and threatened to leave. In return, she said, "he made fun of me because I couldn't speak English. And he said I can't call the police because I can't speak English. And if you want to call *la migra* [ICE], I'm friends with *la migra*. So, I couldn't complain in any way because he had these connections."

Eventually, Maria was put in contact with two local agencies—El Congreso and the Wage Claim Clinic, which formed in 2005.[87] Working with El Congreso organizer Jacinta Gonzalez, Maria filed a civil action suit against her employer. Once in court, the judge calculated thousands of dollars of withheld wages and forced the owner, who was present in court, to repay her. But instead of paying, José fled town.

"Well, I never got the money because he left for Dallas without paying me. He knew he was wrong. That's why he left," Maria said, adding playfully, "and if I see him around here, I'll have to get justice, because I won't leave it like that." Maria quickly found housing and a new job as a line cook at a newly opened Honduran restaurant.

Employers like José weaponized ICE, using the "deportation threat dynamic" to silence and control workers. But José's threat was not enough to curb Maria's ire; rather, she found recourse in El Congreso and the Wage Claim Clinic. Even though she didn't get the money she earned, she was able to escape the exploitative job and achieve some level of vindication and empowerment. At the same time, her experience of being threatened with ICE showed the growing need to protect workers from escalating numbers of deportations. Spanning 2005 to 2009, deportations skyrocketed, from 246,000 deportations to 392,000 per year.[88]

In response, El Congreso decided to reframe its campaign in 2010, shifting from a focus mainly on wage theft issues through a "Know Your Rights" campaign to protecting immigrants from deportations. The newly formed "Right to Remain" campaign meant that the immigrant workers deserved the right to not be surveilled by ICE and local law enforcement and the right to stay in the city they helped rebuild.[89] Stand members still fought for the "Right to Return" to the city and jobs, and El Congreso members began their fight against detention and deportations. Both groups continued to push for workers' rights and to forge multiracial solidarities; El Congreso's social movement framing just expanded.

CONCLUSION

While workers' wages weren't always recovered, people like Denis, Daniel, Maria, and Mateo were still able to join a multiracial movement to help combat labor and civil rights abuses. In the absence of state support, the workers built power through self-reliance as part of grassroots movements. They made ends meet with the resources at hand. Meanwhile, *Mr. Moneybags* bosses like Bimbo and José at El Chaparral were results of the deregulated urban governance that fostered labor abuses while creating a federally sanctioned pliable workforce. Yet, the workers proved they were anything but pliable as they continued to organize against exploitative labor practices.

A disaster situation offers no clear blueprint for quick recovery; however, a disaster situation that allows for unfettered profiteering and exploitative models of recovery instead of oversight and equity paves the way for failure and exacerbates an already aggravated environment. Along with high incidents of wage theft and minimal protections, workers endured grueling labor by day and wretched living conditions by night. The emergence of the esquinas, sites like "Tent City," and street food vendors illustrates how post-Katrina workers exercised their right to the city, operating in the informal sector to make ends meet when no other options became available. Through these everyday practical acts and amid glaring state absence, workers turned to self-reliance, setting up work recruitment sites, makeshift camps, and itinerant businesses as informal, unregulated spaces in an already deregulated city.

Instead of recognizing the value of these informal economies, the state turned to the private sector and philanthropic services to help oversee recovery efforts.[90] Yet, the task proved too complicated for small outsider contract crews like Storm Force in City Park. Billions of dollars of subcontracts went to waste. And restaurant owners, like Rogerio, were overworked and understaffed as they fed thousands of federal workers. FEMA's funds went toward toxic trailers and extravagant cruise ship housing and into the pockets of corrupt developers. Meanwhile, local, state, and federal officials turned to NOPD and ICE officials to criminalize the people who did much of the recovery work, rather than bolster existing, on-the-ground grassroots operations.

These informal spaces played out as sites of resistance and collaboration to combat uneven power structures that kept people locked in exploitative jobs and locked out of opportunities. Linking day laborers, who are often considered too peripheral for collective action due to their ostensible transience and the informality of their work, with street food vendors illustrates how these informal economies that emerged after Katrina played an essential role in rebuilding efforts. And it shows how they built coalitions and worker power with Black New Orleanians who faced similar issues of being locked out of resources and opportunities and left out of efforts to rebuild their own city.

On December 6, 2005, "Mama D" French Cole spoke to a congressional committee about Katrina, giving a message on behalf of her Seventh Ward community.[91] With great fervor, she said, "I beg you all, you know, right now the main thing we need—because I didn't just come with questions, we came with solutions—we need you all to take FEMA and FEMA mama and daddy, and Red Cross and all the rest of them people and just take them somewhere, just get them out of my neighborhood." She continued, "We did not lose our ability to fish. Don't bring the fish to our door, just bring us some fishing poles and some bait. We didn't lose our minds. I don't know why we didn't, but we could have. We lost all of the necessities we need to support our survival. Just give us that. Just give us that, and I promise you, in six months . . . come back, we're going to make you some gumbo."[92]

And, just maybe, Mama D would have been okay with offering up tacos, too.

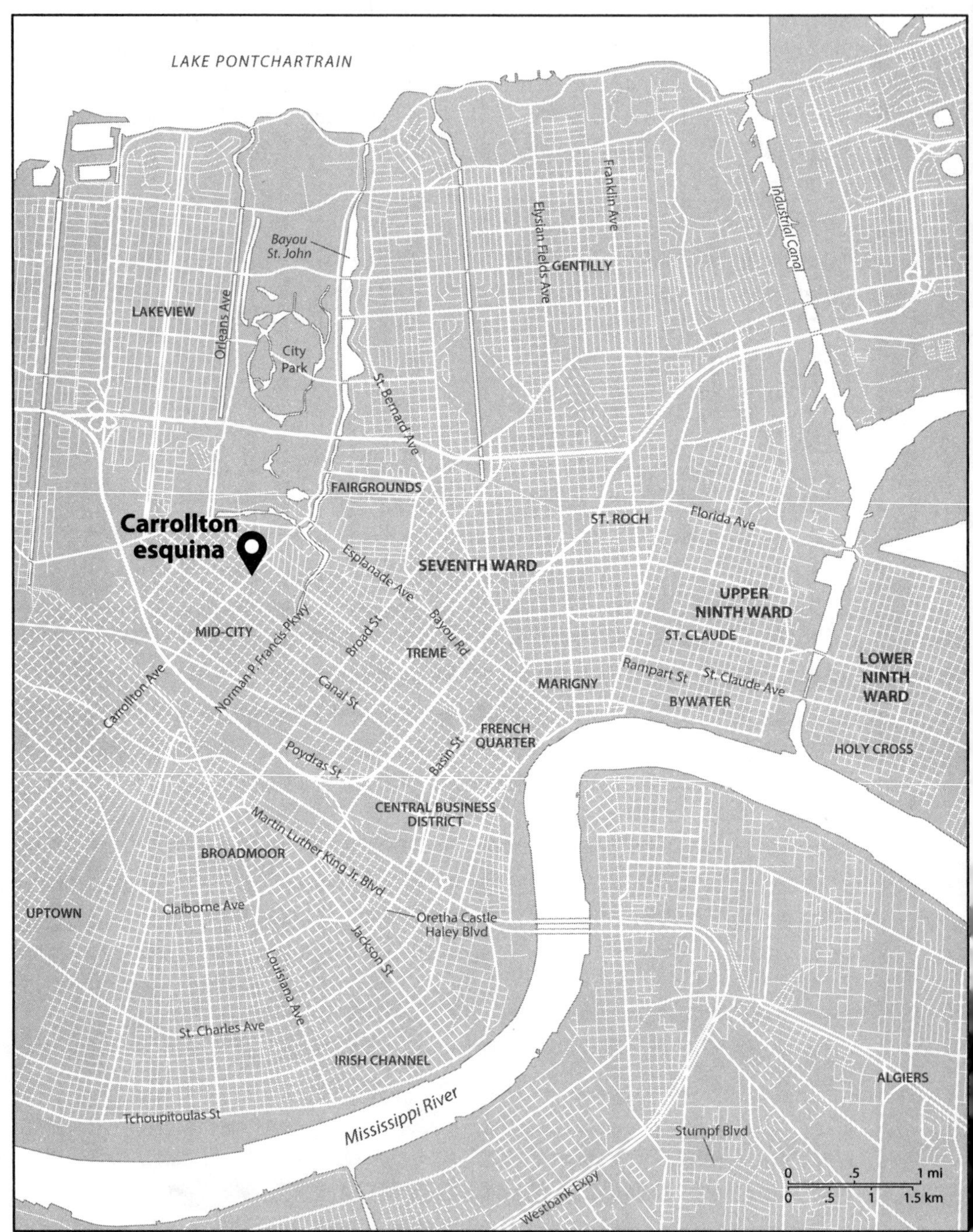

Carrollton esquina in New Orleans.

Chapter 2
Right to Land
Fighting Gentrification and Displacement

People didn't look like me,
but they had the same interests
as me.

— ALFRED MARSHALL,
organizer with Stand with
Dignity, 2020

The struggle began as a
right to land in my country
and continues as a fight for the
right to my new city.

— EL CONGRESO
member from Honduras
at a meeting, 2015

Watanegui consup, lupipati,
lupipami (I want to eat conch
soup; a little for you, a little bit for
me)

— BANDA BLANCA
singer Juan Pompilio Tejeda's
translation of the "Sopa de
Caracol" lyrics

In the Mid-City neighborhood, visits with Denis to the Carrollton esquina often involved negotiating with Home Depot managers over the rights of workers to remain on the sidewalk in front of the store. We won those fights, ensuring that workers could continue to look for jobs in the public space. Located in the heart of New Orleans, halfway between Lake Pontchartrain and the Mississippi River, the Carrollton esquina first emerged a year after Katrina in September 2006, operating outside the newly opened Home Depot that initially functioned as a temporary location for hurricane relief purposes.[1] The Carrollton day-laborer corner's tenure lasted until 2013, when Home Depot eventually closed, making way for a major commercial development in the rapidly gentrifying district.

After Katrina, demographics dramatically shifted in the majority Black Mid-City neighborhood: the white population skyrocketed from 23.2 to 39.7 percent and the "Hispanic" population increased slightly from 10 percent in 2000 to 11 percent in 2019, while the Black population plummeted almost 20 percentage points, from 64.3 to 45.8 percent.[2] Across New Orleans's Mid-City Planning District, the bloated tourism industry and mega-development projects led to rising rents, the demolition of public housing, and the displacement of communities.[3]

Commercial spaces reflected these changes through high-end restaurants and boutique hotels that targeted a wealthier and whiter population. Latin food establishments and bars opened across Mid-City aimed at immigrant communities. Thus, trips to the Carrollton esquina meant Denis and I had a breadth of food options available, including hot lines at Latin grocery stores, a Honduran bakery, and a variety of Mexican restaurants and taco trucks. Yet given these options, Denis's predilections usually led us to his comfort zone—Honduran food at Costa de Tela.

Before establishing themselves in the Mid-City neighborhood, Costa de Tela owners Carmela and her three daughters, Adriana, Olivia, and Caty, initially reconfigured their business from street vending to a brick-and-mortar space in a strip mall in the Broadmoor neighborhood.[4] Tucked into a corner, the restaurant went unmarked except for a Louisiana gaming sign and an outdated green awning with the remnants of the previous restaurant's name, Lebanon, drooping from the storefront's tinted windows.

With capacity at around twenty people (staff included), the restaurant squeezed in about double that amount on a typical Friday night as construction workers filled the bar and restaurant after a long workweek. When Denis and I visited in late mornings in 2011, the space was usually empty except for Adriana and Carmela, preparing foods to a soundtrack of telenovelas or reggaeton blaring in the background.

At Costo de Tela, I was first introduced to the Honduran classic *sopa de caracol*—conch soup—a dish so notable that it has a song named after it. Written by Hernan "Chico" Ramos, made *Billboard*-famous by Banda Blanca, and further popularized by Elvis Crespo and Pitbull, the song is quintessential *punta*—a type of Black Indigenous music that originated from the Garifuna people, thus containing African and Arawak influences. In Banda Blanca's version, a keyboard and drum kit lead into a strong brass overture accompanied by congas that set the beat for the song's first lines: *Watanegui consup, lupipati, lupipami* (I want to eat conch soup, a little for you, a little for me). The melodic refrain blends Spanish with Garifuna and is punctuated by the song's title, "Sopa de Caracol," a chorus repeated throughout.

Made with conch meat (large sea snails), yucca, *guineos* (small green bananas), and bell peppers, the coconut potage resembles a Thai curry but without the spiciness. The seafood dish is also reminiscent of the restaurant's name, Costa de Tela, which is a nod to the northern coastal Honduran region where the family is from—Tela. Some 2,000 miles south of New Orleans, on the northern coast of Honduras, Adriana, Olivia, and Caty's father, Don Carlos, runs a small bar and pool hall just off Laguna de los Micos outside of Tela.[5] As one of the few establishments in the small village, Don Carlos's bar caters mostly to men from the area, many of whom work in either fishing or agriculture. His village sits just across the inlet from a Garifuna coastal village bounded by the lagoon and the Caribbean Sea.

Both Honduran communities—in Don Carlos's village near Tela and in Mid-City New Orleans—face existential threats caused by unfettered capitalism and growing tourism industries.[6] In Honduras, purveyors of tourism industries and big agriculture acquire land across the coastal region, disregarding the realities of poor and working-class communities of color. In Mid-City New Orleans, a trend of public-private partnerships overlooks existing infrastructure and community needs, leading to the development of large-scale projects that displace residents and contribute to increased rental costs. Analyzing land grabs in Honduras alongside megaprojects in New Orleans illustrates how land accumulation connects with displacement and takes place in collusion with market-based privatized systems on a global scale.

Thus, this chapter is about the right to land, and Costa de Tela and Don Carlos's bar offer micro examples that help center a macro examination of the multiple threads that link New Orleans and Honduras: of land grabs and gentrification, displacement and privatization, labor exploitation and over-policing. The central claim of this chapter is that capital accumulation in relation to land grabs is central to these processes of displacement and migration; in both places, narratives of violence or job creation are used to justify these acts of dispossession. Historical examples of capital accumulation set the foundations for contemporary examples of land extraction facilitated by corporate agendas and post-disaster contexts.

Disaster capitalism acts as a backdrop for both New Orleans and Honduras, where speculators, politicians, and planners saw a blank slate that would enable them to use dispossession and exploitive development projects to re-create both places while enriching themselves.[7] In Honduras, Hurricane Mitch in 1998 and then the coup that ousted leftist president Manuel Zelaya in 2009 were the shocks that resulted in austerity measures that gave significant power and land to the elite.[8] These shocks facilitated market-based reforms, the brunt of which were absorbed by poor people and people of color in these regions. Linking labor exploitation with land grabs highlights how both the state and capital, oftentimes working together, fostered precarity in these communities.[9]

While media coverage of Honduran migration often either ignores root causes of migration or narrowly focuses on gang and narco-trafficking violence as the cause of exoduses, this chapter centers the role of privatization and displacement in forcing people to flee from their homes and their ancestral lands. Daniella Burgi-Palomino of the Latin America Working Group argues that displacement due to resistance to large-scale development projects is "documented to a lesser degree" and cites an unnamed Honduran activist who explicitly ties dispossession to the state: "The government's extractivist model drives migration."[10] The state disregards its role in this displacement and the scale of it and instead aligns with violence narratives (gang, narco-trafficking) in order to justify and bolster militarized force. In turn, these militarized forces are used by the private sector as instruments to further dispossess. Due to the depth of corruption and state violence in Honduras in particular, little recourse is available beyond grassroots mobilization and superficial protections from supranational organizations.

Poor and working-class Black communities—in both Honduras and New Orleans—are disproportionately impacted; the same market-based policies buttressed by racialized policing systems continue to disrupt and uproot lives. In Honduras, Black Indigenous communities like Bay Islanders and the Garifuna people are constantly forced to defend ancestral lands from the avarice of tourism speculators. In New Orleans, Black communities have historically borne the brunt of egregious housing policies and have continuously been disenfranchised in terms of land and development.

Groups such as the Workers' Center have pushed back against these acts of displacement through campaigns like the "Right to Remain" and the "Right to Return." In Honduras, groups such as the Black Fraternal Organization of Honduras and the Council of Popular and Indigenous Movements of Honduras have mobilized on a multiracial level to navigate and resist forces of extreme privatization and deregulation to fight for their right to remain. Thus, Costa de Tela is emblematic of these transnational processes—a story of immigrant women pivotal to disaster recovery efforts and a transnational tale of place that surfaces the history and global impacts of capital accumulation, top-down redevelopment, and the resistance.

DEMOLITION, GENTRIFICATION, AND RESISTANCE IN THE MID-CITY PLANNING DISTRICT

Around the same time that Denis left New Orleans in 2011, Costa de Tela coincidentally closed its doors for a brief period. I'd learn later that Carmela and her daughters were still operating clandestinely out of their house in the Broadmoor neighborhood at that time, before reopening again at a new location in Mid-City in 2013.[11] Located just blocks away from the Orleans Parish Prison (OPP) complex, the restaurant's gingerbread trim and vinyl siding blended in with the bail bondsmen centers and residential homes that line Tulane Avenue. On the front exterior, a white sign advertised "Big Tasty Restaurant & Bar." Referencing the strip of English-language commercial spaces when I asked about the name "Big Tasty," the middle daughter, Olivia, chuckled and said, "We thought it'd fit in better."

Inside, the open floor plan allowed space for ample seating, a stage, a lone pool table, and an electronic jukebox. Without fail, upon my many entrances into the space, one of the bar patrons would change the jukebox from Honduran *punta* to music in English (lots of Journey) to welcome me. The interior space, which once housed a bar called Mile High Club, consisted of a built-in brick bar with dark wood trim wrapping the front half of the restaurant and serving as a divider between the customers and the stocked bar and open cooking area.

A view down Tulane Avenue in front of Big Tasty, aka Costa de Tela. Photo by Fernando López, @sentir.con.ojos.

Costa de Tela was a party place, and this reputation fit in with the *le bon temps roule* ethos of the city. On the weekends, the restaurant seamlessly converted into a club with drag shows, karaoke, and reggaeton dance parties. These festivities went late. "On the weekends, I leave at six in the evening and my sister takes her shift," explained Olivia. "A Saturday isn't a Saturday unless it goes until five or six in the morning and then she [Adriana, her sister] closes." Yet the party image was not always favorable, especially for the neighbors living in the area. A white neighbor once wrote on the restaurant's Facebook page, "You are a pox on the neighborhood," and then detailed a grievance regarding noise complaints, trash, loud music, and fighting.[12] When I asked Olivia about the disturbances, she shrugged and said, "We handle it."

Many of the patrons who frequented Costa de Tela also worked on the $1.1 billion hospital built between 2011 and 2015 and located just five blocks south of the restaurant. Bounded by Canal and Tulane Avenues, the hospital complex consists of the University Medical Center and Veterans Affairs Hospital and was built mostly using federal hurricane recovery money. The development was part of a public-private partnership that followed similar disaster capitalism trends of dismantling public institutions in favor of private-public developments. Geographer David Harvey warned in 2008, "A 'Financial Katrina' is unfolding, which conveniently (for the developers) threatens to wipe out low-income neighbourhoods on potentially high-value land in many inner-city areas far more effectively and speedily than could be achieved through eminent domain."[13] And it did, with and without eminent domain. Katrina ushered in disaster capitalism projects that led to the dismantling or defunding of most things public in that city.

To make way for the massive billion-dollar hospital complex, developers demolished or relocated seventy acres of residential and commercial space in the heart of the Mid-City neighborhood while also snubbing the redevelopment of the landmark public Charity Hospital. Charity's iconic art deco–style structure was built in 1939 to serve the city's indigent population.[14] When the massive building flooded during Katrina, a team of 200 recovery workers, including doctors and nurses, pumped out floodwaters and prepared the space for medical use only to be denied reentry by hospital police. Representatives from Louisiana State University (LSU) who ran Charity and had longed for an excuse to shut down the public hospital employed textbook disaster capitalism strategy by declaring (despite major dispute) that disaster damage exceeded 50 percent of the cost of rebuilding (FEMA's requirement for funding a new development).[15]

In an interview with *The Nation*, John Kennedy—who is Louisiana's current Republican US senator and was a Democratic state treasurer at that time—said that when he asked Louisiana State University representatives whether the LSU hospital system could move into Charity temporarily, they replied, "If we do, we'll never get a new one."[16] With support from Governor Kathleen Blanco, the state quickly ushered in plans for the two new massive hospital complexes.[17] At the expense of helping medical officials in the dire post-disaster scenario, politicians colluded with university officials and neglected to reopen the vital public space, only to ensure their new hospital be built. Forty-nine homes and twenty-eight commercial buildings in the major section of Mid-City—just a block away from Costa de Tela—were either moved or demolished through eminent domain, affecting approximately seventy families from the majority-Black neighborhood.[18]

The construction of the massive medical campus spurred gentrification first by displacing families and then by pricing out people as more medical professionals settled in the neighborhood.[19] Subsequently, the Mid-City neighborhood experienced a commercial and real estate boom.[20] To keep up with the hospitals and new businesses, the state invested in a $10 million beautification project on Tulane Avenue, paid for by the Louisiana Department of Transportation, directly in front of Costa de Tela.[21]

Maria, who worked as a cook at Costa de Tela and lived nearby, acknowledged the rising prices surrounding her rented shotgun house located directly in front of the Veterans Affairs Hospital. In 2017, I asked Maria if she would have to move because of the rising prices surrounding her house.

"Looking around the street it seems like everyone is moving," she said. "I haven't had to yet, but I haven't talked to the owner."

Since that conversation, the speculative real-estate price of Maria's shotgun has increased from an estimated $160,000 in 2015 to $240,000 in 2019.[22] Like many of the Central Americans and Mexicans who remain in the area, she faced the risk of being forced out as part of the gentrification processes. Many of the Black and immigrant communities have been uprooted and forced to relocate to New Orleans East, one of the few neighborhoods in which the Black and "Hispanic" populations have increased while the white population has decreased.[23] In the East, crime rates have skyrocketed.[24] A lagging public transit system makes it difficult to get to and from the East, which is ten miles from the French Quarter, the heart of the city's service industry economy where many of these individuals work.

Public officials also saw the development as a way to improve a troublesome zone. Just a block away from Costa de Tela and adjacent to the OPP, the Tulane and Broad Street intersection has carried particular infamy.[25] Writing for the *Times-Picayune* in 2013, Richard Webster referred to the intersection as a "popular destination for junkies and sex workers who take watch over barren street corners after dark" and critiqued the dilapidated motels—remnants of the highway boom of the 1950s—that once lined the street. Webster quoted NOPD officer Ricky Jackson as saying, "The workers [construction workers at the hospital site] get paid Thursday, Friday, Saturday and then they go pick up the girls or guys. Sometimes they come by early morning, pick up a girl and then go to work. It's supply and demand. You see it all the time."[26] Webster's tone cast a cautionary tale facing the hospital development in reshaping the Tulane and Broad corridor.

Yet since Webster's reporting in 2013, with the exception of one motel north of Costa de Tela, which was refurbished and converted into a Los

Angeles–style hotel complete with a chic café, bar, and clothing-optional pool in 2017, the mid-century motels have since been demolished, making way for apartments for wealthier residents, including medical professionals. The vapid design of the new apartment buildings along Tulane Avenue—a far cry from the grandiose and sundry New Orleans aesthetic—is consistent more with the homogeneous design deadening the charm of city neighborhoods across the United States. More importantly, the rates for Mid-City apartments escalated.[27] Rampant crime was used to justify the developments and excessive policing was used to deliver the order, even though the crime was oftentimes perpetuated by these same systems and failures of the state.[28]

By 2017, New Orleans food writer Ian McNulty called the Tulane and Broad corridor a "food frontier" in an article detailing the impacts of the hospital complex. "Those hospitals are still ramping up, but their sheer scale has already thrown much of the surrounding area into flux," McNulty noted. "One change is a tide of small eateries drawn to their periphery, which are giving a once desolate stretch the feel of an anything-goes frontier for food."[29] While addressing this so-called frontier, McNulty also brought attention to the remaining spaces that targeted Spanish-speaking immigrant communities, like Ideal Market, a grocery store located in between the hospital development and Costa de Tela.

Prior to Katrina, Ideal Market had one corner store that predominantly served the Black community. Since 2005, the owners, who are Palestinians, expanded Ideal Market to include six chain stores across Louisiana.[30] After Katrina, the owners maximized the potential of this growing Spanish-speaking immigrant population, swapping out Blue Runner beans for Goya brand, expanding its marketing on Spanish-language radio stations, and hiring Central American and Mexican immigrants to work as cooks in their kitchens and as cashiers in their stores. Denis and I dropped in weekly to get to-go plates of *caldo de res* (beef stews) and fresh-made tortillas from Ideal's weigh-your-plate buffet.

Thus, McNulty inadvertently drew attention to this tension in which, as Black residents were displaced, Central American and Mexican immigrants moved in as unintentional actors in these displacement processes. In many cases, the fruits of their construction job labor contributed to the displacement and dispossession. Ipsita Chatterjee identifies these processes through "spatialities of exploitation" in which "networks of labor" are "usurped" to reproduce what she calls "landscapes and lifescapes of accumulation." Here, "thefts of space" happened to Black and immigrant residents who were forced out of the spaces they made meaningful.[31]

The same economic forces that drew the owners of Costa de Tela to New Orleans and brought in their clientele—rebuilding efforts, the hospital projects, and a growing service industry economy—were the same forces causing the gentrification that priced them out. In this sense, the post-Katrina disaster capitalism system that fostered the arrival of immigrant workers who continued to do the city's unregulated and underpaid jobs was the same system that was pushing them out by bankrolling private megaprojects and displacing residents. As these gentrification projects expanded, law enforcement and ICE increasingly became instruments to control poor and working-class people of color. Yet, as the next section illustrates, grassroots organizations like the Workers' Center strove to build multiracial solidarities to combat these spatialities of exploitation: Black New Orleanians forced out of public housing fought for the right to the jobs to rebuild their former homes, and, as part of the "Right to Remain" campaign, Central American and Mexican immigrants fought against a surge of ICE raids and deportations to fight for their right to stay in the city they helped rebuild.

TREMÉ: A HUB OF BLACK CULTURE AND MULTIRACIAL POLITICAL ACTION

In New Orleans's historic Tremé neighborhood, located just two miles east of Costa de Tela, the wall of a usually vacant commercial space displayed a new mural when I drove by in 2017. The facade featured a gray banner with the restaurant's name, Tremé Market, in the center of a royal blue base coat. A palm tree hand-painted brown and green alongside three white birds in flight set the scene for the rest of the mural, which showcased a motley carte du jour of Honduran, Mexican, and New Orleans dishes written in cursive along the sides. Tacos, pupusas, and *pollo con tajadas* (fried chicken and fried plantains) joined Crescent City specialties like *yakamein* (a rich and brothy beef and noodle soup), icebergs (Kool-Aid slushies), fried chicken, hot wings, and hot tamales.

I entered the dimly lit restaurant, which featured an unexpected wall of Hollywood action photos and framed movie posters decorating a spartan eating section. As I ordered a sack full of *nacatamales*—the Central American version of the versatile cornmeal dish—I learned that the Black-owned restaurant employed a Honduran chef, and according to the restaurant manager, the owner wanted to celebrate the neighborhood's "intermixed cultures" as well as showcase his own celebrity as a B-list actor in New Orleans's burgeoning (and exploitative) film industry.[32] Just six months later, the royal blue tropical mural was painted over with an alabaster beige, an erasure of an ephemeral space and a symbolic whitening of a rapidly changing city neighborhood.

The "redevelopment" of the Tremé serves as an emblem of gentrification, the growth of a tourism-centric economy, and the consequent displacement of cultural contributors, exploited for profit in the tourism industry.[33] There's even a David Simon television show about it. Tremé, which is the southernmost part of the Mid-City Planning District, experienced a dramatic demographic shift after Katrina: the Black population dropped from 92.4 percent in 2000 to 56 percent in 2017; meanwhile, the white population skyrocketed from 4.9 to 35.6 percent, and the "Hispanic" population grew slightly from 1.5 to 5.1 percent in the historic Black neighborhood. These changes were ubiquitous across the Mid-City Planning District, a stark example of post-Katrina malfeasance and failed policies that favored developers whose plans forced out poor and working-class people.[34]

Half a mile southwest of the Tremé Market sit the offices of the Workers' Center at 217 N. Prieur, an address I often shared during my attempts to recruit day laborers to attend El Congreso's weekly meetings held there. Since 2007, the camelback shotgun house headquartered the offices of each of the three Workers' Center organizations—Stand with Dignity, El Congreso, and the National Guestworker Alliance (which changed its name from Alliance of Guestworkers for Dignity around 2007). Three days a week for almost a year, I met Denis in front of the shotgun each morning before organizing at the day-laborer corners and on Wednesday nights to help prepare for the weekly meetings.[35] Part of my duty was to order food, which, in the early stages, was provided for meeting attendees and paid for by El Congreso. The food selection alternated between Domino's Pizza and catering from Julia, a member of El Congreso who brought trays of Mexican stewed beef, rice, spicy salsa *verde*, and salad. Free food helped bring people to the meetings, filling the stomachs of some who were unable to afford adequate meals due to low wages and limited work.

When Denis left New Orleans in 2011 to return to Honduras, I continued working with lead organizer Jacinta Gonzalez, who shepherded El Congreso through its shift from a "Know Your Rights" campaign at the esquinas to a broader "Right to Remain" campaign.[36] The reframing went from solely protecting against worksite exploitation to focusing on the increased number of deportations by the Obama administration and the growing collaboration between local law enforcement and ICE agents in the city. Spanning 2005 to 2011, deportations climbed sharply, from 246,431 to 390,442 per year, and these deportations paralleled an increase in Honduran migration.[37] Louisiana ranks fourth (behind Arizona, California, and Texas) in number of deportations since ICE was established in 2003, with the numbers of deportations peaking between 2011 and 2014.[38] Since 1927, New Orleans has hosted the headquarters of the "New Orleans Sector" of the Border Patrol, which currently spans 694 miles of coastline across the Gulf region. The southern Field Office for Immigration and Customs Enforcement is also located in New Orleans and covers a jurisdiction of five states. The federal footprint of the Department of Homeland Security looms large in the Crescent City.

Thus, El Congreso's shift to "Right to Remain" also meant much of my work went from fieldwork at the esquinas to office work, calling in A-Numbers (alien registration numbers) to help families of detained immigrants, accompanying immigrants for check-ins at the ICE field office, and driving the growing numbers of El Congreso members to the weekly meetings. From 2011 to 2012 the number of El Congreso members expanded from 40 regular attendees to well over 200 people. Instead of free food at meetings, Honduran street vendors began selling food outside of the nearby churches and gymnasiums to better match the membership growth.

As Stand members and other Black New Orleanians fought for the "Right to Return" to the city, El Congreso members began their fight for their "Right to Remain." Like Chatterjee's "spatialities of exploitation," these campaigns bridged the concepts of labor exploitation and land grabs, each incorporating a lens of analysis intersecting the fight for workers' rights and against displacement—from gentrification to deportation. Efforts to combat these "spatialities of exploitation" played out in direct actions that unified seemingly competing interests in respective campaigns led by Stand and El Congreso members.

The Section 3 Campaign and the Intersectional Approach to Worker Rights

In 2011, Stand members began a local-hire campaign to draw attention to community members left out of the decision-making for the reconstruction of the B. W. Cooper Public Housing Development, known as the Calliope Projects until 1981. The former public housing project located on the western edge of the Mid-City Planning District was demolished to make way for mixed-income housing, now called "Marrero Commons."[39] Mostly built between 1939 and 1969, the brick structures of the Calliope Projects had replaced wooden shotgun houses on the 192-acre lot, providing dense housing for working-class New Orleanians.[40]

As the city declined in the 1980s due to a plummeting tax base, market-based economic restructuring, and an oil bust that led to over 13.2 percent unemployment (6 percent higher than the national average), violent crime increased, particularly at B. W. Cooper. Nevertheless, rather than address root causes of this crime, politicians and developers added it to their list of justifications to demolish the area.

Their desire came true after Katrina. At the behest of the Department of Housing and Urban Development (HUD) and the Housing Authority of New Orleans (HANO), and much to the chagrin of residents, activists, and historic preservationists, the City Council voted unanimously in 2007 in favor of the demolition of the "Big Four" public housing units (three of which were located in the Mid-City Planning District) to make way for mixed-income housing.[41] The United Nations called for an immediate "halt" to the public housing demolition and for a redevelopment plan that protected the poorer and predominantly African Americans displaced by the disaster.[42] The City Council haughtily snubbed the UN's warnings.

Before demolition, some experts contended that renovation of the public housing units—which housed 5,146 people, the vast majority Black tenants—would have been the most efficient way to mitigate the housing crisis that left the majority of New Orleanians displaced.[43] Pre-existing predatory and discriminatory practices already plagued housing access for Black working-class residents, from high rent prices and low home-ownership rates that far surpassed national averages to housing discrimination that impacted a staggering 77 percent of Black renters.[44] With the public housing units gone, the mixed-income units built in their place replaced only 10 percent of the units demolished.[45] Poor and working-class people of color had no place to return and were forced to relocate. Immediately after Katrina, thousands of people wound up living in encampments that lined a half-mile stretch along Claiborne, in City Park, and at Duncan Plaza in front of city hall.[46]

When efforts to block demolition of the public housing failed, Black New Orleanians sought the right to work on these new development sites. Alfred Marshall, who eventually became an organizer with Stand, joined other B. W. Cooper residents who lived in the initial remaining 25 percent of the public housing and were locked out of their neighborhood redevelopment jobs, which were mostly going to white and immigrant workers. Residents of B. W. Cooper, such as Toya Ex Lewis, who also became an organizer with Stand, were even trained by HUD through a construction apprenticeship program but still were not hired. At the same time, some B. W. Cooper residents were also prevented from being hired due to felony records, yet another structural barrier through hyper-criminalization of Black communities.[47]

"I was born in Charity. But I came out of Brick City [B. W. Cooper]," is how Alfred introduced himself in our interview in 2020. Explaining how he became linked with Stand, Alfred said that the lead organizer, Colette Tippy, first approached him about collaborating with Stand. "She came up to my door asking if she could talk and I said, 'Hey white lady, that's fine, but I'm in a meeting right now, can you come back another time?'" he explained. "She said 'OK, sure I'll leave you a card and contact you later.'"

Soon after that, they began to educate themselves about federal housing policies and to strategize particularly around the 1968 HUD Section 3 Act, which stipulates that 30 percent of HUD-financed jobs must go to low-income local hires.[48] These informal meetings became the launching point for the campaign and the impetus for Alfred's own foray as an organizer with the Workers' Center.

"After three months I found my family," Alfred said about the Workers' Center and his immigrant colleagues. "People didn't look like me, but they had the same interests as me."

While El Congreso met every Wednesday night in the shotgun house in the Tremé, Stand members met on Tuesday nights to plan campaigns. At 217 N. Prieur they developed member-led strategies around the Section 3 policies. Then they began attending HANO meetings, putting pressure on the HANO director to audit Gibbs Construction Company and allow residents to monitor HANO's compliance.[49] The audits found what was expected—contractors did not hire local residents, and discrepancies in pay abounded.

In one example, white building framers made eighteen dollars an hour, compared with immigrant framers who made just fourteen dollars. As the evidence accumulated, Stand members increased pressure on both HANO and the developer, Larry Gibbs. A surprisingly amenable Gibbs told contractors that he was stopping the project until all contractors hired at least 30 percent local residents and increased wages.

Alfred said, "That night people were getting phone calls, 'Hey, do you wanna work, do you wanna work?'" Contractors also raised workers' wages.

In August 2011, Gibbs told the *Times-Picayune*, "But I don't think anyone appreciated what Section 3 was about. I don't think we did. Until this job."[50]

By organizing, educating, and operating through a multiracial framework, Stand members directly addressed the complex layers of disenfranchisement plaguing the post-Katrina milieu. The campaign fostered some levels of collaboration and negotiation with the developer *and* with the HANO director. Moreover, the campaign did not scapegoat immigrants; rather, immigrants forced accountability of the federal government's own policies while fighting for fair wages and for their right to these jobs on the lands on which their homes were demolished.

The Section 3 campaign intersected these spatialities of exploitation by drawing links between labor exploitation (worker disenfranchisement) and land dispossession (demolition of public housing). These links carried over to struggles for place for immigrant workers and their families and informed campaigns led by El Congreso that happened concurrently with Stand's Section 3 campaign. For example, in the next year, Stand members were arrested in solidarity in an El Congreso–led campaign against ICE raids, a direct action that took place from 2011 to 2013 to support the "Right to Remain" campaign.

Fighting ICE with Multiracial Solidarities

El Congreso's collective decision to shift from "Know Your Rights" to "Right to Remain" was a practical move. Discussing the origins of the campaign, lead organizer Jacinta Gonzalez stated that some people expected immigrant workers "to come, rebuild, and then go because they are migrants and, well, they just come and they go."

"What happens when people stay? And what happens when people feel ownership over their city?" she asked, rhetorically. "So that was the concept [of "Right to Remain"]—you can have participatory democracy in action, not because of citizenship, not because of votes, but because of sheer participation and pressure and power."

The "Right to Remain" campaign began in 2011 as an effort to end a collaboration between the Orleans Parish Prison (OPP) and ICE. ICE would issue an "immigration detainer," colloquially referred to as a "hold," by which ICE called on local jails and prisons to "hold" an immigrant for an additional forty-eight hours beyond their release date, allowing extra time for ICE agents to come to OPP to apprehend immigrants to initiate deportation proceedings. The process rendered already overloaded and corruption-plagued law enforcement officials at OPP as de facto immigration officers.

The OPP first moved in 1931 from its historic location in the Tremé neighborhood to its current location at Tulane and Broad—just a block away from Costa de Tela—on urbanized swampland, which was developed to take on the expanding city.[51] In the next ninety years, the OPP earned notoriety as one of the worst jails in the United States, monitored since 2013 under a perpetual federal consent decree for its countless cases of inmate deaths, suicides, abuse, and neglect.[52] After Katrina, over 600 imprisoned people were left behind in the OPP for up to four days with no water, food, or ventilation after the city was devastated.[53]

The "holds" and collaboration with ICE seemed like a small frog in a big, contaminated pond until El Congreso drew attention to two cases in which Sheriff Marlin Gusman held one individual for 91 days and another for 160 days, well beyond the forty-eight-hour stipulation. In February 2011, El Congreso leaders coordinated a twenty-four-hour prayer vigil in front of the OPP and a subsequent federal lawsuit against Sheriff Gusman (*Cacho v. Gusman*) for violating rights of due process and deprivation of liberty.[54] Thus, the "Right to Remain" campaign emerged from the members' experiences and understanding of what was happening on a local level.

"We started to really look at the mechanics of it," Jacinta said. "To be honest, no one was really doing that. Every time you would go to a national conference, everything was about Secure Communities. And it was very much centered on policy and DC lingo. But it didn't really get to what we were seeing on the day-to-day."

At the same time, because of the Workers' Center's multiracial scope, attention was drawn to the sheriff's office that went beyond just immigrants' rights to address the city's high incarceration rates and mistreatment of prisoners. Members of Stand met with El Congreso leaders to discuss their respective experiences with criminalization; they connected by detailing incidents of racial profiling and detention.

"ICE holds weren't only about migrant rights, but it was one of the many steps the sheriff and the City Council could take to decrease the city's addiction for incarceration," Jacinta explained. El Congreso members, like those in Stand, were able to grasp the complexities and nuances of this disenfranchisement and reach a multiracial analysis of the impact of state-sponsored criminalization on poor and working-class communities of color.

Yet even though El Congreso eventually won the lawsuit, Sheriff Gusman continued with the immigration detainers. After another egregious holds abuse case at OPP—a Honduran immigrant mother, Delmy Palencia, was held forty-one days—and after two more years of strategic organizing (which included a women's group talking to the sheriff's wife), El Congreso successfully pressured Gusman to end the holds in August 2013, making New Orleans the first southern city to adopt the noncompliant stance.[55] El Congreso members invited Gusman to their weekly Wednesday night meeting, chanting "Si se puede" (Yes we can) as the sheriff put on his newly gifted black-and-white El Congreso T-shirt in front of over 250 members at the meeting. One of just five white people in the space during the meeting, I stood against the wall on the side of the main stage in my usual location as a steadfast gofer. When Gusman approached the front of the meeting, he made an extra effort to shake my hand, nodded, and said, "Thank you." I wanted to say, "I'm just the driver." Even though the effort had been entirely directed by El Congreso, there is still a tendency to see gains in democracy or freedom as gifts given by white people.

While El Congreso won a major victory locally, it still faced ICE raids occurring at unprecedented levels. By the summer of 2013, it became clear that ICE had escalated its searches and agents were using racial profiling tactics to detain people, raiding spaces like apartment complexes, grocery stores, laundromats, and parks. One major raid took place at Ideal Market—the grocery store located just one block from Costa de Tela—when ICE agents blocked the store parking exit and indiscriminately stopped store patrons. After grocery shopping in August 2013, Ernesto, a member of El Congreso, attempted to leave the Ideal parking lot, but ICE agents forced him out of his car. Handcuffed and lined up with seven other men, Ernesto reported watching as an ICE agent kicked another man in the knees who tried to flee. Ernesto was eventually taken to a detention center to face deportation procedures.[56] An innocuous task like grocery shopping became a site of intimidation and fear.

As cases like Ernesto's grew, so did individual consultations, a free service offered to El Congreso members after Wednesday night meetings. Consultations during this period exceeded 100 per meeting and involved organizers documenting cases for follow-up testimonies, tracking raids, assisting with wrap-around services like doctors' appointments and ICE check-ins, and strategizing. By 2013, after Denis's departure, El Congreso had also hired more organizers to join Jacinta—Jolene Eberth and Fernando López. Jolene moved from Florida with experience working with Immokalee farmworkers. Fernando, originally from Mexico, had been living in Arizona and working with campaigns in Maricopa County.[57]

After going through a member's paperwork from his ICE release in September 2013, El Congreso organizers discovered that ICE agents had accidentally disclosed a New Orleans–based pilot program called the "Criminal Alien Removal Initiative" (CARI). The clandestine program, which had been underway for almost a year, involved indiscriminate raids across the city, coordination with local police, and the use of mobile biometric fingerprinting as a racially charged guess-and-check method to determine the immigration status of people.[58] Writing for *The Nation*, Zoë Carpenter called it a "Stop and Frisk for Latinos."[59]

El Congreso organizers and members quickly mobilized to plan a direct action, setting the date for November 14, 2013.[60] In the days leading up to the event, I joined El Congreso members and their families at the 217 N. Prieur office to plan the action and prepare materials. Members painted dozens of protest signs, made large fabric banners, and constructed a giant papier-mâché protest puppet depicting a villainous ICE director. On the day of the action, over 200 Workers' Center members and community leaders, equipped with the posters, banner, and puppet, met in front of city hall chanting "Ní una más deportación" (Not one more deportation) and "Sin papeles, sin miedo" (No papers, no fear) and then marched to the front of the ICE field office on Poydras Street in the downtown Central Business District.[61] When ICE officials failed to acknowledge the protesters, the direct action moved to the streets, blocking off the busy six-lane intersection of Poydras and Lasalle Streets for almost an hour. Police eventually intervened and, as part of the act of civil disobedience, arrested eighteen El Congreso members and four community leaders, including Alfred and another Stand member, Austin.

Once the arrests happened, I immediately drove Jacinta to OPP, attempting to beat the police van there, and witnessed firsthand Jacinta calling Sheriff Gusman, an unlikely bedfellow, to let him know about the situation. Although they had been adversaries just months prior, Jacinta's leverage with the sheriff and his growing critique of ICE helped ensure the quick and successful release of the twenty-two individuals, without charges. The action helped draw attention to the CARI raids, garnering national media coverage and even galvanizing support from US Congress member, Cedric Richmond, who wrote a letter condemning the raids.

Protesting the CARI raids in 2013. Photo by Fernando López, @sentir.con.ojos.

Addressed to the acting director of ICE, Richmond stated, "Profiling any race is not the American way and no one should be subject to unethical pursuit; especially not while accompanying your son at his school bus stop, while attending weekly Bible study meetings, or while purchasing food for your family at the local supermarket."[62] The CARI raids ended in January 2014. Two years later, as part of a federal consent decree, the NOPD's collaboration finally ended with ICE through a no-bias policy in 2016. Like Gusman, New Orleans police chief Michael Harrison attended El Congreso's meeting to address a cheerful crowded and put on the black-and-white El Congreso t-shirt.[63]

Fighting for the right to the city, Stand's organizing at B. W. Cooper and El Congreso's "Right to Remain" campaign demonstrate how building a strong, multiracial organizing base enabled the people most impacted by exploitative policies to fight against formidable state and private entities. In response, community members drew from their everyday experiences of dispossession and displacement, operating *both* outside and within state apparatuses to shape cities on their own terms. Pressuring developer Larry Gibbs and Sheriff Gusman—neither of whom are protagonists here—to just do their jobs correctly also enabled these communities to build leverage with these individuals. At the same time, these actions set precedents for future movements in New Orleans and beyond.

Stand and El Congreso members, with seemingly distinct experiences in post-Katrina New Orleans, connected their struggles and made concrete demands that better addressed their everyday needs. Acting collectively, they were able to shape the city on their own terms. Making these links on a local level is essential to building power to fight from the bottom-up against exploitative institutions and processes. Tracing examples of urban development and displacement, from Costa de Tela to Don Carlos's bar in Honduras, underscores how similar patterns of accumulation through dispossession materialize globally.

TELA: TRACING LEGACIES OF DEVELOPMENT AND DISPLACEMENT TO HONDURAS

While conducting fieldwork in Tela in 2015, I stayed in a hotel just blocks from the Caribbean Sea. It was a welcomed reprieve from weeks of bus travel along dusty roads visiting families across Honduras. I was surprised by how much Tela, a coastal city with a population of just over 100,000, reminded me of a smaller version of New Orleans, but specifically a New Orleans in sweltering July: largely unhampered by tourist hordes; horns and percussive sounds resonating from high school marching band practice; terra-cotta rooftops protecting colonial architecture from an ominous hurricane season; and street vendors ambling through open-air restaurants with offerings that ranged from necklaces (in New Orleans, Mardi Gras plastic beads; in Tela, plastic conch pearls) to alcohol (in New Orleans, Jell-O shots; in Tela, *gifiti*—an herb-infused elixir popular among the Garifuna people).

No doubt eating "southern soul food"—ribs and mashed potatoes—at a place called "the Bungalow" helped me link the places, too. Serving New Orleans flavors alongside Honduran dishes seemed like a perfect fit, considering the restaurant owner, Newman Taylor, who passed away in 2016, grew up with Jamaican Honduran parents just outside of New Orleans. Born in 1963, Newman eventually settled in Tela, working various jobs, including as a chef aboard an international ship, before opening the Bungalow in 2011. A handwritten "Apple Pie" sign in English alongside an announcement for weekly karaoke lured me in; Newman's generosity and charm kept me drinking beer and talking about New Orleans longer than I should have, especially considering my early morning the following day.

After the serendipitous southern meal at the Bungalow, I stopped by La Ensenada Resort, a gated hotel and convention center built in 2005. I was interested in La Ensenada's connections to the United Fruit Company—the resort had purchased land and derelict buildings previously owned by the company.[64] For much of the twentieth century, Tela was a main hub for United Fruit, serving as the headquarters for its railroad subsidiary, Tela Railroad Company.[65] "El Pulpo" laid the framework for corporate imperialism as one of the first giant agribusinesses and paved the way for government corruption and spatialities of exploitation that continue to plague the northern coastal region.[66]

At La Ensenada, a large metal fence fortified by a forest of thick palm trees lined the periphery of the resort. Surrounding the compound, yellow-painted buildings joined refurbished cottage houses that once belonged to United Fruit. Historian Ronald Harpelle referred to these types of United Fruit housing as "the white zones," which he defines as "planned communities constructed to house the families of managers, mechanics, engineers, and other skilled workers of European descent."[67] It seemed a version of the white zones remained.

The next morning, Don Carlos sent a driver, Antonio, to meet me for the twenty-kilometer ride to his village. As we left the city, the landscape quickly transitioned from industrial to rural homogeneity, with palm tree groves consuming the roadside. Planted in meticulous rows, the individual reddish fruits grew in dense, pumpkin-sized clusters and resembled a cross between an acorn and a cherry. United Fruit first introduced palm oil to Honduras in 1937 as an alternative to bananas during a blight.[68] Tanya Kerssen explains that peasant-led movements in the 1960s pressured the Honduran government to distribute land to small cooperatives to cultivate palm oil.[69] But by the 1990s, market-centric agrarian reform transferred much of the arable flat land from small palm oil cooperatives to the major corporations like Grupo Jaremar and Grupo Dinant.

Production of coffee, which is the country's top food export, also expanded significantly during this economic restructuring, yet, unlike palm oil, coffee production was still mostly farmed by small-scale landholders, like Denis and his family. Modernization reforms helped develop roads in rural mountainous areas where coffee grew, but not to the scale implemented by the banana industry, which had already established infrastructure along the flat coastal regions connecting nearby ports and cities.[70] This existing infrastructure facilitated the shift from bananas to palm oil in the northern coastal regions in the 1990s.[71] By 1998, Hurricane Mitch further exacerbated this shift as disaster capitalism logics took shape and wealthy landowners capitalized on the vulnerability, especially along the coast.

When the hurricane hit, Chiquita lost 100 percent of its banana crop. Instead of replanting for the next season, many of the plantations closed their banana operations, and the lands were replanted with palm oil.[72] From 1996 to 2014, palm oil production grew by 30 percent.[73]

Palm oil is in over 50 percent of all processed foods, ranging from Oreos and instant noodles to peanut butter. Honduras ranks eighth in the world in palm oil production and third in Latin America (behind Ecuador and Colombia), producing 300,000,000 kilograms of palm oil annually.[74] US food industries have increasingly become dependent on palm oil, further feeding the demand. Scholars like Kerssen increasingly draw attention to the role of palm oil industries in forcing migration and displacement as wealthy landowners take over most of the arable coastal land.[75]

The level of corruption and corporate kickbacks linked with politicians and palm oil executives is reminiscent of the United Fruit Company's ability to manipulate and maneuver the government in the company's favor. In her research on "narcopoliticos" (the connection between narco-traffickers and politicians), Karen Spring notes how politicians collude with developers to create fronts that channel money from inflated government contracts. In her work, Spring cites a testimony from a former palm oil plantation owner turned informant who flipped for the DEA to testify against Tony Hernández, who was sentenced to life in prison in 2019 in the Southern District of New York on charges of narco-trafficking and murder.[76] Hernández is a former Honduran congressman and brother of Juan Orlando Hernández, president from 2014 to 2022, who was found guilty in a US federal district court for drug trafficking and arms.[77] Vestiges of cronyism and corruption abound.

Leaving the luxury of the paved Calletera 13, Antonio and I turned onto a dirt road leading to a small town. After a few bumpy miles, Antonio said, "It's a factory," pointing to the threshers, tanks, and fruit pressers all connected through an oxidized conveyor belt used to produce the palm oil. We stopped in front of a row of worn-down bungalow houses with the same character as the white zones at La Ensenada. "Those were from the United Fruit," explained Antonio. "Now the [palm oil] factory managers and their families live there." I later confirmed that the San Alejo Company, part of the Grupo Jaremar Corporation, bought up many of the plantations formerly owned by the United Fruit Company, expanding its monopoly to 14,500 hectares in the Tela region.[78] In a loan application, the corporation used violence and job creation as justifications for the expansion of its land and to secure $20 million in financing from a private investor.[79]

For the rest of the drive, the small car's pace was at the mercy of the narrow dirt road filled with potholes, small ravines, and the occasional herd of pigs. Don Carlos's village seemed to emerge suddenly from the palm frond monotony. Approximately fifty houses, an open-air school, a municipal building, and his bar lined the main road. Nets were hung out to dry, strewn across trees in front of homes where people sat, tending to their patios or cleaning equipment. As we parked, Don Carlos approached us from a modest portico with a roof just large enough to cover three pristine pool tables. We introduced ourselves and then immediately called Don Carlos's eldest daughter, Adriana, back in New Orleans, to let her know I had made it safely. We made small talk about his bar and his role in the village.

"Like Adriana and them have Costa de Tela, I have my bar," he said. "People come from all around."

I asked about the background of the village. He pointed down the road. "We used to be a fishing community because we are so close to the ocean and the lagoon," he said. I later learned that hunting and fishing restrictions had destroyed the livelihoods of many of the fishers in Don Carlos's village.[80]

"I want to show you something," he said. As we strolled farther down the main street in the Honduran summer heat, a river ran parallel to us about 100 yards from our path. The waterway seemed small and innocuous with some children splashing on the bank as a woman washed laundry. Most of the houses looked empty, except for a few newer builds on stilts. As we came closer, Don Carlos explained that floodwaters had devastated the strip in November 2013 when a landowner undammed a tributary to divert the waters from flooding his palm oil fields and intentionally flooded the small village instead. As the water levels began to rise, the newspaper *La Prensa* reported that town officials from the village filed a police report against the illegal rerouting of these waters, but the prosecutor did nothing to protect the town. Almost all the people were evacuated—266 people in total.[81] No one was killed, but the water devastated the northern part of the village.

As we walked toward the lagoon, Don Carlos signaled toward a building buried in sediment that reached as high as the front doorknob. "That is where I had my pool tables," he said, pointing to what once was the patio of his former bar but now looked half-swallowed in quicksand. Tops of furniture peeked out above the dirt as faded Salva Vida beer advertisements drooped from the wall. He next pointed to a cinder-block house on a corner and told me that it was Adriana's old house. It was buried in soil and sand. The estuary, where the river meets the lagoon, went from being a source of prosperity and livelihood to an imminent and volatile force created by the agro-industry and exacerbated by the destruction of wetlands.[82]

"No one can live here. She has nothing to come back to," he said despondently.

Don Carlos's former bar abutted Laguna de los Micos, a 150-square-mile lagoon that separates his village from the Caribbean Sea, just three miles away as the crow flies. The lagoon provides sustenance for much of the biodiversity in the coastal region and serves as a valued resource for the nearby Afro-Honduran and campesino villages. After spending the next day at Garifuna villages located across the lagoon from Don Carlos's village, I learned the extent of the impact of the fishing regulations.

Immediately upon arriving at the Garifuna villages, I randomly met Junior, a Bay Island Creole, which is a group of English-speaking Afro-Honduran people originally brought to work on banana plantations in the late nineteenth century. Junior eagerly walked me around the sleepy village, which consisted of thatched-roof huts, no electricity, and small restaurants specializing in fresh juices and fried whole fish with plantains. Black and Indigenous communities, such as the Bay Island Creoles and Garifuna, established thriving fishing settlements along the coastal regions of Honduras. These communities developed rich cultural traditions in food, dance, and language, leading to their recognition as a UNESCO "Masterpiece of the Oral and Intangible Cultural Heritage of Humanity" in 2001. Despite this prestigious acknowledgment, the culture and well-being of these communities remain inadequately protected and safeguarded.[83]

Wearing a red polo shirt with the blue, yellow, and white Chiquita Brands logo, Junior explained that the survival of his communities was in jeopardy because of fishing regulations that had destroyed the local economy.

"But that's the real problem," he said, pointing down the beach at a giant complex of tall buildings fortified with a massive iron gate.

The encroaching Indura Beach and Golf Resort, a high-end hotel and resort that boasts its occupation of twenty-six miles of Tela Bay, has been an ongoing struggle for the Garifuna people since the 1990s. Indura, which ironically means "Honduras" in the Garifuna language, is a mega-development sponsored by the Honduran government and private businesses, with partial funding by the Inter-American Development Bank.[84] These stakeholders justified the land grabs by deeming Garifuna land use as unproductive, reinforcing job creation, and highlighting the potential of increased tourism to the Garifuna communities.[85] The government justified the development by claiming the resort would bring in 6,000 direct jobs and 18,000 indirect jobs.[86]

Here, spatialities of exploitation play out through the false promise of job creation in the tourism industry used to expropriate lands while concomitantly outlawing small-scale fishing, an industry that has sustained Garifuna, Bay Island Creoles, and coastal campesinos for centuries. The initial development of Indura included filling in 216 acres of the lagoon, destroying a significant amount of the wetlands in the lagoon and the surrounding Jeannette Kawas National Park.[87] While fisher communities are scapegoated as perpetrators of the wetland devastation, resorts are greenlighted to build more golf courses and ecotour adventures.

The latest land grab effort against the Garifuna communities occurred in 2014 when local military officials violently evicted people from their beachside villages, citing eminent domain.[88] Junior described the event in detail, explaining how the military police woke him up in the middle of the night and forced him out as they set fire to and destroyed his beachfront hut. No homes were spared that night. Many people, like Junior, rebuilt their homes; others fled. The state-sponsored violence for the sake of private companies has been successful as thousands of Garifuna people have since migrated to the United States.[89]

Pressure came from international organizations to challenge the Honduran government's support of these violent land grabs. An Organization of American States (OAS) group called the Inter-American Commission on Human Rights ordered the Honduran government to return land to ancestral owners, which the government refused to do.[90] When climate change was officially recognized in 2018 as a driver of migration by the UN's Global Compact for Migration, the Honduran government flouted international pressures to address this systemic issue.[91] Most recently, in 2020 the OAS anti-corruption body called the Mission to Support the Fight against Corruption and Impunity in Honduras, which had major success in bringing down two powerful Hondurans from 2015 to 2020, was refused a contract renewal by the Honduran Congress, which claimed the group had overstepped its power. The OAS General Secretariat called the end of the program a "negative step in the fight against corruption and impunity in the country."[92]

As supranational powers—UN designations and OAS oversight programs—offer limited recourse, the Honduran government instead doubles down on privatization programs. Beth Geglia illustrates how "model cities" initiatives, aka Zones for Economic Development through Employment, operate as autonomous regions run by private entities on Honduran lands. The latest target is called Crawfish Rock, a Bay Island Creole fishing community on the island of Roatán, just eighty-five miles off the coast from Tela.[93] The Zone for Economic Development through Employment program was crafted at a think tank founded by the grandson of Milton Friedman (the mastermind of the rise of neoliberalism) and funded by the big-tech architect behind biometrics systems like Palantir, one of the biometrics systems used by ICE to regulate and surveil immigrants. Ronald Reagan's son Michael served on one of the advisory councils.[94] The spawn of privatization is alarming and ruthless and runs deep.

When communities fight back—and they do, relentlessly—they are met with violence, repression, and more subtle forms of retaliation.[95] The retaliation has lasted since the 1990s. Jeannette Kawas National Park was named after an environmental activist who defended the park surrounding Laguna de los Micos from the expansion of palm oil. After Kawas was murdered in 1995, the Inter-American Commission on Human Rights declared the State of Honduras responsible for her death. Her case, *Kawas-Fernandez v. Honduras*, set legal precedent for governments in the Americas to protect at-risk human rights and environmental defenders, yet it has had little impact. Likewise, immediately after filing a lawsuit in 1997 against the Tela Municipal Authorities for granting investors "erroneous deeds" in their quest to build Indura, three of the leaders of the Land Defense Committee of Triunfo de la Cruz, a Garifuna community outside of Tela, were murdered; the cases remain unresolved, but the incident sent a message of intimidation throughout the nearby communities.[96]

More recent groups have been successful in their resistance efforts, despite murders of and death threats against organizers.[97] Groups like the United People of the Agúan and the Council of Popular and Indigenous Movements of Honduras have successfully organized small agricultural cooperatives to protect workers from private developments.[98] The Black Fraternal Organization of Honduras has been one of the loudest voices in fighting corruption, land grabs, and state violence as well as in advocating for food security issues.

In the Agúan Valley, 100 miles southeast of Tela, organizing efforts, led by Berta Cáceres, were successful in blocking mega-projects like the construction of the Agua Zarca Dam, a joint project between the Honduran company Desarrollos Energéticos SA and the Chinese-owned Sinohydro.[99] On March 3, 2016, Cáceres was brutally killed in retaliation for her organizing work.

Roberto David Castillo Mejía, the US military–trained and former director of Desarrollos Energéticos, was found guilty of her murder in 2021.[100] The future of community-led development in Honduras is grim, not because of apathy but because of fear of death by government-backed security forces. Five Garifuna men were kidnapped in Triunfo de la Cruz in July 2020; one of the daughters of the kidnapped men lives in New Orleans.[101] Overall, more than 100 activists have been murdered in Honduras since the 2009 coup that ousted Zelaya.[102]

Ubiquitous retaliatory measures filled with graft, cruelty, and violence ensure that private sector industries can operate without regard for the people and the environment and demonstrate the lengths the Honduran private sector and government will go to quell opposition to exploitative models of development. The garrisoned walls around gated resorts create an appearance of luxury and safety from the poverty and violence as these development projects build upon the neocolonial legacies of the United Fruit Company, occupying the same lands and infrastructure to establish their own cultural and political hegemonies while undercutting democracy. People like Don Carlos and Junior have little choice but to be resilient, constantly rebuilding their bars and huts, as these spatialities of exploitation play out with impunity.

CONCLUSION

Tracing the story of the two food establishments—Costa de Tela in Mid-City and Don Carlos's bar in coastal Honduras—enables us "to see food as a reflection of sociopolitical relations that are much broader than what is on our plates."[103] Starting with the *sopa de caracol* dish at Costa de Tela helps situate the Afro-Honduran cultural origins of this important coastal tradition that centers the migration processes of the people who share and produce these foodscapes. Adriana and her family's restaurant in New Orleans and Don Carlos's bar near Tela are connected on a macro level: networks of capital-driven development and single food commodity markets that build on historical precedent of accumulation through dispossession.

Beyond the familial ties and the *sopa de caracol* is a tale of people struggling for their right to land amid extractive industries that dominate development models. Like El Congreso's "Right to Remain" framework, the Honduran resistance consists of campesino, Black, and Indigenous–led organizations that have fought doggedly against exploitative models of development. These examples deepen understandings of "right to the city" frameworks, particularly how people operate within and outside the state to shape a place. These case studies also underscore limitations of "liberal-democratic frameworks" of "right to the city" applications when relying on entities like the United Nations and the OAS. Aimed at the state level, liberal-democratic frameworks are symbolic, incremental, and easily defanged or flouted rather than transformative and power-building, led by the people most impacted.[104]

Food establishments are inevitably about places and the people who make those places meaningful. And places are dynamic and constantly changing as people come and go. Restaurants close, menus adapt, signage adjusts—all examples embedded in this chapter. Yet too often injustices emerge when uneven power structures determine profit-driven visions of development and dictate who can fit into white reimaginings and sanitized tourist sites. Cultural spaces, neighborhood blocks, public housing, and coastal villages are demolished just to add another golf course or shiny new complex. Meanwhile, narratives of violence or job creation are used as a means to justify these "thefts of space" and do little to acknowledge, let alone fix, the systemic failures that foster and perpetuate these systems.[105] Structural issues of poverty, mass incarceration, and dispossession are not solved or even ameliorated; rather, they are excuses used to further marginalize people or to hide behind gated walls, creating a false sense of security.

During an El Congreso meeting in 2013, which addressed the growing number of ICE raids taking place in the city, a member stood up in front of the audience in the packed church gymnasium and proclaimed, "The struggle began as a right to land in my country and continues as a fight for the right to my new city." The audience members erupted in applause. With the ICE raids plaguing New Orleans, it was difficult to grasp the complexity of his statement. Nevertheless, I jotted the comment in my notes and sat through the rest of the meeting. Going to Honduras in 2015 helped me to better interpret what he meant. Following the stories allowed me to connect these dots between people and places to make more legible the web of uneven capitalist systems as well as the powerful resistance that emerged.

In June 2016, a group in New Orleans called Los Indignados de New Orleans (The Indignant of New Orleans) marched in transnational solidarity demanding an end to impunity and corruption in Honduras. Waving protest signs and banging pots as part of a *caceroloza* (a form of popular protest), Honduran immigrants marched from the Mid-City neighborhood to the Tremé. One of the handmade signs read "Our remittances sustain the Honduran Economy." Often these remittances go toward purchasing land in their home country, because lack of access to land is a driver of poverty and immigration.[106] For example, Denis purchased seventeen acres of land in Honduras to cultivate coffee prior to his return in 2011. When I visited the family of Sofia, a Honduran street vendor based in New Orleans who sold food at El Congreso meetings, her formerly landless and itinerant family proudly showcased a modest plot of land they purchased with remittances Sofia had sent back.[107] The land is used to cultivate small red beans for home consumption and to sell at market. After my visit with Sofia's mom in 2015, she sent me back to New Orleans with a five-pound sack of freshly harvested beans. Sofia beamed with pride, knowing that her investment provided her family some degree of self-sufficiency. Even as land rights are constantly threatened, land access is central to people who have left and who may want to return.

Understanding the cultural and everyday realities of a place (use value) is vital, because too often value is based solely on speculative price (exchange value), thus fostering this insatiable, capitalist desire for bigger and more. Redistribution of lands and investment in public institutions would be an important start, or *lupipati, lupipami* (a little for you, a little for me), as the song "Sopa de Caracol" puts it.

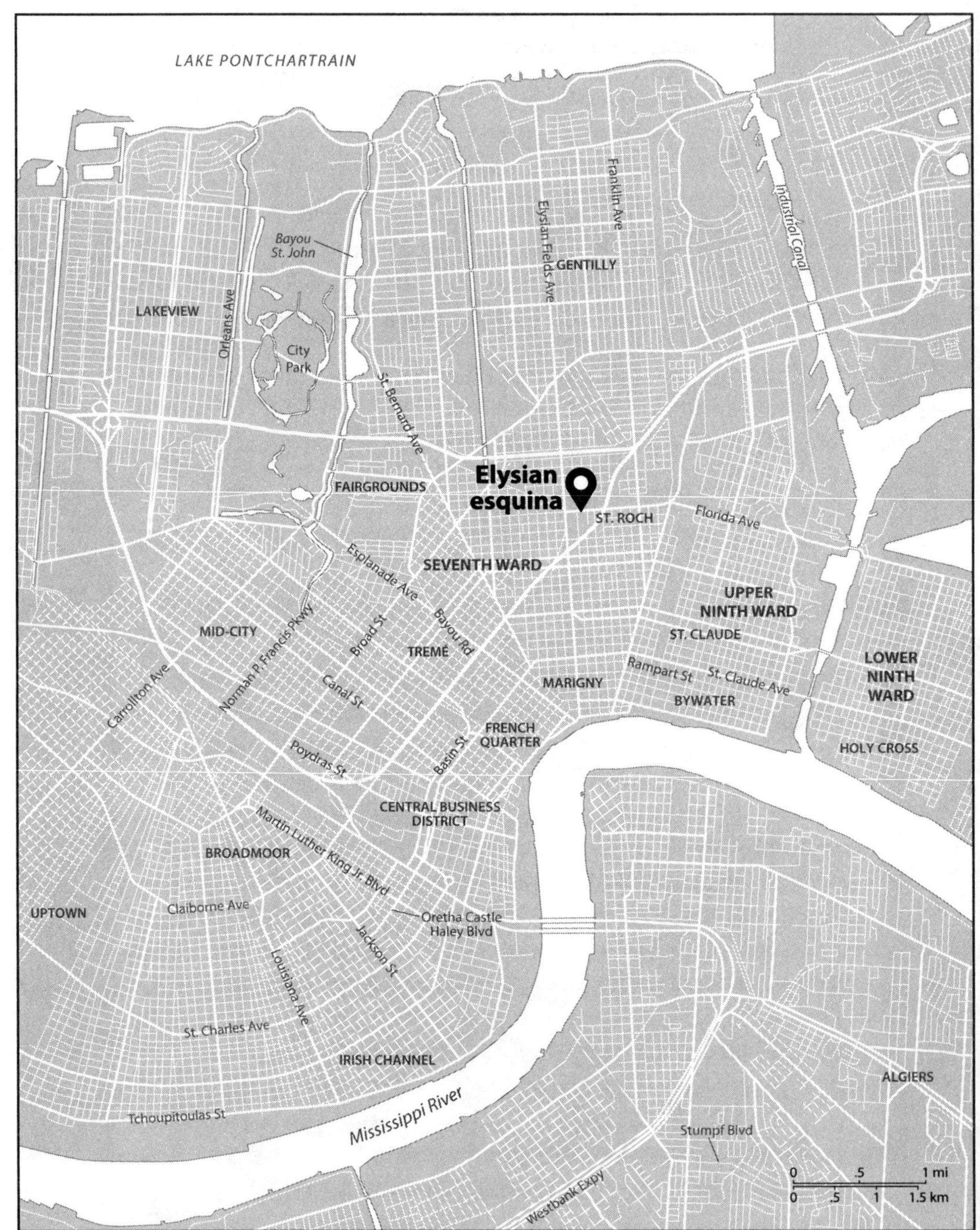

Elysian esquina in New Orleans.

Chapter 3

Right to Culture

Navigating Crackdowns on Street Hustles

If it's not a cycle of imprisonment,
it's a cycle of debt.

— TOYA EX LEWIS, former Stand with Dignity organizer, 2020

We challenge this idea that the culture serves the City while the City doesn't serve the Culture. Harassment & restriction of street culture.

— WENDELL PIERCE, on Twitter, in response to the city's proposed permits for vendors, 2012

They are the instruments through which the human imagination is smashed and shattered. Insurrectionary moments are moments when this bureaucratic apparatus is neutralized.

— DAVID GRAEBER, *Revolution in Reverse*, 2007

Talk about undocumented, these are undocumented people! When you're talking about sanctuary, you gotta have sanctuary for Black people, too. It's the same thing under a different name; we're all being separated from our families.

— ALFRED MARSHALL, referring to impacts of fines and fees on poor and working-class Black people, 2020

Beneath the Elysian Fields Avenue overpass, which spans Florida Avenue, dozens of day laborers congregate at the base of five mature live oak trees in front of a Lowe's Home Improvement. The esquina goes mostly unnoticed by passersby because it sits adjacent to the overpass and is accessed by a road that feeds only into a derelict junction and an industrial rail yard. Of the five major esquinas that emerged after Katrina, the Elysian Fields day-laborer corner is the largest and most complex, and it's the only esquina where Denis recommended that I stay in the car during most of our visits. He'd cautiously whisper, "Dicen cualquier cosa" (They'll say anything). Given his experience working and organizing on the corner, it was enough to keep me in the car. Instead, I'd watch from the driver's seat after grabbing some food from Taqueria DF, a lonchera parked on the access road close by.

Like many restaurants and taco trucks in New Orleans (and elsewhere), the food establishment carried a Mexican name—Taqueria DF—yet the lonchera was staffed by Honduran cooks who made a mix of Honduran and Mexican dishes. In 2011, the nondescript, white-painted single-axle trailer had two concession windows with awnings open on either side. The lonchera hitched to a silver Dodge Ram, which held a trash can and other supplies in its bed. Three Honduran women nestled in the eighty-square-foot kitchen, working side by side, almost in dance-like fashion, taking orders, making change, and preparing foods. With the griddles constantly running and the hot plates warming *guisos*, the compact setting turned into a sauna in the sweltering and relentless New Orleans heat.

One of the perks of the Elysian Fields esquina was the proximity to Taqueria DF and the *baleadas* made there. Denis claimed they were the best in the city. Until I moved to New Orleans, I had never heard of a baleada but learned quickly about the dish's significance and variations. Legend has it that the baleada was popularized in the coastal Honduran city La Ceiba in the 1960s by Doña Tere, a single mother and street food vendor. In the early twentieth century, Italian immigrants like the Vaccaro family—who lived in New Orleans and built the banana company that became Standard Fruit—brought flour with them to Honduras to make their pastas and breads. Hondurans, who were more accustomed to corn, yucca, or plantains for their starch, began to experiment with the wheat flour at home. With her food stand, Doña Tere merely popularized the baleada her mom made that she grew up eating.[1] Now the dish is ubiquitous.

A baleada is a uniquely Honduran meal served as breakfast but often offered all day. The variations range from a baleada *sencilla* (simple) and baleada *mixta* (mixed) to a baleada *con todo* (with everything) that can include anything. The shell of the baleada starts as dough made from flour, baking powder, water, and fat (oil, butter, or lard) initially formed into a shape resembling a mozzarella ball. When ready, the cook stretches the dough evenly to form a large, flat circle with an approximately six-inch diameter that is placed on the *comal* (griddle or skillet) to fry. Once it has browned on either side, the thick and flakey tortilla resembles a mix between a burrito shell and naan.

The baleada *sencilla* is filled with refried red beans, crema, and crumbled Honduran cheese and then folded over.[2] *Mixta* is a *sencilla* but with scrambled egg. And *con todo* specifies a bit more complexity—meat, scrambled egg, and oftentimes avocado. At Taqueria DF, Gloria knew my order—baleada *con todo* with salsa *verde*. The tangy crema and the velvety avocado cut the saltiness of the tender meat and rich beans, providing a filling lunch for a meager four dollars.

At the Elysian Fields esquina, I observed lots of action from my driver's seat, often while eating a baleada *con todo*. On one occasion in 2011, I watched from my car as Officer V.—the only Spanish-language speaker in the New Orleans Police Department at the time—ordered food from Taqueria DF. As he made his order, the conversation between the women cooking and Officer V. seemed good-natured—at least at first. In contrast, the day laborers immediately took some distance from the police officer, moving toward the much-needed shade of a live oak tree that towered above. I kept my eyes on Officer V., who dominated conversation with his Colombian-accented Spanish—a distinction from the speech of the mostly Honduran and Mexican day laborers. After about ten minutes, the women handed him a plastic bag with a Styrofoam container. He reached for the bag through the concession window and paid with a handful of cash; as they made change, Officer V. laid a piece of paper on the stainless steel counter, walked a few feet back to his patrol car, and left.

By that point, Denis had returned to the car and sat with me eating his own baleada *con todo*. He turned and looked at me square in the eyes and said, "Les dió un ticket" (He gave them a ticket).

"A ticket?" I asked in disbelief.

"Sí," he said as we approached the lonchera. The women were angry. It turned out that the ticket was a parking citation because the truck was in violation of a policy that, at the time, required food trucks to move from their location every thirty minutes. The women knew the rule, just like the majority of other food truck operators across the city knew the rule, but few followed it because there was rarely any enforcement and the terms were so egregious. Thirty minutes was hardly enough time to prepare a single dish, let alone make a living.

Out-of-touch policies beget erratic enforcement, which breeds injustice and mistrust, especially in poor and working-class communities. But such policies and regulations began to be enforced as part of a general aim to maintain "order" in the post-Katrina normalization period between 2011 to 2012, taking particular aim at cultural purveyors—from street food vendors to musicians—who encountered hyper-policing amid an already precarious livelihood.[3] Through the mayor's newly formed "Office of Cultural Economy," culture became something inherently tied to economic utility and an "engine of capital development," thus prioritizing exchange value of culture for market return and a tourist gaze over use value, which was shaped and defined by local people's everyday consumption.[4]

Viewing culture vis-à-vis its economic productivity engenders a hierarchy of culture, determining whose culture fits and whose doesn't.[5] Regulation is created to exclude, and the consequences can be dire, putting undocumented people at risk of deportation and Black people at risk of exacerbated charges. Thus, right to culture refers to the right of individuals to produce culture in the interests of their communities and in response to their communities in a way that reacts to what is taking place on the ground and is defined democratically from the bottom up.

This chapter is about the regulation of street vendors and the right to culture, centering on how crimes are created through bureaucratic means.[6] Focusing on how Central American and Mexican immigrants' somewhat new forms of food culture and cultural production fit within Black-led cultural institutions that shaped the city's core, I argue that the criminalization of immigrant street food vendors mirrored the criminalization of Black cultural producers, particularly at second line parades and at-home side hustles.

This chapter is also about the resistance—how people, especially women, navigated these regulations, organized, and created alternative systems that resisted formalization. Street food vendors operated by asserting insurgent rights that took shape because these groups were denied legal pathways due to structural barriers, racialized legislation, and white spatial imaginaries that defined top-down policymaking.[7] In response to this criminalization, Workers' Center subgroups—El Congreso and Stand with Dignity—shifted their scope to address these issues, particularly through a focus on the fines and fees through campaigns like "Right to Remain" and NOLA Shakedown.

Throughout the chapter, the term "street food vendors" is defined broadly and encompasses a range of enterprises, from pop-up bars and barbecue grills to taco trucks and tamale vendors, and includes any form of vending that eschews licensing and permitting.[8] For this chapter, I include many of the lonchera owners along with itinerant street vendors because at that time, many lonchera owners operated without proper licensing and disregarded the stipulations of the "food truck" policy in place at the time.

THE PIVOTAL 2010–2012 ENFORCEMENT AND RESISTANCE CONTEXT

In 2011, six years after Katrina devastated the city and the year I began with the Workers' Center, city officials under the Mitch Landrieu administration began to aggressively enforce oftentimes antiquated city policies that had been mostly overlooked for years. At the same time, by request of the Landrieu administration, the Department of Justice submitted a report that revealed major corruption and civil rights violations by the NOPD. By 2012, a consent decree—considered the most expansive consent decree in the United States at the time—was put in place, promising sweeping reforms for the police department.[9]

The Obama administration deported a record-breaking 391,953 people in the same year.[10] The Secure Communities initiative, implemented during the Bush era in 2008, had cemented a partnership between ICE officers and local law enforcement. While the program purported to deport only individuals with major criminal offenses, 79 percent of the deportations under Secure Communities were of people with low-level offenses and no criminal record.[11] With a ticket for trespassing or for parking too long in one spot, vendors risked deportation.[12]

By the time Denis returned to Honduras in November 2011, my role shifted from driver and corner visitor to dutiful factotum under Jacinta Gonzalez, the lead El Congreso organizer. My new duties reflected the larger reframing of El Congreso, which had moved from a "Know Your Rights," labor-oriented campaign to an anti-deportation campaign focused on the right to remain. With Denis gone and an increase in deportations and ICE presence, El Congreso leaders sought to reframe their campaign to combat deportation threats while also addressing the worker exploitation that still permeated the city. It wasn't that exploitative labor abuses had miraculously ended; rather, workers continued to be exploited *and* criminalized.

Instead of going to the corners with Denis, I'd do direct accompaniment. Meaning that I'd go to court to help people navigate municipal, traffic, and district court hearings and assist them in dealing with other outstanding issues identified through the *consultas* (individual meetings), which took place after each Wednesday night meeting. I had to iron my shirts for court appearances, and I spent a lot of time at a desk helping locate people who had court dates or who faced deportation. Accompanying individuals to help them take care of fines and fees from traffic and municipal court became a branch of the "Right to Remain" campaign.

At the same time, the work of Stand with Dignity also expanded from a sole focus on housing and worker rights to include the fight against criminalization of the poor and working-class Black community. By 2012, Stand enjoyed major victories on local and national levels that included Section 3 policy enforcement, wage increases, job mobility, and a training policy for local workers on publicly funded construction projects. Yet, Stand organizers realized that many of their members and extended community were locked out of jobs and housing due to felony records and arrest warrants from outstanding fines and subsequent fees that had accrued from minor municipal and traffic violations. Thus, as the city tightened up surveillance and criminalization of poor and working-class communities and as ICE beefed up its deportation regime, the Workers' Center subgroups mobilized and reframed their priorities to reflect these shifts.

Street vendors like Mateo individually noted the increased enforcement in New Orleans, each commenting that officers who used to purchase food from them instead gave warnings that they would start enforcing regulations. In some cases, police officers assisted the vendors in figuring out how to get licensing. In 2011, in anticipation of reforms from the consent decree, Police Chief Ronal Serpas sent Officer V. to Nashville, Tennessee, to train under the "El Protector" program to improve services for non-English-speaking communities.[13] When he returned, Officer V. launched New Orleans's own version of "El Protector," with the goal of building trust in Vietnamese- and Spanish-language neighborhoods instead of "focusing specifically on enforcement measures."[14]

In an interview with me in 2018, Officer V. spoke highly of the program and explained how it focused more on outreach with communities and on cultural awareness and language training with police officers. He also assisted city hall's permitting process by doing "test runs" with Spanish speakers to navigate the system in place.

Second line buckjumping in the Upper Ninth Ward.
Photo by Fernando López, @sentir.con.ojos.

"El Protector has an umbrella that covers many things, so it's not only public safety," he said. "It's actually survival. And that is survival: getting that permit." However, as the aforementioned example of Taqueria DF and the case studies in this chapter show, despite the El Protector program, enforcement measures remained in place, and acquiring permits was not always that easy: the bureaucracy, language barriers, and inspection fees often proved to be a deterrent for many vendors who had established consistent clientele and who were used to the freewheeling nature of the post-Katrina milieu. And, often, Officer V. was the enforcer, not the protector.

Further, in 2011 the city also increased enforcement by revising policy and regulating the city's second line parades, a long-standing cultural tradition led by New Orleans's Black communities. Second lines are parades that run throughout the year, usually on Sundays, and include brass bands, brightly colored and coordinated outfits, and buckjumping-style step dance and are hosted by different Social Aid and Pleasure Clubs.[15] Second lines emerged from the jazz funeral tradition (the main line) when outside spectators joined the jazz funeral (forming the second line) to fill the streets with music and dancing. The tradition dates to the nineteenth century, when Black New Orleanians established benevolent societies and Social Aid and Pleasure Clubs during segregation as a financial support to defray health care costs amid a racialized and insufficient health care system.[16]

At each second line parade, dozens of street vendors sell food and drink to the parade-goers, offering up a range of items from barbecue pork sandwiches and bottled water to cocktails served from makeshift bars set up in the beds of pickup trucks. Some vendors interweave through the crowds, parading through the streets with wagons filled with ice-cold beers hidden haphazardly below bottles of soda and water. Other vendors remain stationary, posting up on the neutral ground (median) slinging sausages and burgers from grills.

While each parade has a set of stops at neighborhood bars during the roughly four-hour-long trek, the vendors provide an important service for the hundreds and sometimes thousands of parade participants. Most notably, they coordinate with the Social Aid and Pleasure Clubs and are self-organized. Nevertheless, in 2011, the mayor's advisor on cultural economy negotiated with parade organizers and initially sought to charge a $500 yearly fee for each vendor, require vendors to clean up litter around their post, and prohibit the sale of alcohol.

Like the process of formalizing policy for taco truck owners, some second line vendors were on board with the move to sanction vendors, even if it meant more paperwork and the prohibition of some sales. Tired of shirking police, this echelon of vendors sought more degrees of formality and no longer wanted to operate under a penumbra of precarity. Other street vendors—immigrants and Black New Orleanians alike—preferred the figurative shadows precisely because structural barriers had locked them out of formal systems due to language barriers, ceaseless bureaucracy, felony records, undocumented status, warrant attachments, and histories of worker exploitation. Fear and mistrust in these systems came from a combination of corruption, hyper-surveillance, and criminalization plaguing the city. Instead, street food vendors imagined alternatives to these formalized economies by building infrastructure and support systems that self-organized and relied on a collective need rather than on an outside and inconsistent policing system that disproportionately impacted communities of color.

Oftentimes people enter the informal sector as street food vendors because they are unable to access jobs in the formal sector, they need flexibility in order to supplement income, they need to take care of family members, or they can make much more money on their own.[17] While informal economies force people to take on more risk in terms of purchasing equipment, lack of stability, and being ticketed by law enforcement, these economies also provide autonomy, help to reinforce community ties, and offer efficient systems of serving familiar, accessible, and affordable foods. Despite these vulnerabilities, and in part by taking advantage of these systems, vendors in the informal sector create networks and systems of self-reliance to forge their own economic and cultural spaces that defy capitalist structures perpetuated by a tourism sector.[18]

When city authorities opt to revise rather than relax or jettison policies, case studies in this chapter show how such policy revisions can become too specific and contingent, failing to reflect what's actually playing out on the ground.[19] This increased regulation produces and exacerbates vulnerabilities, and the enforcement of these policies is erratic and racialized.[20] In New Orleans after Katrina, overtaxed police officers were tasked with regulating communities who already self-regulated. Complaints stemmed from business owners who claimed to be encumbered by sporadic competition and from white transplants who clutched their pearls over trash in the streets or over noise from short-lived brass bands and bounce music playing in their block.

Outside of New Orleans, these expectations of laissez-faire as status quo may seem extraordinary and, perhaps, illicit; nevertheless, this freewheeling spirit is defined by the people, is what shapes the local culture, and is what services largely poor and working-class communities. Because immigrant street food vendors and second line vendors provide for local populations, these informal economies have, thus far, defied commodification; precisely because they serve a New Orleans–based public—oftentimes outside the tourism zones—they avoid pandering to a tourist gaze.[21] These cultural productions resist capitalist notions of profit and accumulation that can be controlled and appropriated.[22]

LONCHERAS AND FOOD TRUCKS

"We got our first truck in 2008. It was easy then," said Iris, a Honduran immigrant who has operated taco trucks across Louisiana. "Now there are so many inspections, it's so much money, it's so exaggerated." Taco trucks that arrived in post-Katrina New Orleans from places like Texas and New York introduced a relatively new mode of selling food in the Crescent City, operating itinerantly and efficiently to serve cleanup crews and reconstruction workers who had limited access to nourishing and affordable meals.

Immediately after the storm, the loncheras ran on generators and had their own potable water tanks, which allowed hot foods to be prepared onsite, a reprieve from the prepackaged meals distributed by the Red Cross

A vendor serving baleadas from her lonchera. Photo by Fernando López, @sentir.con.ojos.

and even tamale vendors. These taco trucks provided an essential service that often goes overlooked in terms of disaster recovery measures. With new languages and new cultures, they also represented a growing and lasting immigrant presence in the southern metropolitan area.

While the City of New Orleans, with some exceptions, tolerated the loncheras, understanding their integral role in the recovery efforts, neighboring Jefferson Parish Council, led by council member Louis Congemi, passed an outright ban on taco trucks in June 2007. The youngest child of Sicilian immigrants who often celebrated his blue-collar upbringing in political campaigns referred to the loncheras as "unsightly remnants of the makeshift conditions" left over from Katrina.[23] Comments like Congemi's illustrate how legislators viewed working-class immigrant communities as a threat to the middle-class white suburban status quo that dominated Jefferson Parish.[24]

The ban made national news. *Los Angeles Times* reporter Miguel Bustillo articulated the double standard: "In the parking lot of a drive-thru daiquiri bar that sells frozen White Russians in plastic to-go cups, Fidel Sanchez is running an illegal enterprise that's too unwholesome to be tolerated, according to politicians here in suburban Jefferson Parish." Bustillo's statement captured the irony of these policies, which he called "thick with racial undertones." An à la carte, laissez-faire approach of lawmaking meant drive-thru alcohol purveyors (a tradition that began in the state in 1981) were permissible, yet taco trucks were "unsightly" and "makeshift."[25] In an attempt at their own defense, Jefferson Parish Council members labeled the food truck ban as a zoning violation, an assertion that was shot down by city planners.[26] Then Jefferson Parish officials used health and safety conditions as a justification for the ban, even though the health department reported that they had found no problems with sanitation.[27]

Meanwhile, in Orleans Parish, the 2011 "city normalization" period also coincided with the growth and popularity of "gourmet food trucks." Following food truck crazes in places like Los Angeles, Austin, and Portland, these self-propelled kitchens became ubiquitous in New Orleans with clever names, trendy dishes, and art that matched the food served.[28] Owners of these trucks, oftentimes middle-class and white, had the wherewithal to understand and navigate city policies as well as the social media dexterity to keep followers abreast of their latest moves and menus.[29]

The loncheras did not quite fit into these "gourmet food truck" imaginaries; nor did they seek the same type of mobility or acclaim as the gourmet trucks. Rather, the loncheras relied on an established clientele—a Central American and Mexican base—and operated territorially, strategically parking near their respective day-laborer corner. Unlike gourmet food trucks, which set up shop in various neighborhoods and tapped a catering, private party market, loncheras didn't really change locations. The lonchera menus also remained relatively homogeneous with similar selections of Honduran and Mexican foods, including a range of tacos, burritos, baleadas, *taquitos*, plates of carne asada, and *menudo* specials. Handmade corn tortillas or a charred green onion and jalapeño lagniappe with a plate of tacos were examples of the few differentiating touches between vendors.

Just before Denis's departure in November 2011, Gloria from Taqueria DF at Elysian Fields bought her own lonchera. She named her new venture

Taqueria Las Delicias after her small town in northern Honduras. The turquoise-and-white-painted trailer was an upgrade to the former truck and featured two concession windows on one side and a stainless steel standing bar assembled just below the concession windows, spanning the length of the trailer. The Honduran-owned and -operated lonchera featured Mexican dishes on a ready-made orange menu; a makeshift paper menu hung just to the side with a list of available Honduran dishes and specialty meats for the tacos.

After multiple disputes between Gloria's crew and Lowe's authorities who claimed that Taqueria Las Delicias obstructed traffic and impeded entry to the home improvement store, Gloria moved her lonchera approximately 700 feet north to the Florida Avenue junction under the overpass—out of sight but still close enough to the esquina. As local law enforcement, including Officer V., stepped up their systems of policing loncheras and ticketing day laborers for trespassing violations, ICE agents also beefed up their operations, focusing on the esquina where, in one case, they performed a sting operation and violently arrested an El Congreso member.[30] With these threats from store security, ICE agents, and police officers, it was an easy decision for Gloria and her team at Taqueria Las Delicias to move from in front of Lowe's to the more clandestine space in the derelict lot a block away.[31]

As the precarity of loncheras grew and gourmet food trucks continued to emerge, it was clear to Orleans Parish policymakers that updates needed to be made to the byzantine food truck policy. In 2011, the policy on the books restricted food trucks from being within 600 feet of schools or restaurants, allowed trucks to remain in one place for only forty-five minutes (and they could not return to that place in the same day), prohibited mobility in the French Quarter and Central Business District, grouped food trucks within a large vendor category (including flowers and souvenir vendors), and limited the number of vendor licenses to 100.[32]

Opposition came mostly from the restaurant industry. Citing sanitation issues and unfair tax advantages, the Louisiana Restaurant Association propelled opposition to food trucks and helped maintain archaic laws that had not been updated since 1956.[33] However, some opposition came from folks who saw the food trucks as a harbinger of gentrification, following what was culturally trendy on a national level, rather than what was happening on the ground locally. Jules Bentley of *Antigravity* magazine engaged the distinction between gourmet food trucks and other itinerant food vendors left out of the discussion—second line barbecue trucks and taco trucks banned in Jefferson Parish. Just a month before the first vote, Bentley caustically asserted, "These food trucks provide a way for high-tech newcomers to avoid having to deal with or even speak to New Orleanians; they're another layer of twee West Coast culture superimposed atop what's left of our city, to make it more comfortable for well-off 'young creatives.'"[34]

Nevertheless, a growing contingency of gourmet food truck owners became understandably disenchanted by the limitations of the policy and, in turn, began to organize under the New Orleans Food Truck Coalition. Much of this leadership came from Rachel Billow, owner of La Cocinita, which opened on November 19, 2011.[35] The coalition first organized in 2012 with the goal to update the policy and support the "growth and success of food trucks and other mobile vendors in New Orleans. Founded by food truck owners, our group is a diverse collection of vendors, consumers, restaurateurs, community activists, neighborhood organizations, and more."[36] When I searched the long list of coalition members, I found no mention of lonchera owners.

Taylor Jackson, the coalition president at the time, said that he made multiple visits to lonchera owners inviting them to participate and provided accessible information in Spanish, but they always opted out. It made sense. Taco truck workers may have feared that participating in a campaign for improved food truck rights could draw attention to their or their clients' immigration status, potentially leading to legal consequences and risking their livelihoods.

City officials were on board to liberalize the food truck policy to provide a more even playing field for the growing number of food truck operators. Led by council member Stacy Head, who worked alongside the coalition, the City Council unanimously passed an update to the food truck policy in April 2013; however, the policy was vetoed by Mayor Landrieu due to what he dubbed as potential "unconstitutionality" of the revised policy. In a convoluted letter, Landrieu expressed that the policy didn't go far enough to liberalize the procedures.[37]

Over the next few months, the City Council made adjustments and removed language regarding distance between food trucks and restaurants—the key complaint expressed by Landrieu. Council members passed the new policy, which increased the number of permits to 100 food vendors, expanded the amount of time in one spot to four hours, and allowed food trucks to sell in the Central Business District (but still prohibited sales in the French Quarter).[38] The updated food truck ordinance also maintained some restrictions, like prohibiting vendors from operating within twenty feet of any intersection or within three feet of a driveway and requiring liability insurance to cover $500,000 in damages. The changes officially went into effect in January 2014, and the updated policy coincided with the opening of the "one-stop shop," a program aimed to streamline the process to access licensing for four sectors of city hall's jurisdiction: the City Planning Commission, the Historic District Landmarks Commission, the Safety and Permits Department, and the Vieux Carre Commission.[39]

The one-stop shop was developed under the Landrieu administration as a method to streamline customer service issues for licensing and permits and was implemented in March 2013. As part of the "El Protector" program, representatives from city hall asked Officer V. to test out the program for Spanish speakers. "They wanted to do a trial run to see if a Hispanic could go into city hall, find his way, and get a permit," Officer V. explained. He continued, "So, I chose a candidate and I said, 'Look, you need to see if you can go get a permit.' He said, 'Yeah,' and I said, 'I'm just going to follow you. If we can't figure it out, we'll figure it out.' And it was about signage and it was about getting to the office you were supposed to go [to]. Because city hall can be confusing." As a result of the test run, they posted more signs to guide people in the right direction. He added, "City hall loved it because they didn't have to have an interpreter." Officer V. made it sound easy.

In July 2014, as part of my factotum work with El Congreso, I unintentionally did my own reconnaissance to test the one-stop shop. Jacinta asked me to help Magda, a member of El Congreso, license her own lonchera.[40] When I first met Magda back in 2012, she was already well-versed in the politics, culture, and de facto and de jure spatial governance of operating a lonchera in the New Orleans area. Originally from Santa Bárbara, Honduras (the same department as Denis), Magda arrived in New Orleans in 2006 to work in disaster cleanup efforts. She bounced between jobs in the formal sector, working as a gas station attendant, to jobs in the informal sector, cleaning houses through a family-run business and selling foods from loncheras.

After her sisters arrived in 2007, the family team embarked on their lonchera venture, renting their first truck in 2008. The sisters opened the truck strategically at the cross intersection of Tupelo Street and North Claiborne Avenue, a main thoroughfare in the Lower Ninth Ward. The lonchera offered freshly cooked meals in the food desert left dry by post-Katrina negligence.

In 2012, the father of Magda's teenage children was tragically murdered in his home in Honduras. No motive was determined, and no one was caught. Fearing for the lives of her two teenagers, Magda sent for them to come to New Orleans. They arrived in 2013 and reunited with their mother and her sisters in their home in Chalmette, the seat of St. Bernard Parish, located southeast of New Orleans. From 2013 to 2014, almost 100,000 children and youth arrived in the United States as "unaccompanied minors," fleeing violence and poverty in Mexico and Central America.[41] While her children adjusted to life in New Orleans, Magda realized she needed more flexibility with her job and decided to open her own lonchera.

With the new food truck policy in place and the one-stop shop open, it seemed like an ideal time to get licensing. I checked out the online resources for the one-stop shop, which posted a useful checklist and clear guidelines for opening a food truck, but at that time, these resources were available only in English. I roughly translated the instructions for Magda, and she and I made an appointment to visit the one-stop shop in person.

A few weeks later, we arrived at the one-stop shop, taking a ticket from the queue system machine. We sat briefly in the waiting room until the loudspeaker announced our number, and a friendly clerk summoned us to her cubicle. I interpreted as Magda asked for clarification around the certificates required from the health department and the fire department. Operating a lonchera prior to 2011 didn't require these certificates, but given the precarity and increased enforcement, Magda knew she had to get the right permitting and keep her business aboveboard.

Over the next eight months, Magda and her business partner, Juan, worked diligently to get their newly purchased lonchera—a twelve-by-six-foot 2012 red stainless-steel trailer—up to par.[42] A quiet man in his mid-forties and originally from Mexico, Juan had been living in New Orleans since before Katrina and is a naturalized US citizen. He had taken the day off from his job as an ice vendor in St. Bernard Parish to help Magda with the paperwork. The truck would be in Juan's name because he had the Louisiana driver's license required to procure the food truck permit. Together, Juan and Magda had invested slightly over $20,000 in preparing the truck, paying fees, and getting the correct certification to meet the one-stop shop's standards.

On March 30, 2015, Magda contacted me saying that she and Juan had completed the health department and fire department inspections and were ready to get the licensing. I met them at City Hall the next week, and we returned to our post in the waiting area of the one-stop shop. During this time, Juan and Magda proudly showed me their white binder filled with pages of bureaucracy, neatly organized between the plastic hole-punched sheets. As required, they had a page dedicated to four photos of the red lonchera, which looked shiny and new.

The clerk gave us more paperwork to fill out, all in English. I asked Magda the name of the business.

"Taqueria La Duranguense," she and Juan said in unison.

"A Mexican name?" I said, looking curiously at Magda.

"Nobody knows about Honduran food," she said, laughing.

As the clerk called us up to her cubicle, Magda grasped the white binder, which signaled both pride and protection. When the clerk asked for a specific document, Magda found it immediately—the copy of the driver's license, the occupational license, the certificates, and the proof of insurance with liability coverage of at least $500,000. She was so prepared.

Then, the clerk asked for the pictures of the future Taqueria Duranguense. Magda quickly turned to the page with the four photos of the trailer pasted neatly below the plastic guard. The clerk took one look at the photos and asked about the axle. According to the policy, food trucks must have two axles. Taqueria La Duranguense had only one. That was a big hurdle. We briefly convened. Juan was certain he could have someone weld another axle on the front of the trailer. No problem.

We reported back to the clerk, only to encounter the next hurdle: it must be a "self-propelled" vehicle to qualify for the permit. This detail came as a bit of a surprise. At that time, "self-propelled" vehicles were not listed on the requirements on the checklist—just the size regulations and the double-axle requirement (which we had overlooked). Up until that point, I had not even considered there to be a distinction between a trailer and a truck. This hadn't been on any of the food truck ordinances. As this information registered, I had to interpret the upsetting news to Juan and Magda. They were devastated.

Seeing our frustration, the clerk sent us to the director of the one-stop shop. We walked about fifty feet to her spacious office overlooking downtown New Orleans. The director was friendly enough, asking Magda and me to sit in chairs in front of her desk and grabbing a third chair from another room for Juan; Magda immediately showed her the photographs of the trailer.

"Can they still get a food truck license?" I asked.

The director shook her head. Because it was not self-propelled, the city could not provide a license. She and I spoke quickly, back and forth, in English. Juan and Magda sat blindsided. I interpreted the key parts to Juan and Magda, but they were lost behind a barrier that went beyond language. This barrier included a wall of bureaucracy with entirely too many rules and too much paperwork, which were so far from the objective—making tacos, burritos, baleadas.

The apologetic director said that the existing taco trailers had been grandfathered in before 2013. Seeing the shocked looks on Juan and Magda's faces, the director admitted, "We don't have enough staff to regulate these licenses."

We went into the hallway, where I interpreted that last bit of information. The calm-tempered Magda shook her head angrily, fists clasped, face red.

"Sapo," she exclaimed. But she was not talking about the director. "El es un sapo," she repeated, calling out Officer V., the bilingual officer, as a "snitch." I knew what Magda meant as soon as she said his name. Limited city resources for licensing inspections might have created a gap in enforcement oversight; nevertheless, Officer V. still wielded regulatory authority at his discretion. Like the case with Gloria at Taqueria DF, Magda had also experienced the duplicity of Officer V., "El Protector."

We left city hall. Magda said she would investigate getting a license out of Houma, a small town located about fifty miles southwest of New Orleans in Terrebonne Parish. She had heard it was easier to get licenses there. I said I would contact a couple of people in New Orleans to see if there were any other options. Magda followed up with me a couple of months later. I expected her to tell me that she had purchased the license in Houma. But she instead had sold the trailer to Gloria for $5,000, a loss of $15,000 (plus the time spent on the bureaucratic rigmarole). Because Gloria had the existing truck, she could grandfather the new trailer in under that license. Four years later, Magda was able to ultimately get a license from outside the city and operate a highly successful lonchera enterprise with a fleet of trailers run by her and her sisters.

The experience with Juan and Magda was traumatic and devastating on several levels. One, in Magda and Juan's noble attempt to follow all the rules, they were ultimately encumbered by a newly invented rule that was rife with racial undertones: the majority of loncheras *are* trailers and *all* the gourmet trucks are self-propelled. The distinction between trailer and truck, something that had not been on the policy books before, suddenly became a deal-breaker. In the widely celebrated effort to liberalize the outdated policy, policymakers drafted a new exclusionary policy that harkened back to antiquated times. At least the racialization of the Jefferson Parish ban was explicit when prohibiting loncheras; instead, Orleans Parish buried exclusivity underneath layers of sticky red tape targeting a specific type of vendor—Central American and Mexican.

Second, turning down the invite from the New Orleans Food Truck Coalition and being absent from the negotiating table shouldn't have meant that the needs of the lonchera owners weren't met. Even though the realities of their situation were clear (they used trailers), policymakers intentionally and egregiously excluded the loncheras. Policymakers generated yet another level of precarity with a new regulation in a move that marginalized an already vulnerable community and further cultivated depths of mistrust in these systems.

Third, more regulation meant more opportunities for enforcement, which put the owners and their clientele at further risk. While the "El Protector" program aimed to build trust in communities and not focus on "enforcement" measures, the face of El Protector was one who had already sown seeds of mistrust and inconsistency within the Spanish-speaking communities. Officer V. proudly portrayed himself as El Protector of the Hispanic community, positioning himself in a clearly patriarchal position. And he had some fans—Mateo who ran a lonchera in Central City held Officer V. in high regard: "I think that the New Orleans police have been very tolerant with Latinos who have a business and we owe this to Officer V." Nevertheless, his type of erratic enforcement was precisely what street vendors sought to avoid. As the city aimed to liberalize its policies, they instead created more methods to criminalize. With the heightened surveillance and increased enforcement from the NOPD and ICE, the inconsistent enforcement entailed severe consequences.

FREEWHEELING STREET VENDORS

For almost two years, from 2013 to 2015, a church sidewalk served as the metaphorical line in the sand between two street vendors, Sofia and Susana, as they sold food at separate stands outside of the weekly El Congreso meetings.[43] One could hear Susana crooning a deep, raspy "Chicharrones con yucca" on one side of the church entrance, while Sofia bellowed a higher-pitched "Taquitos, tamales, elotes" from the other side. The two vendors often tried to eclipse one another and win over clientele. Despite having seemingly similar backgrounds and livelihoods and almost identical menus, Sofia's and Susana's respective stories demonstrate the contingencies at play in how people navigate space and place.

In this section, I look at street vending, first through a case study of dueling Honduran street food vendors and then through snack vendors known as "Candy Ladies" to show how individuals navigated the informal sector in the years after Katrina. Many street vending jobs have become increasingly racialized and criminalized, as vendors are required to have state-sponsored documentation to operate and subsist. For undocumented people, pathways to legalization, of both businesses and people, are oftentimes too expensive, too bureaucratic, or impossible because of political obstacles. Moreover, obstructions to obtaining this type of licensing—red tape, language barriers, racial profiling—perpetuate fear among immigrant communities. In response, individuals defy these systems of bureaucracy, asserting agency to create highly efficient, versatile, and oftentimes lucrative means to cultivate their own legitimacy and networks through these street vending operations.

The Dueling Honduran Street Food Vendors

Originally from Honduras, Sofia had limited job opportunities to help provide for her family, who lived in extreme poverty in a remote town called Esquipulas del Norte. As Sofia was growing up, her mother generated income through an at-home sewing business. To support the family, which included seven siblings, Sofia and her mother also sold food—baleadas and tamales—itinerantly at bus stations in the Copán region, a tourist zone located in western Honduras, before moving across the country to be closer to Sofia's former in-laws. When her mother was diagnosed with osteoporosis, Sofia knew that she needed to earn more money to take care of her family. Facing limited job options in Honduras, Sofia left her three young children behind with her ex-mother-in-law and migrated to New Orleans in 2007. Over the next five years, Sofia settled in the Mid-City neighborhood, began work in the hotel industry, and had two more children, born in New Orleans.

In Sofia's absence, her ex-mother-in-law raised the three older children on a small farm near the town of Tocoa. Once narco-traffickers took over the area, it was no longer safe for them. When a relative was killed on the family farm, the threat of further violence forced Sofia's children to flee for their safety. With the help of her ex-husband, who stayed behind in Honduras,

Sofia sent for them to come live with her, paying a coyote around $10,000 to bring them on the long journey to New Orleans through Mexico and across the border. Sofia's three oldest children, by this point teenagers, arrived in New Orleans in 2013 and, like Magda's children, were among the over 100,000 unaccompanied minors who arrived in the United States from Central America.[44]

After arriving in New Orleans in 2007, Sofia had worked steadily as a hotel housekeeper, earning low wages while working long hours with no benefits. In 2013, with five children to support in New Orleans and her mother remaining in Honduras, Sofia had to pick up extra work to bring in more income. She began supplementing her eight-dollars-per-hour income in the hotels with her street vending hustle, her preferred trade. Sofia increasingly relied on her cooking skills, drawing from her street vending background to make and sell food itinerantly, almost exclusively at El Congreso meetings. She and her sister sent her mother in Honduras some remittances, which she invested in land to grow red beans, which are harvested twice a year. The income generated from the bean production sustained Sofia's aging mother and supported her nieces and nephews in school.

In Sofia's pursuits as a street food vendor, she never tried to get a mobile vendor permit, preferring the safety of the church grounds at El Congreso meetings. Language barriers, misinformation, tax issues, and quotas prevented her from even attempting the bureaucratic process. While there is no specification that a person must be a US citizen to officially license their business, oftentimes people like Sofia *prefer* to remain in the shadows to avoid having their name and business registered with the government. Their undocumented status begets their clandestine business, and informal economies become optimal given the flexibility, independence, and potential to earn a stable income. Nevertheless, the risk remained—a ticket for trespassing or being pulled over for a traffic stop (undocumented people cannot get a driver's license in Louisiana) could lead to deportation.

Unlike Sofia, Susana had more mobility and faced less risk given her immigration status. Susana became a naturalized US citizen through her Puerto Rican husband, who passed away in 2018. Originally from Juticalpa, Honduras, Susana bounced between Juticalpa and the port town of La Ceiba throughout her youth, spending most of her time learning to cook coastal foods typical of that region. When Susana was in her early twenties, she followed friends and relatives in northern Belize to work as a housekeeper and in a restaurant. After Hurricane Mitch devastated the region in

1998, jobs were scarce because there was no tourism due to the damaged infrastructure.

Soon after, Susana moved to the United States, first to Philadelphia, where she worked in kitchens, ranging from fast food chains to a Mexican restaurant. She alternated between cooking and doing dishes but always yearned to make her own food. While living in Philadelphia, Susana met her husband, Raul, a US citizen and army veteran who was born and raised in Puerto Rico. After living in Philadelphia, Raul and Susana decided they wanted a change of pace, so they moved back to Belize, where they purchased a home and ran a small restaurant.

Raul and Susana lived comfortably in a small coastal town until Raul was diagnosed with cancer. They maintained their home in Belize but moved to the United States, where Raul could get better medical care using his veteran's benefits. They ended up in New Orleans, where Susana's brother had settled after Katrina. Susana procured a catering license through a friend who owned a restaurant in New Orleans. I first met Susana when she sold plates of *pollo con tajadas* at the Pelican League soccer fields in City Park. Since 2011, Susana had sold food at the park most Sundays, but she lost her place at the fields because she had to miss a few weeks due to obligations with her church and to take care of her ailing husband. She was disappointed to lose her vending spot; however, she acquiesced, given the fact that the league had clearly devised a de facto system to self-organize. Susana picked up other gigs across the city, selling foods at church events, small festivals, and El Congreso meetings.

In 2015, Susana received notice that she received her green card through her marriage to Raul. She could finally work in the United States legally, providing her much more mobility to navigate the bureaucratic systems of the city, especially compared with Sofia. Because of her legal status, she could access various resources in New Orleans, from health care to a driver's license. While she was not without her own challenges (especially considering Raul's declining health), she could navigate the city with more mobility and less fear.

In 2011, around the same time Denis left, El Congreso attendance expanded considerably, from around 40 members at the weekly meetings to approximately 200. The meetings quickly outgrew the shotgun house on North Prieur Street and the organizers had to locate larger spaces, often churches, to hold the assemblies. The rise in membership reflected the growing numbers of people detained and the arrival of unaccompanied minors. Immigrants needed support and were impacted by increased criminalization and deportation threats.

El Congreso meetings began at 7:00 p.m. each Wednesday and varied in structure and content. At some meetings, organizers updated members on key legislative events and built awareness around campaigns, or members gave testimonies of a loved one detained. Sometimes leaders from other grassroots organizations, like the Black-led Stand with Dignity, discussed their struggles and called for collective action. As a result of those meetings, dozens of May Day marches, vigils, protests, and policy-oriented campaigns transpired.

When the meetings ended around nine o'clock each week, El Congreso leaders had food catered and ready for the members; meanwhile, organizers stayed late conducting *consultas* with members who needed support. These *consultas* involved members seeking assistance in translating official documents, dealing with immigration detentions, fighting wage theft cases, and, like in the case of Magda's lonchera, arranging for interpretation during appointments. The *consultas* filled an essential service for the members while also helping to build trust and garner a firsthand understanding of everyday issues immigrants face.

As the number of members grew, so did the demand for a more efficient way to feed people. Both Susana and Sofia started selling food to supplement the limited food that El Congreso leaders provided. By 2013, El Congreso grew so large that it quit providing food, leaving just Susana and Sofia selling food before and after the meetings. These gatherings were integral to both Sofia's and Susana's sources of revenue.

Every Wednesday, beginning in 2013, Sofia and Susana arrived around four o'clock to set up. They put together their respective pop-up tents and folding tables, essentially mirrors of one another, with similar Honduran dishes spread across the plastic tables. As the two women assembled their stands, they made no eye contact with each other, operating as if the other wasn't there—Susana on the left side of the church entrance with her team of family members keeping her company and helping collect the payment; Sofia posted on the right, often operating with a neighbor friend who plated foods.

The setup included large, stainless steel pots, ziplock bags with servings of *mango con chile*, a variety of tamarind and dulce de leche–flavored candies, and small coolers warming already prepared baleadas and *taquitos*. Each vendor had her respective assembly lines ready to arrange beds of fried plantains topped with fried chicken or chicharron, cabbage, *chismol* (Honduran *pico de gallo*), and dressing packaged neatly in Styrofoam containers. Coolers filled with cold sodas and bottled waters doubled as seats for customers. Sofia always had a bucket of *nacatamales* wrapped in banana leaves neatly stacked and ready to serve from a twelve-quart stainless steel stockpot.

"It takes four to five hours to make the tamales," explained Sofia, indicating the long preparation process for the evening fare. "I make the tamales the night before and leave them prepared. I make the rest of the food the day of the meeting. I fry the chicken last."

As demand for this food increased, so did the tensions between the two women. When the organizers for El Congreso received complaints from both vendors, they decided they no longer wanted to play mediator and asked the women to alternate weeks. Sofia and Susana resisted at first but then agreed to the terms. With the help of El Congreso organizers, they readjusted, alternating Wednesday night schedules. They even began attracting non–El Congreso members, often Mid-City neighbors who caught on to the weekly tradition and popped in for a plate of Honduran food.

Susana kept up her other side hustles, catering mostly as part of church events; meanwhile, after unrealized dreams of opening a lonchera, Sofia set her eyes on a more permanent venture: a booth at the Westbank Flea Market. The women remained a central part of El Congreso's tenure, providing an essential service of sustenance and familiarity as people organized to fight for their right to remain in the city.

When I asked Sofia whether she had ever had any run-ins with law enforcement, she said, "Thank God, no, never. But that doesn't mean I wasn't worried, that I wasn't careful." The rise in the informal economy added an extra layer of risk, yet it also allowed people like Sofia and Susana to take care of their families. In New Orleans and elsewhere, informal economies are increasingly ubiquitous, providing a hustle to help individuals and families make ends meet. This informal sector work has become central to the economy, especially for poor and already disenfranchised groups.

Food Culture as Part of the Movement

While Sofia and Susana kept El Congreso's base fed at the weekly meetings, the members of Stand with Dignity held potlucks for their meetings, which fell on Tuesday evenings at the North Prieur office. Longtime Stand member Williana was often the ringleader in orchestrating the menus and preparing her southern classics. With a long history of cooking in kitchens across the city and as part of her own food vending side hustle, Williana could adeptly plan out a meal for a large group.

In 2016, the Workers' Center's ten-year anniversary brought together members of Stand with Dignity, El Congreso, and the National Guestworker Alliance. I was asked to help Williana transport her food from her home in Marrero Commons (formerly the B. W. Cooper Public Housing Development) to the Workers' Center office. As we headed over, I hit the brakes too quickly, and one of two trays of peas toppled over, leaving a fetid brown stain on the vehicle's carpet. Left with only one tray of peas for the large celebration, Williana kept a raised eyebrow on me all evening. Six years later, she still playfully held that grudge, giving me a stoic look when I reminded her of the event.

"Oh I remember your heavy foot on those brakes," said Williana. "I bet it still stinks, doesn't it?"

Born and raised in the St. Thomas projects, a public housing development in the Uptown area, Williana grew up watching her mother cook New Orleans classics like smothered chicken, stuffed bell peppers, and red beans and rice. Her first job was in a small restaurant on Tulane Avenue, and she has since worked off and on as a house cleaner and in the food service sector. "Between food and cleaner's work, that's what I know."

In Marrero Commons, Williana identifies as a "Candy Lady," which refers to her hustle of selling snacks in the neighborhood, a long-standing tradition in New Orleans and across the South. The origins of the "Candy Lady" tradition stem back to Rose Nicaud, an enslaved woman whose unique drip-coffee preparation style forged a pushcart business in the French Market in New Orleans. Rose Nicaud's legacy is linked with other Black enslaved women who made and sold street foods like praline candies and cala (fried rice fritters) on Sundays, a mandatory rest day in Code Noir guidelines. Licenses at the time were available only to white people and free people of color, but the hustle was worth the risk, potentially allowing enslaved women to save enough money to buy their own freedom.[45] Although there is less food preparation at home (people mostly sell prepackaged snacks), contemporary Candy Ladies adapted from these traditions of creating home businesses to help sustain their families and supply foods in underserved neighborhoods.[46]

Recognizing the limited food options in Marrero Commons, Williana decided to create an ad hoc at-home business selling snacks, drinks, and prepared meals to help make ends meet. The Candy Lady hustle allowed her the flexibility to take care of her four grandchildren, who lived with her.

"I would sell cookies, cold drinks, honey buns, Vienna sausage, Ritz crackers, pig lips," she explained. "At first, I started off going to Family Dollar, buying little cakes and pies, and now I find myself going to Sam's buying big boxes with the full bottles of pig lips, the jars of pickles."[47]

On most weekends she'd make homemade supper plates filled with fried chicken and red beans or mac and cheese with fried fish and sell the orders to hungry neighbors.

Like Sofia and Susana, Williana was able to provide culturally relevant foods for her family and neighbors. At Stand with Dignity meetings, Williana made sure members were fed and had access to home-cooked meals as they met to plan Black-led housing justice actions, fight criminalization, and support labor campaigns. Her foods became tantamount with the movement.

One afternoon, Williana was stopped by an NOPD officer while riding her bike with a friend. Because Williana had a warrant for a traffic violation fine, the officer picked her up for questioning. Rather than book her, the officer asked Williana about drug dealers in the neighborhood.

"Well, you're the police," she said. "You should be telling me about drug dealers that I don't know about."

"You're the Candy Lady, so you should know them all," the officer replied.

Williana was shocked by the incident. She said that when the officer told her it was against the law to sell the food without a license, she responded with, "Baby, all I'm doing, just going to the store, get stuff for people that's not able to make it to the store. And all they are doing is paying me my money back. Now what's wrong with that law? Helping other people."

The officer let her go, but Williana was shaken by the incident.

Members of the Stand community, like Williana, often had fines and fees from municipal or traffic violations that had added up over time and turned into a warrant or prevented them from getting a driver's license or applying for some jobs or even public housing.

In Williana's case, the police clearly knew she had an attachment, which was issued by the court for her failure to comply with the traffic court's fines and fees system. Williana lived with this vulnerability and could be stopped by law enforcement at any moment. For people who have access to resources, hiring a lawyer or going to a courthouse to take care of these charges is a piece of cake. For others, mistrust of the criminal justice system and other structural barriers make this poverty-crime-induced bureaucratic process extremely daunting. Thus, helping people to handle these charges was imperative to protecting people from erratic enforcement.

Shakedown and Bias-Free Policing Relief

The fines and fees system exacerbates economic and racial disparities and often causes more harm to communities than the original offense. Thus, similar to the way that El Congreso organizers moved toward helping members handle outstanding fines and fees as part of the "Right to Remain" campaign, Stand with Dignity leaders sought out a streamlined method for members to wipe these aggravated charges away.

"A poor person goes and finds out what they owe [from a traffic or municipal violation], then realizes they can't make more payments; they get a fee on top of the fine, and then find a job, and then find out they have an attachment for an arrest," explained Stand organizer Toya Ex Lewis. "We knew that we didn't want criminal background to be a barrier to employment."

Stand began planning processes to relieve these poverty offenses in 2016. After a year of planning, Stand with Dignity developed the NOLA Shakedown Warrant Clinic in 2017.[48] Stand's vision for the clinic was, "We believe a new system is possible that addresses the root causes of systemic injustice and uses public resources to provide and facilitate full and fair employment and overall wellbeing for all New Orleanians."[49] Stand with Dignity spearheaded the grassroots program, partnering with local community organizations, the city attorney's office, and the Orleans Public Defenders. Working with El Congreso, Stand brought in interpreters to facilitate the services for the Spanish-speaking community.

Legal allies helped get local traffic and municipal court judges on board like Judge Robert Jones and Judge Desiree Charbonnet. The judges finally reckoned with and acted on mitigating the damage done by this structural violence and systemic failures. "This is to address the difficulty many of the indigent defendants have paying fines and fees and then avoiding arrest because of that," Charbonnet said in an interview with *The Advocate*. "These are misdemeanors, public intoxication, trespassing, disturbing the peace, not the crimes that place terror in our hearts when we read the newspaper every day. People had cases stemming 10 years back and they pretty much stayed out of trouble all that time."[50] During the first clinic, Judge Jones even agreed to stay as long as people were in line. They wiped fines and fees until one in the morning.

In total, the first NOLA Shakedown Warrant Clinic relieved people of over $1 million in fines and fees. Stand with Dignity also saved the city approximately $1 million in incarceration costs.[51] Other more invisible results of the expungement were unquantifiable. For example, in the most egregious case, one Black man had accrued $23,000 in fines from a traffic infraction in 1989, which was reduced to a $9 fee. Over that time, he had his license taken away in 1997 and lived two decades in constant fear of being pulled over whenever he risked driving. No longer saddled with this criminal justice debt, the man planned to apply for a job with the Regional Transit Authority—a public sector job he couldn't previously access because of the warrant.[52]

The fines and fees system privileges people who have access to capital and instills fear in those who don't by putting financial barriers on poorer residents who must choose between paying criminal justice debts or providing for family and paying household bills.[53] It locks people out of certain jobs and housing opportunities. For people like Williana, it can mean being plied by police for intel. For undocumented immigrants, fines and fees from trespassing while vending food can lead to arrest and deportation.

Stand with Dignity hosted two NOLA Shakedown Warrant Clinics, both of which were highly impactful but served as mere Band-Aids on a hemorrhaging problem. The organizers recognized these limitations and made broader demands at the systemic level: (1) Make all municipal fines equitable and based on ability to pay; (2) abolish all fees and court costs added to underlying fines; and (3) prohibit jailing people for poverty offenses. The New Orleans branch of the Vera Institute of Justice, a research and policy nonprofit, made simultaneous demands to eliminate certain fines, fees, and outstanding warrants for failure to appear and published reports to support these demands. In 2019, the institute successfully sponsored a city-level resolution to end the unjust "user fee" system, which relied on funding from the criminalization of poorer communities.[54] *Times-Picayune* reporters Matt Sledge and Bryn Stole described the system as "squeezing blood from a turnip."[55]

Despite El Congreso's efforts, the issues related to discriminatory policing persisted and extended beyond the elimination of fees. Even with the consent decree clearly prohibiting the NOPD from taking law enforcement action based on immigration status, including stops or field contacts, the NOPD was slow to adopt the "bias-free policing" policy.[56] Since 2014, El

Congreso has pressured the NOPD to revamp its immigration policy, citing discriminatory policing cases, including investigations into residents' immigration status during routine interactions outside grocery stores and homes. In an interview with *The Lens*, Workers' Center lawyer Julie Mao said, "The overarching concern we have is, it's very much an 'enforce federal policy' rather than a bias-free policy."[57]

Part of this pressure resulted in a criminal justice hearing at City Council chambers on March 26, 2015, which included testimonies from El Congreso and Stand members—and ICE administrators. The hearing date coincided with the year-and-a-half deadline of an unanswered Freedom of Information Act request that the Workers' Center had submitted to ICE during the civil disobedience action against the CARI raids in November 2013.

"Everything lined up really well because before the criminal justice hearing we went to ICE to deliver the lawsuit. We decided we'll file it that same day and make it into an action," said El Congreso organizer Fernando López.

Before the hearing, the group of 100-plus Workers' Center staff, community supporters, El Congreso members, and Stand leaders arrived at the ICE office. The gathering congregated at the main entrance of the Hyatt House on Poydras Street, a privately owned hotel that houses the ICE regional headquarters on the third floor. At the action, ICE administrators refused to formally receive the letter to file the lawsuit, so the members left a copy with reception. Then the group marched one block away to city hall holding stenciled signs reading phrases such as "Not 1 More," "No Más Redadas" (No more raids), "NOPD Stop Assisting ICE in Deporting Reconstruction Workers," and "Workers Are Not Disposable."

At the City Council hearing in the council chambers, the 100-plus people from the action made their way through the metal detectors at the front of the building, filling the hallway as they waited to file into the seating area of the chambers. In the rear left corner of the audience section, three ICE officials sat attentively, clad in stiff suits. The legal team from the Workers' Center, along with members from El Congreso and Stand, provided testimonies detailing their encounters with ICE raids and instances of racial profiling. Subsequently, representatives from ICE presented their perspectives.

"It was a public spanking on ICE," said Fernando López. The City Council members agreed, particularly Latoya Cantrell and Jason Williams, who organized the session.

By 2016, the city passed a "Bias-Free Policy" resolution focused on cooperation with immigrant communities rather than perpetuating bias against individuals. The policy explicitly prohibited officers from inquiring about an individual's immigration status. "El Protector" was nowhere to be found in these policy changes.

In the face of the criminalization of individuals from poor and working-class backgrounds, leaders from Stand with Dignity and El Congreso responded proactively, pursuing optimal solutions to address the needs of their members. And that work continued with other informal sector organizing, recognizing the needs of hustle workers. At the grassroots level, Southern Project Hustle, Toya Ex Lewis's project that centers "Black working-class hustlers," builds power through popular education and cooperative strategies. Southern Project Hustle takes an intersectional approach with a focus on gender to celebrate the "unrecognized and unseen" labor of Black women in New Orleans to build an alternative economy focused on collectivity.[58] Flea markets like Dix Jazz Market and the Westbank Flea Market have emerged in the post-Katrina context as safe havens for people like Sofia to formalize their street food hustles with licensed food stalls. Some people remain in the shadows operating at their own risk.

CONCLUSION

The 2011 normalization period was meant to bring order to New Orleans after instability in the post-Katrina recovery. But order mostly entailed more enforcement and more bureaucracy, which either created new regulations that took aim at cultural producers or had a homogenizing effect on culture. Or both. Regardless, the enforcement functioned erratically, disproportionately impacting poor and working-class communities. Street food vendors took on risk by continuing with their precarious informal economies and faced a parasitic fines and fees system that could lead to exacerbated charges—incarceration, deportation, trumped-up charges (having to plead guilty)—or to paying an aggravated fine rather than provide for the family. Programs like "El Protector" sought to mitigate some of this enforcement and hyper-policing, but the slated El Protector had already fomented mistrust in the communities he was meant to protect. A bilingual traffic cop cannot suddenly shape-shift into a community engagement officer. It's like a butcher joining PETA.

To liberalize regulations, legislators created crimes by creating more red tape, like the outright ban on trailers in Magda's case. The question became, Liberalize for whom? As Jules Bentley aptly queried, "Where was food truck advocacy then [when Jefferson Parish banned taco trucks]? Again, maybe those weren't the right kind of food trucks—not serving the right kind of food to the right kind of people."[59] Preference for gourmet trucks resulted in policy that reflected a whitewashed imagery of self-propelled trucks, one that matched national trends—mirroring what's happening in Portland more than local realities: an array of loncheras that introduced new foods and played an important role on the grassroots level in the recovery of the city.

Unpacking these stories unveils the layers of gendered factors at play. In many cases, women like Sofia, Susana, Magda, and Williana turned to street vending because of better wages, easier access to street vending jobs, and the sheer enjoyment of producing and sharing one's culture. The flexibility to take care of children while street vending was also attractive and helped the women save on childcare. For Magda and Sofia, their reproductive labor even expanded into Pierrette Hondagneu-Sotelo's concept of "transnational motherhood" in which they responded to family needs back home in Honduras while also providing for their families in New Orleans.[60]

These case studies demonstrate the à la carte approach to the question of whose culture fits into the social fabric of the city and push back against the white spatial imaginary vis-à-vis the tourism industry that shapes much of the redevelopment strategies and policymaking of the post-Katrina milieu. It is a complex story that often gets overlooked—one where the vendors who fed workers who helped cleaned up after Katrina and then settled in the city intertwined with the story of the economies that emerged in Black cultural spaces like second line parades and Candy Ladies, hustle economies that help with finances and sustenance.

Tracing the relationship between food, cultural producers, and regulation of street food vendors through fines and fees illustrates how Black and immigrant street food vendors asserted insurgent rights that responded to *their* culture and provided an integral service for *their* communities. It shows how people created new cultural economies, building on old traditions—outdoor markets and street vendors—as well as introducing new methods of selling foods to make ends meet. Second line vendors make pork chop sandwiches and sell Heinekens to *their* customers. Honduran lonchera workers make baleadas for *their* immigrant clientele. Candy Ladies sell snacks like pickled pig lips to *their* neighbors. These foods are not produced for a tourist gaze, and they don't fit national fads of what's trendy to eat. These street food vendors provide services in food-insecure areas from grassroots places; they keep the movements fed, hydrated, and . . . spirited.

Chapter 4

Right to Space

Creating Food Stands and Markets in the Suburbs

You know, I felt like I was in my Mexico. It felt like, well, Mexico in these spots called the *tianguis*.
— JUAN JOSÉ, former taqueria owner at La Pulga, 2017

One could easily outfit a 1950s kitchen—perhaps even an entire apartment—with one Saturday morning shopping spree in Algiers.
— SHELLY N. C. HOLLE, "Will West Bank Wonders Never Cease?," 1997

We live in a world, after all, where the rights of private property and the profit rate trump all other notions of rights one can think of. But there are occasions when the ideal of human rights takes a collective turn, as when the rights of labor, women, gays and minorities come to the fore.
— DAVID HARVEY, "The Right to the City," 2008

I just think everybody wants a chance to be given a chance. I mean, if I was in their country and I needed help, I would want their help too. What I do is I put myself in other people's shoes and say, "If this was me, what would I want?" and if I know that I would want this help, then that's the way I try to go about helping people.
— ANGELA DIX, owner of Dix Jazz Market, 2017

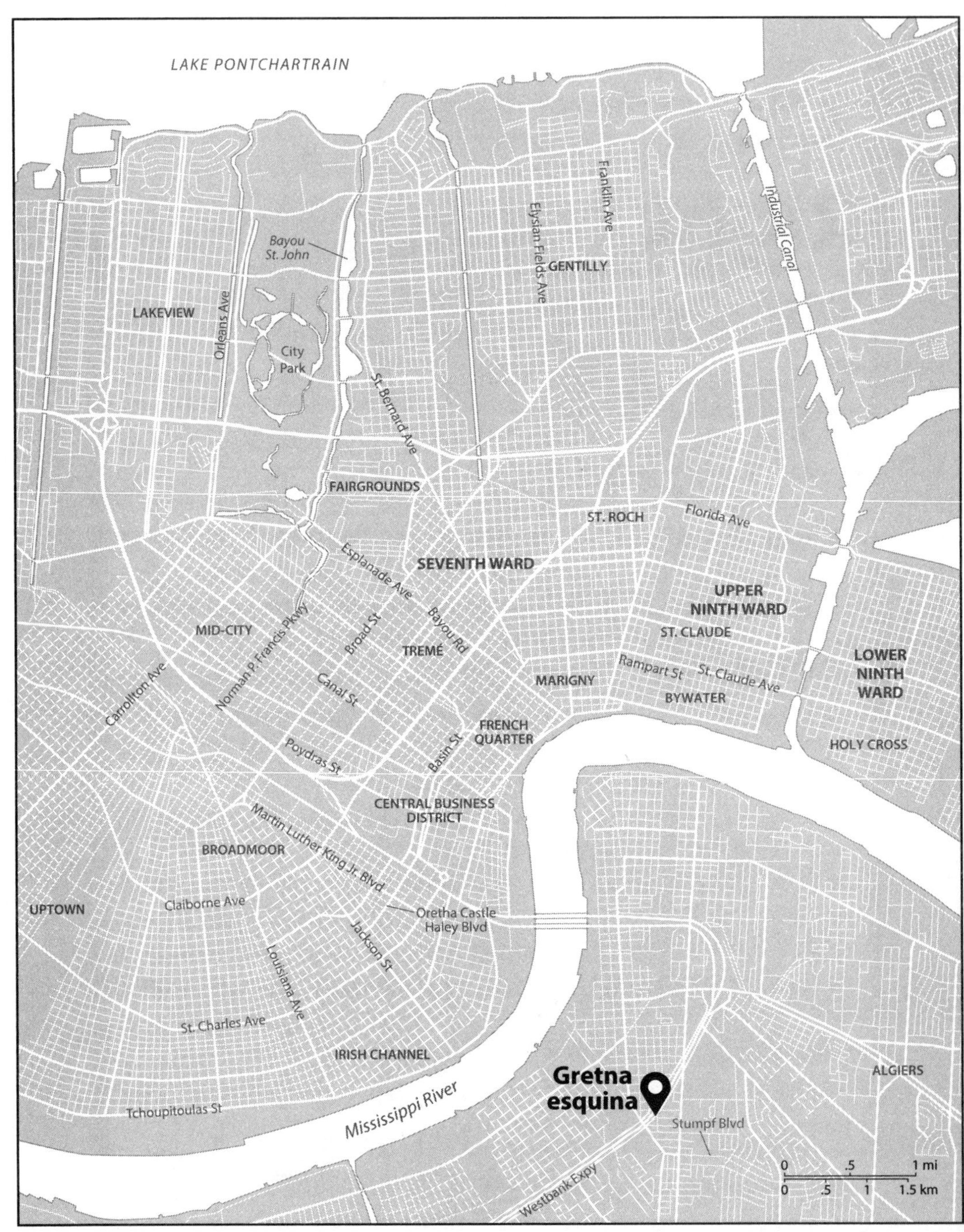

Gretna esquina in New Orleans.

Denis and I spent most of our time at the Gretna esquina, the most organized of the five main day-laborer corners in the New Orleans metropolitan area. Located across the Mississippi River on the "Westbank," reconstruction workers established the esquina in the immediate aftermath of Katrina in the small town of Gretna, the administrative center of Jefferson Parish. The parish, which delineates the western and southern suburban borders with Orleans Parish and makes up part of the New Orleans metropolitan area, hosts the state's largest "Hispanic" population at 19 percent.[1] From 2005 to 2011, the Gretna esquina went from a traffic imbroglio in front of Home Depot on the bustling Westbank Expressway to a designated area with a heavy-duty steel frame canopy tent, eight turquoise-painted picnic tables, trash cans, a bike rack, and a portable toilet all nestled under the I-90 underpass.[2]

The new space, which officially opened on January 31, 2011, saw a promising collaboration between Mayor Ronnie Harris of Gretna and El Congreso, led by Denis and Jacinta. Gretna city officials realized that ticketing day laborers for soliciting work was ineffective because their labor was needed and their method of looking for work was legal in the public space. Instead, the city opted for what Mayor Harris called "safe streets based on inclusion."[3] Home Depot donated the materials, and the day laborers built the tables. Contractors looking for hire could pull through the underpass with ample space to park and negotiate with workers. It was a rare win-win-win-win situation, and it emanated from listening to the needs of workers and adapting to what took place on the ground. The city even hosted a ribbon-cutting ceremony at the esquina.

Because the space served as Denis's home base when he was a day laborer, he had already established relationships with many of the men, whom he also recruited to attend the weekly Wednesday night El Congreso meetings. When Denis first arrived in New Orleans, he lived in Gretna near the esquina, but after he started working with El Congreso, he moved to Metairie. "It's just cheaper," he said when I asked why he lived in the suburbs. Denis's foundations at the Gretna corner made my acceptance easier, and my role was more legible because the men could also associate me with El Congreso meetings. My increased interactions, especially compared with those at the other esquinas, also meant I observed more of the everyday exchanges that took place during our visits.

"Vas a querer ver esto" (You'll want to see this), Denis said one day, knowing my interest in food. A car rolled in and a pair of women quickly exited, tending to a makeshift kitchen revealed as the hatchback door swung open.

As the men swarmed the car like a pit crew, the women swiftly served foods in Styrofoam containers. One woman took orders and collected payment as the other dished out over a dozen orders of *pollo con tajadas*, portioning out beds of fried green plantains and shredded cabbage topped with pieces of seasoned fried chicken, *chimol*, tangy tomato sauce, pickled onion, and *aderezo* (roughly, Russian dressing). It was a fast, clandestine, and highly coordinated delivery service to provide a quintessential Honduran dish to the workers.

Typically, a contractor put in an order for his crew with a trusted and favored vendor, requesting enough to feed his team members plates of satisfying lunches. Often, the vendors doubled the number of orders to have extra plates to sell to the day laborers at the corner who were not part of the crew. The Gretna esquina was a safe and easy spot from which to distribute the food, given the large space, which spanned approximately two-thirds the size of a football field and offered a guaranteed customer base.

Who sold food on what day depended on varying levels of convenience, networking, and crew leaders' preferences. For Sara, who was a longtime El Congreso leader, convenience and demand sent her from working solely on construction sites to the streets to sell food.[4]

"Food, well, it's a business that sells," she said when I asked her in 2017 how she ended up in food service. "What is made one day [on the construction site] can be made in three hours selling food."

Originally from Olancho, Honduras, Sara did not grow up making food. "I was an accountant," she said matter-of-factly about her former job in Honduras, "but that profession isn't valued here. You have to find a way to survive because life is very hard here."

She got her start by selling food in her neighborhood and delivering to the nearby Gretna corner, where Honduran workers sought out her plates of *pollo con tajadas*. She explained that because there was such a high demand for the foods that it was not competitive.

"Each person has their own people," she said. "Where we lived, we sold to our friends from our country."

When I asked how she learned to cook, I naively expected a romanticized story of a grandmother's kitchen. Instead, she sheepishly clarified that she never learned to cook in Honduras.

"I learned it all here," she said. "I just go to the Internet and there I search how to make it, all the ingredients, and then I prepare it."

Along with pop-up vendors like Sara, other food options flank the Gretna esquina, ranging from a corner store and a dive bar to two Vietnamese

A view of a fruit stand in the Algiers *pulga*.
Photo by Fernando López, @sentir.con.ojos.

restaurants and a taco stand called Taqueria Sanchez. Because of the ban on taco trucks in 2007, there were no free-roaming loncheras in the area; however, La Pulga, the colloquial name for the triad outdoor market that comprised the Algiers Flea Market, the Algiers Mini Mart Flea Market, and Dix Jazz Market, became a privately owned space where, with the right permission, loncheras and other itinerant street vendors could station themselves.

Just one mile northeast of the Gretna esquina, La Pulga thrives on a busy intersection near the I-90 overpass in the Algiers neighborhood. Located in Orleans Parish, just on the edge of Jefferson Parish, La Pulga is open only on the weekend and is busiest on Sundays. The bustling market, which has been in business since 1970, consists of makeshift booths, made of basic plywood infrastructure, that line dirt paths. The individual booths at La Pulga offer a range of items, from tchotchkes and soccer jerseys to live chickens and leather handcrafted goods.

Most notably, over thirty food booths fill Dix Jazz Market's section, almost exclusively offering Latin American specialties. The Black-owned market, run by Angela Dix, became a hub for Central American and Mexican food vendors in the aftermath of Katrina. When Angela initially purchased the property, she planned to use the land to build a restaurant; however, because the space had become so central to the immigrant community, the food vendors approached her asking her to allow them to continue to sell food. She obliged—rather than build her own restaurant, she helped them build out their stands to better serve the thousand customers each weekend.

Following La Pulga's model, Tri Cung opened another flea market with his uncle in 2017, located two miles southwest of the Gretna day-laborer corner. Often referred to as "La Nueva Pulga" or "La Pulga 2," the open-air market has two official names: 1) Nawlins Flea Market and Food Truck Park and 2) Westbank Flea Market. For consistency, I'll use Westbank Flea Market.

From the expressway, the chain-link-fence-enclosed market with a red corrugated roof looks more like a single-story storage unit center than an open-air market. The prefab walls, made of plywood, aluminum, and steel, along with the concrete floors, offer fixed-size and rainproof booths for the dozens of vendors. A range of barbershops, haberdashers, antique dealers, and food stalls fill the units. The food vendors distinguish their booths by decorating their spaces with tapestries, flags, and artisanal handicrafts that reflect their country of origin. Speakers blaring Honduran *punta* music or Mexican corridos indicate further hints of patriotism.

Opting for a more stable food vending opportunity, Sara opened her own stall, Golosinas Sarita, in the spring of 2017 in the Westbank Flea Market. She wanted a more consistent space for her growing clientele. And she wanted to have a licensed business rather than run the risk of being ticketed for her street vending hustle. Instead of delivering foods to the Gretna day-laborer corner, the contractors came to Sara's booth on the weekends to pick up orders or eat at one of the tables in front of her kitchen. During the week she continued her construction work and prepared for the weekend food sales.

Like at the Gretna esquina, the managers of La Pulga and the Westbank Flea Market adapted to what already existed by working with immigrants who, despite their precarious status—often undocumented, unlicensed, or with language barriers—actively produced and shaped their own urban spaces. These collectively produced spaces were forged in response to necessity, which was initially legitimized not by the state but by demand from their communities.[5] Given the opportunity and oftentimes advanced by unexpected alliances, these individuals moved to formalize their operations by cooperating with local and state governance.[6] These "unexpected spaces" show how collaborations took place as a way to navigate and legitimize otherwise precarious operations in locations beyond just the New Orleans city limits and into Jefferson Parish.[7]

Spanning the Mississippi River, Jefferson Parish borders over half of Orleans Parish and includes small suburban cities like Gretna, Kenner, and Metairie, stretching south to small fishing and shrimp communities along the Gulf of Mexico. The 1950s postwar context of highway construction, festering racist sentiments stemming from the desegregation of Orleans Parish schools, and new technology to drain water out of swamps set the stage for the development of the Jefferson Parish suburbs. White flight helped Jefferson Parish boom, and devastation from Hurricane Betsy in 1965 further exacerbated the influx of white people into the suburbs.

At the same time, this white flight also included Honduran immigrants who worked in the banana industry and lived near the wharves in the Lower Garden District. In the mid-twentieth century, the neighborhood was dubbed "El Barrio Lempira" because of the large Honduran community and the ubiquity of services targeting the Spanish-speaking community, from movie theaters to corner stores and restaurants. The Honduran white flight, particularly to Kenner, created the foundation for Jefferson Parish to contemporarily boast almost 80,000 "Hispanic" people and the highest percentage in the state.[8] Affordable and available housing also helped cement that status.[9] The Williams Boulevard thoroughfare in Kenner exemplifies this growth, encompassing a long strip of Latin American restaurants with some Chinese, Middle Eastern, and Southeast Asian food establishments scattered in between.

Drawing from a spatial analysis of interactions that took place beyond the city center and the tourist zones, this chapter provides insight into the Greater New Orleans area. Matching trends across other cities, suburbs in Jefferson Parish have radically diversified, deviating from the stereotypical twentieth-century white picket fence, middle-class white family.[10] Gentrification and the proliferation of short-term rentals in New Orleans neighborhoods have pushed people out due to lack of affordable housing. Poorer and working-class people of color, like Denis, can access more affordable and, oftentimes, more spacious homes in the suburbs. Nevertheless, racialized policies like the taco truck ban still exist, and Jefferson Parish overwhelmingly supported Trump in the 2016 and 2020 elections.[11] Hence the unexpected spaces that take shape, in which alliances take place where people collaborate and make space together.

In the case of the Gretna esquina, rather than criminalize day laborers for seeking out work, city officials actually worked *with* the day laborers to produce the space together. At the flea markets, the owners of the open-air markets embraced the demand by responding to the popularity of these Latin American food vendors and creating formalized ways for the vendors to sell their goods. The markets helped to legitimize hustle economies and those behind them, like Sara, who began selling food itinerantly. For some vendors, having the financial capital to open a restaurant was too far out of reach, and the flea markets offered an affordable, familiar, and semipermanent setting to sell their foods.

Thus, this chapter, which spans 2011 to 2018, is about establishing the right to space by forging unexpected alliances. It traces how individuals moved from the informal sector to more formalized operations to mitigate precarity and allow for a more stable livelihood in an established market. The case studies illustrate how La Pulga and the Westbank Flea Market served as important hubs for the immigrant community to provide a familiar method of vending, one that brought to mind the open-air markets ubiquitous in Latin America. The markets also served as incubator spaces for small businesses to test recipes and build capital for future endeavors. And they presented job opportunities and provided community for other marginalized groups. As these case studies show, unexpected alliances emerged in these spaces, bringing together unlikely bedfellows who recognized demand, located mutually beneficial resources, and built collaborative solutions together.

FLEA MARKETS, FOOD HALLS, AND LA PULGA: OPPORTUNITIES AND UNEXPECTED ALLIANCES

New Orleans food writer Ian McNulty called the markets a "destination for Latin American cooking."[12] Juan José, a taqueria owner, likened La Pulga to "los tianguis," or the open-air markets in Mexico.[13] Food writer Helen Freund called the markets "longtime cultural meeting points for the city's Latin American community."[14] Tri Cung referred to the Westbank Flea Market as a "culinary center."[15] Traditionally, the term "flea market" or *pulga* (flea) refers to places to sell and purchase secondhand goods; yet, the gastronomic fare propelled the appeal of La Pulga and the Westbank Flea Market far more than their everyday bric-a-brac.

"Food hall," perhaps, provides a more serviceable name, yet that term is rife with undertones of gentrification, especially in the context of post-Katrina New Orleans. The food-hall revival has grown across the United States in the twenty-first century, and cities such as New Orleans are quick to invest in this form of redevelopment, offering tax credits and community development block grants while doing little to ensure that these markets don't contribute to displacement.[16] Food halls can serve as a generator space for start-up vendors but oftentimes carry an overhead cost out of reach for many vendors who lack capital to pay and maintain fees.

For example, the St. Roch Market, an upscale food hall located in the highly gentrified St. Roch neighborhood located in the Upper Ninth Ward, charged $10,000 in startup fees, then a subsequent 30 percent monthly charge on all sales with a minimum monthly payment of $4,500. Left vacant after Katrina, the St. Roch Market, which was built in 1875 and modernized with WPA funds in 1937, historically served the working-class neighborhood as a fish market offering an array of fresh seafood and prepared foods such as po'boys. In the public-private agreement where the city invested $3.7 million of FEMA money to rehabilitate the former fish market, the white transplant developers who won the bid started out leasing the 6,800-square-foot space from the city for $3,500 per month, a sum that grew to a $6,500 maximum over the course of their ten-year contract.[17] The grant terms under the HUD Community Development Block Grant Disaster Recovery program required that 70 percent of the space be used "to benefit low and moderate-income residents."[18] The objective was not met until new management took over in 2023, when longtime vendor Kevin Pedeaux assumed leadership and made the market more affordable and equitable for vendors. Before the shift, the market was a key symbol of gentrification, an image that's hard to shake.[19]

In 2015, during the parade that spanned the city in observance of the tenth anniversary of Hurricane Katrina, Ecohybridity, a dance troupe organized by artist Kai Lamumba Barrow, targeted the St. Roch Market in an act of civil disobedience. The market had become a symbol of the predatory actions of developers (and the city). Ten Ecohybridity troupe members, dressed in all white, entered the front space, positioning themselves in between the cast-iron columns that buttress the twenty-five-foot ceiling.

As part of the dance performance, Ecohybridity admonished the developers for contributing to displacement and the loss of community in the neighborhood. After their choreographed dance, the participants said in unison, "This used to be a fish market," and, in a clear rebuke, they dumped a dead fish on the market's epoxied floor.[20] While the St. Roch Market has tried to defend its business by highlighting its efforts at hiring a local workforce, developing apprenticeship programs, and matching price points (a nine-dollar po-boy) with other food establishments, its space serves as easy fodder for critics of predatory capitalist models enabled by the city.

In many ways, the comparison of the St. Roch Market and the flea markets is apples and oranges—the flea markets are open only on the weekends, they are located on the outskirts of the city (so they are not tourist destinations), they serve completely different demographics, and they don't sell alcohol; while the St. Roch Market occupies a historical space owned by the city. However, each market provides a similar model that formalizes the process for pop-up food vendors and serves as an incubator space for burgeoning, often immigrant-owned businesses.

Juxtaposed with the St. Roch Market, the flea markets offer an alternative paradigm, one that is built from the bottom up and is informed by grassroots vendors who work with the owners of the individual markets at rates that are affordable and on terms that are collaborative.[21] Because the flea markets don't fit neatly within a national food hall trend or zoning models that are easily regulated, the flea markets, particularly La Pulga, face their own criticism that comes largely from local governance and indignant neighbors.

The Algiers Flea Market began in 1970 when Oscar Lacinak opened his garage door, assembled some tables, and sold antiques. Noticing his successes selling some sought-after sundries like candelabras, New Orleans Saints swag, midcentury dish sets, pottery, and clocks, Lacinak joined forces with Laton Weinberger, rented more spaces in his yard, and gradually grew out the makeshift market. In 1975, Betty Grandbouche opened a snowball stand alongside tables filled with knickknacks next door to Lacinak and Weinberger. By 1997, the maze of makeshift booths swallowed up Lacinak's home. "I got a nice house here, but you can't see it for the junk," he once said.[22]

As the market expanded, so did critiques from neighbors and city officials. "I should be filing suit against them for interfering with my livelihood," said Betty Grandbouche in the summer of 1985 in response to a group of homeowners in the Algiers neighborhood who attempted to sue her and the flea market's other two owners.[23] Fed up with piled-up trash, increased traffic, lowered property values, and "unsanitary acts" (people urinating behind trees), the homeowners association filed an unsuccessful lawsuit with the aim of shutting down the market. The New Orleans City Council cited the owners for violating zoning laws and illegally using city property, forcing the owners to cut back on parking and restricting market operations to just the commercial zoning areas.[24] Betty Grandbouche, who operated her section of the flea market from 1975 until her death in 2015, pushed back against the claims, stating that she paid $400 per month for cleanup and security in the neighborhood block. The owners withstood the complaints and continued expanding.

In its early stages, the flea market served as a food vendor hub, particularly for the growing Vietnamese community. On its website, the popular Vietnamese American restaurant Pho Tau Bay proudly announces that it "operated a stand in the Algiers flea market until 1982."[25] The expansion of the Algiers market corresponded with the fall of Saigon in 1975, and the New Orleans metropolitan area became an important resettlement area for 2,100 Vietnamese refugees.[26] The family of Pho Tau Bay's owner, Tuyet Cao, owned thirteen restaurants in Saigon. After fleeing Vietnam, Tuyet and her husband, Karl Takacs (an American GI who was stationed in Vietnam, where he met Tuyet), decided to carry on Tuyet's family tradition and opened the booth in the Algiers market. Once the owners earned enough capital, they opened a brick-and-mortar restaurant on the Westbank Expressway, located just a half mile from the Gretna day-laborer corner, until 2015 when they relocated across the Mississippi River to Tulane Avenue.

With some exceptions like Pho Tau Bay, the Algiers Flea Market remained predominantly a traditional flea market until after Katrina, when thousands of Central Americans and Mexicans settled in the city. Food stalls selling *pollo con tajadas*, baleadas, and tacos emerged alongside the tables of antiques and mass-produced goods, providing an important space for the new immigrant community while also facing continued criticisms from neighbors and city officials. Some flea market owners also complained. "They're ruining the market," said the outspoken Betty Grandbouche in 2014 during an interview for *Vice*. "I have tried my best to keep them off of that lot."[27]

While Betty Grandbouche saw the Central American and Mexican community as a threat to her section of the market, Angela Dix fully embraced the new immigrants. Prior to Hurricane Katrina, Angela Dix's family ran a chicken and seafood restaurant in the Central City neighborhood in New Orleans.[28] When the restaurant was destroyed by Katrina, Angela's family sought out land on higher ground to rebuild their Creole-style restaurant. In 2007, her father purchased the land adjacent to the Algiers Flea Market, which was on a derelict, overgrown lot with no infrastructure. Angela's initial goal was to build out their restaurant and have vendors rent spaces to sell goods around their restaurant. But as immigrant food vendors, such as Imelda of Gorditas Zacatecanas, were forced to close or turned away from the adjacent flea markets, they asked Angela if they could build on her newly acquired land.

"It flourished into eleven restaurants later on, so it was like, 'Okay I'm not doing my restaurant.' It's not even my market, meaning it's not my food; it's their niche. And so, I've just started to work with them to help them build their business," she said, adding, "I'm a landlord."

After clearing out the overgrowth and putting gravel down, Angela's focus turned to helping the vendors build out their booths. The vendors pay a $100 weekly rental fee per space, which they construct to their liking. And even though she speaks very little Spanish, Angela facilitates that process.

"I took them to Home Depot and we just built the buildings," she said. "At the beginning, we were all just like, 'OK, we're all in this together.' So I just built one at a time."

She helped vendors create a fee schedule so they could finance their own construction, and they worked together to build out the spaces with each vendor deciding the scale they sought. Angela provided the electricity through a generator and water through a shared spigot. By 2013, the individual booths were constructed out of plywood with Gorditas Zacatecanas, a Mexican-owned stand, opening as the first major food stall in the Dix Jazz Market section of La Pulga.

It is easiest to imagine the markets at La Pulga as sections of a rhombus-shaped city block. The Algiers Flea Market occupies the northwesternmost corner, the Algiers Mini Mart Flea Market is in the northeastern corner, Dix Jazz Market takes up the southwestern corner, and the parking lot, which is owned and run by Angela, occupies the southeastern corner. Except for a few Central American stands in the Algiers Flea Market, the majority of La Pulga's approximately thirty food vendors are managed by Angela.

At Dix Jazz Market, Gorditas Zacatecanas operates like a stand-alone restaurant and spans two sections of the market. Divided by a corridor, one side of the stand focuses on the fruit-based beverages—*licuados* (smoothies), milkshakes, fruit cups, *raspados* (shaved ice), *rusa* drinks (mix of citrus, chili, and grapefruit soda), *mango con chile*, and an array of aguas frescas (fresh juices)—and the other side focuses on variations of gorditas and tacos with over fifteen types of meat, vegetable, and cheese fillings.

Mismatched chairs and tables provide ample seating on the fruit-stand side. A sit-down counter wraps around the eating area of the gordita stand. A condiment bar filled with salsas, cucumbers, and charred jalapeños sits adjacent to the walk-up window where the food orders are taken. The colorful, open-air stall features a large hand-painted sign that towers above the green walls decorated with fake tropical plants and fruits that line the exterior; smaller menus handwritten on bright posterboard are hung throughout. The entire space sits atop a wooden platform with the two sections covered by a shingled roof.

Imelda, the matriarch of the family who runs the stand, which opened in 2011, explained that they opted for the food stall in La Pulga because of the lonchera ban in Jefferson Parish.

"It would have been easy to have a lonchera before," she said. "But they took away the permits, right? We wanted to sell daily, but my husband said, 'No, they don't allow for the permits. We'll waste on a lonchera.' And for what? It's better how we are."

For Imelda and others in a similar position, La Pulga became an alternative to a pop-up business or a lonchera model. Even though the market is limited to weekends, it allows for an established operation in a well-known and accessible market with low overhead. For a weekly set rental fee and with minimal red tape, vendors can build out their own space to cater to the thousand patrons who visit weekly. When I asked Imelda if she wanted to open her own brick-and-mortar restaurant, she said, "Let's see in the future. But the truth is, I don't think so because there's so much cost, just a lot, yeah. We better stay with Angela, yes."

At Dix Jazz Market, some vendors operate out of a single window; meanwhile, others, like Imelda, have expanded their booths, building what equates to a small restaurant open on Saturday and Sunday. Xiomara, the Honduran owner of Delicias el Jamo, explained that opening her restaurant in Dix Jazz Market made much more economic sense. Named for the Honduran iguana *jamo*, which is occasionally featured on the menu, Xiomara's stand sits along the western side of the market and consists of a kitchen and seating area equipped with four picnic tables. A television hangs in the top corner of the dining area, providing a large enough screen for passersby to peek in to catch the score of the latest soccer game. The booth is built with plywood supported by two-by-fours and has a wooden platform floor and a shingled roof.

Xiomara explained that when she first moved to New Orleans from Florida, she lost money she had invested in a restaurant in New Orleans when the landlord forced her to make a $5,000 down payment and cover outstanding utility bills. Because the restaurant was such a mess, Xiomara also had to hire a second person just to help her clean the space, sapping more capital.

When she sold only one plate of *pollo con tajadas* in a week, she realized that was it. "I lost all my money," she lamented.

La Pulga provided more opportunities and covered the basics, like "the water, who throws out the garbage," she said. "You pay the owner; it's like a restaurant. Everything is paid for."

The open-air market has its struggles, too. The few shingled roofs are reinforced by blue tarps and provide little coverage from inclement weather. On rainy days, the dirt-lined pathways quickly turn to mud, and larger booths like Gordita Zacatecanas and Delicias el Jamo provide the only shelter. Wooden planks serve as refuge from puddles that checker the uncovered corridors. Public bathrooms are also limited. Running water comes from a single spigot that supplies each of the booths through above-ground hoses. And zoning laws are, at best, nebulous and, at worst, ignored; and just like the pre-Katrina days, neighbors complain about trash and parking.

To avoid complaints from neighbors and to appease state officials, Angela runs a generous but tight ship. After enclosing her space with a chain-link fence, she dedicated half of her lot to parking, building a small shack where she collects a fee from each carload of people. At the market, she prohibits the sale of fireworks, firearms, knives, drugs, tobacco, pirated media, stolen goods, and pornographic materials. The strict policy reflects a raid that took place in the market in 2010 when ICE officials confiscated 16,000 items of counterfeit merchandise valued at $256,171.[29] While the state government has attempted to push back against the market, Angela has diligently fought to maintain the market and justifies the space on the same terms as a weekly farmers' market or a weekend festival. Angela requires her vendors to purchase a Special Event Occupational License from the City of New Orleans, and each booth must have a fire extinguisher.

Angela's work with the vendors also extends beyond the market. "What she's not telling you is that she has a non-profit organization where she goes to help them find houses and bring kids to school," Angela's close friend and market assistant, Victorine, explained. "I witnessed her doing that all the time—finding houses, bringing women to the hospital." Pointing across the parking lot at Angela's truck, Victorine said, "Belongs to all these people."[30]

On the few occasions when her vendors have had encounters with ICE or there have been threats of raids in the city, she reached out to me with questions. I would connect her with El Congreso organizers, who linked her with resources. "I want so much for my vendors," Angela wrote in a follow-up email with me. "I wish them nothing but the best, and my only regret is I wish I were in a position to assist more of them in achieving their personal and financial goals."

Angela's original vision for her family-owned chicken and seafood restaurant completely shifted to adapt to the needs of the growing immigrant community. Without speaking Spanish—though she's learning—Angela has since worked hard to gain trust and to support the vendors in her market, meeting their needs, building community, and navigating bureaucratic processes.

On top of managing the dozens of vendors in Dix Jazz Market, Angela has also provided what equates to wrap-around services for the vendors, which Victorine referred to tongue-in-cheekily as a "non-profit." Rather than seeing the overgrown lot solely through the lens of profit, Angela and the vendors imagined a more collaborative space built through this unexpected alliance. After being excluded in the other markets, the immigrant vendors were bold to approach her. And she was bold to accept their request.

Compared with the growing trend of food halls, the flea market offers an alternative paradigm to those costly public-private projects—a grassroots effort that emerged in an unexpected space that brings together Black New Orleanians' cultural traditions with new Central American and Mexican immigrants. The story of La Pulga also builds on a long tradition of open-air markets that serve as an incubator space for start-up businesses like the owners of Pho Tau Bay. For newly arrived immigrants, it is an important and affordable space with low barriers of entry. In Imelda's case, it has also served to formalize her family-run food stand when other options, like loncheras, were banned or restricted. Thus, operating on the outskirts of the city, legitimized through community demand, and formalized by a weekend festival license, La Pulga managers have successfully navigated bureaucracy and asserted their right to space.

WESTBANK FLEA MARKET AND BUILDING COMMUNITY IN UNEXPECTED SPACES

Like La Pulga, a similar tale of unexpected alliances helped shape the Westbank Flea Market's scope. "The food vendors kept coming to us. It grew from them," said Tri Cung, manager of the Westbank Flea Market. By opening the market, Tri and his uncle wanted to repay the generosity they had received when they arrived as immigrants to New Orleans. He noted how challenging it was to be immigrants in a new country, navigating an entirely new place. With the help from family and friends, they were able to adapt and make space by being innovative and scrappy. "Without help from outside resources, we might not be where we are today."

Part of that generosity came from Betty Grandbouche at the Algiers Flea Market. "Oh, she was great, very helpful." When Tri and his family came to the United States from Vietnam in 1981, much like the owners of Pho Tau Bay, they got their start as vendors in Betty Grandbouche's Algiers Flea Market.

"My love for other cultures branched out there. It's where we got our first opportunities and got our small business started. We sold tennis shoes, another uncle sold home decor, artwork, dollar-store items [like] household products. It provided us the platform to dip our toes in. In the Algiers market, we rented a little house-like structure on the corner and set up every weekend. Even my grandfather was out there with us," Tri said. "We wanted to pay it forward and create a platform for people to share things like artwork and foods."

Located on a four-acre lot in Harvey, in Jefferson Parish, the market sits on a concrete slab and contains two large metal shade structures, two storage shelters painted blue with red garage doors, and one office building with bathrooms. Within the fenced-in area, two entry gates open to a large parking area that accommodates customers, vendors, and even food trucks.

Completed in 2017, the space began as a traditional flea market where an array of vendors—selling anything from antiques and vintage T-shirts to cowboy hats and used electronics—could use the storage units to stash their goods in between weekend sales. The concept of the market shifted as food vendors requested more spots and the space quickly turned into a flea market *and* a food hall. At times, they tacked on "food truck park" and "pop-up spot" to social media advertisements, too.

"It came about because we were out there and thought it would be nice if we had some food out here. People selling different household items. You know what, we could really use some food out here," Tri said. "It was really that simple."

The Westbank Flea Market first made major headlines when it hosted the Pho Festival in June 2018. Members of the Vietnamese American community joined forces to host the event, which brought together Catholic and Buddhist Vietnamese religious communities who had settled on the Westbank.[31] Tri saw great opportunity to showcase the vast Southeast Asian cuisines based in Jefferson Parish. Yet, aside from the onetime Pho Festival and despite the market being managed by Vietnamese Americans, the only Southeast Asian business at the Westbank Flea Market was run by Tri's uncle, who built a hydroponics garden to grow and sell lettuces and herbs from raised beds.

"When we left our country, everyone lived in poverty; food was scarce; opportunities were scarce. The idea that one person could manage a farm and feed thousands of people really intrigued my uncle," Tri said. "And it was a nice balance with the prepared foods."

The uncle was unable to maintain it after some time because he was occupied by other tinkering projects. And, though Tri's uncle trained an employee to take over the garden and shift to only producing and selling hydroponics, the uncle and new hire ultimately switched to growing items in regular soil. The hydroponics vision was short lived and, instead, they turned the focus to the vendors.

Since opening in the spring of 2017, food vendors either established their kitchen and seating area in the individual storage units or, like the approach at Dix Jazz Market, built their own stalls under the metal shade structures. Venecia, the Dominican owner of El Recoqueo DR, was among the first to open her stall in one of the storage units. She began as a street vendor working out of her home to prepare plates of *arroz con gandú* (rice with pigeon peas) served with either fish or beef. Like Sara, she delivered the dishes to workplaces, mostly selling food to fellow Dominicans. But she constantly sought out a permanent location.

"Then I heard the [radio] announcement," she said, laughing warmly. "And I just went there. . . . And I saw it said 'New Flea Market.'"

She immediately called the owner, Tri, and asked what it would take to get a stand. When she told him what kind of food she sold, he was pleased because none of the vendors sold Dominican food. She said, "I was motivated to see the opportunity that they were giving to everyone. For us to grow there. To demonstrate our culture."

When Sara shifted from selling her Honduran food at the Gretna day-laborer esquina, she opted to construct her own stall under the open-air roof, building a U-shaped bar out of plywood with a seating area in front. Behind the bar, Sara prepared her famous *pollo con tajadas* along with other Honduran classics. Sara said she chose the Westbank Flea Market because it was "modern."

"It is different from the others," she said. "The space is super-comfortable; it is spacious; it has public bathrooms; it's very clean."

Given it is a recent construction, the Westbank Flea Market provides protection from inclement weather and offers amenities, including a public bathroom plus gas and water supplied to each booth.

Ivan, the Mexican co-owner of Antojitos Garibaldi, had a somewhat different origin story at the Westbank Flea Market because he initially wanted to open at La Pulga. After having worked in a range of kitchens, Ivan sought to formalize his catering hustle in which he prepared food for events like quinceañeras and weddings and, like Sara, for construction crews. Carlos, a roofing contractor originally from Mexico, explained, "I ask Ivan to prepare food for my crew, of course. I always find him wherever he is. He makes foods from Mexico that I like."

Because of this growing demand, Ivan initially wanted to open his food stall at Dix Jazz Market.

"We wanted to open it there. But we couldn't do it because of the economic barrier," he said, noting that he didn't have enough capital to pay for the materials to build out at the scale he wanted. "Then a few months ago, a friend told us, 'There's a new flea market, would you be interested in it?' I said yes."

Ivan and his partner (business and romantic), Gilberto, opened their Mexican restaurant in the spring of 2017. Located next to Venecia's Dominican stand, Ivan and Gilberto decorated their storage unit with traditional Mexican handicrafts, colorful serape tablecloths, traditional straw hats, and red, white, and green streamers that matched the three-by-six-foot Mexican flag hanging on the interior wall.

Ivan, Venecia, and Sara joined together with other Latin American food vendors to share their culture while making ends meet. At an affordable price ($150 per weekend with all utilities included), the Westbank Flea Market provides them a secure space to formalize their operations and gives their customers a destination on the weekend. Like Angela Dix, who acquiesced to the immigrant vendors at La Pulga, Tri Cung completely shifted the framework of his flea market concept to adapt to the desires of the food vendors, thus creating an expansive market that showcases a range of mini-restaurants and unveils a microcosm of a changing city, all under one roof.

These unexpected alliances took shape organically, in many ways in response to local exclusionary policies like the Jefferson Parish ban on loncheras and as a sanctuary for street food vendors who sought to formalize their precarious economies amid growing fears of an increasingly vindictive and reactionary federal anti-immigration state under the Trump administration. In the case of Ivan, the Westbank Flea Market also served as a refuge for his LGBTQ "family," providing a space for employment, serving as a moneymaker to support the transgender immigrant community, and offering a means to increase visibility of members of this community in their efforts to assert legitimacy and right to space.

When I first met Ivan in 2012, he was working as head cook at Norma's Bakery, a Honduran grocery store with a small restaurant and bakery located in Mid-City. Behind the enclosed buffet line, Ivan, wearing a toque blanche and white apron, took orders from the Spanish-speaking customers hungry for the black beans, *arroz amarillo*, *caldo de res*, pork chops, and other typical foods that filled the chafing dishes. After a few visits to Norma's Bakery, Ivan, a gregarious character, portly in build with long, dark hair worn in a ponytail, recognized me as one of the few white people that frequented that space at the time.

During each visit, our interactions increased and consisted mostly of small talk. In one early encounter, he asked candidly, "¿Eres gay?" (Are you gay?)

Caught off guard, but quite amused, I nodded my head: "Yes."

He chuckled. "I thought so," he replied, adding the "Me too" that I'd anticipated.

From that moment, Ivan and I had a connection. Anytime I showed up with a friend, he gave me a wink and asked, "Is that your girlfriend?" Always ready with the mischievous quip, he'd say playfully, "¿Porque no?" (Why not?) or "Que linda" (How pretty).

In my first of many interviews with Ivan, he welcomed me into his small apartment on the first floor of a house near Norma's. It was clean and simple with a corner dedicated to the Virgin Mary.

"You can be Catholic and gay," he said with a side-eye, adding, "I want to show you something."

I indulged him, following him into his room. He pushed aside a makeshift curtain unveiling a collection of flashy, sequined dresses, boas, and wigs next to his everyday jeans and button-down shirts. He pulled out each dress, explaining to me the drag persona that went along with each outfit. "This is Selena," he said, holding a sequined purple dress.

Ivan is originally from Potrero Nuevo, a small municipality in the coastal state of Veracruz, Mexico. He came to the United States in 2003 because of the lack of jobs in the region and the antigay sentiments of his town.[32] Ivan knew he was gay from a young age but understood that in his rural community, being gay was frowned upon. Because he faced such antigay sentiments and had few opportunities for work, he and his partner at the time decided to leave their families and friends behind. Destination: Dothan, Alabama, a semirural town with a population of about 60,000. Considered the "Peanut Capital of the United States," Dothan is in the southeastern corner of the state, just north of Tallahassee, Florida. While it was hardly the gay metropolis they envisioned, friends connected them with work in the area.

Ivan explained that while living in Dothan, he developed his drag persona, Ivette. "It all began in a thrift store run by the Catholic Church," he said. "There was an older lady there, and she knew that I was always looking for dresses. And when a new shipment of used dresses would come in, she would put a few aside for me if she thought they would fit." He pointed to a dress in his apartment. "This one is from Dothan. I really like it."

After four years in Alabama, Ivan and his partner broke up, and Ivan decided to leave Dothan. New Orleans was still deep in recovery from Katrina, and Ivan knew people who had moved there for construction jobs. Given New Orleans's openness to the LGBTQ community plus all the costumes, feathers, and overall flamboyance of the city, it had already popped up on Ivan's radar as a potential destination. When he arrived in 2007, he immediately began work in the rebuilding efforts, but he didn't enjoy the construction work. "It wasn't for me," he said, shaking his index finger. Ivan shifted to the food service sector, selling prepared foods to construction sites and bouncing around between kitchen jobs across the metropolitan area. Working back-of-house in mostly Honduran-owned restaurants, Ivan added his own Mexican twists to the Central American menus.

"I follow him everywhere," said Carlos, who first found Ivan when he worked in a Honduran restaurant near the racetrack in New Orleans. "The one time I lost him, I quickly found him again. I heard his voice in the kitchen. You can't miss that voice."

Ivan laughed when I relayed what Carlos said. "Ivan!" he yelled, mimicking Carlos's deep voice. "He really does follow me everywhere."

In 2013, I first saw Ivan perform a show as Ivette at a Mexican restaurant on Elysian Fields Avenue. Dressed in a sequined red dress with flowing black hair, Ivette moved gracefully through the tables, lip-synching the words to a Celia Cruz song. Ivette passed my chair, brushing my shoulder, and headed toward the table next to us, which was full of Norma's Bakery employees. The crowd erupted, clapping and whistling. The show continued with Ivette as the solo performer, singing six songs as three different personas: Celia, Selena, and Paquita la del Barrio. More people trickled in as the night went on. After the show, Ivan, back in his regular jeans and button-down, greeted our table, proud of the performance and the crowd. He said he'd let me know when the next show would be.

"I put on the first gay beauty pageant in Louisiana [for the Spanish-speaking community]. And you didn't even make it," he said, reemploying that side-eye. In 2014, the "Miss New Orleans Latina Gay" pageant took place at the Copacabana Club, a "Latino nightclub" located in Metairie, just west of New Orleans in Jefferson Parish. He said at first the owners of different clubs were "taken aback" when he approached them to host a gay beauty pageant. "They told me that Metairie was not prepared for a beauty pageant, that I would have to go to New Orleans where they have Decadence," or "gay Mardi Gras." Ivan's friends feared for the safety of the LGBTQ community—many of whom are trans *and* undocumented—if the show was hosted in the conservative suburb. Nearby New Orleans's libertine spirit was much better suited for all the gaiety and drag.

But Ivan was committed to Copacabana and pushing the limits in Jefferson Parish, where he also resides. "When someone tells me I can't be somewhere, I latch on anyway. I won't settle for no . . . because we all have rights. And they have to treat you with your rights, you know? As a citizen, as a person. It doesn't matter the sexual orientation. You are who you are, and people have to learn to respect."

Copacabana owners remained supportive, and the show stayed in Metairie. Ivan had no sponsors at that point, and he needed money to buy decorations, prizes for the contestants, and for his own costume. Ivan ultimately bankrolled that first pageant by selling his homemade tamales.

"Pageants aren't cheap," he said. "People think I make money. That's not the case." With the tamale money, Ivan was able to procure the supplies and pay a DJ. "We filled Copacabana that night. It's a big place." He gloated.

Over the next couple years, Ivan and I maintained some communication via text message or at an occasional El Congreso meeting, where we would catch up. I knew he had left Norma's Bakery in late 2014 to work as a line cook in a local taco chain. He wanted to participate more in El Congreso, but his work schedule made it difficult for him to attend the Wednesday evening meetings.

At that point, Ivan's organizing with the LGTBQ immigrant community had also moved beyond drag shows and pageants. Because undocumented LGBTQ immigrants are at the intersection of two marginalized groups, everyday challenges are compounded; ineligibility for most public services means health care access and education are oftentimes inaccessible. It's bleak but a reality in a society imbued with anti-immigrant sentiments and that ostracizes anyone who veers from heteronormativity. It's heightened in the southern suburbs *and* within the Spanish-speaking community, which tends to be overwhelmingly Catholic or evangelical. Already fleeing their families back home because of rampant anti-LGBTQ sentiments, the people in this community face the extreme violence that persists in the United States, from hate crimes and sexual abuse to state violence through detention and solitary confinement.

Having a community means everything. Ivan saw his community as something more intimate. "More than anything we use 'family' because here in this country many of us are immigrants; many do not have family," he said. "And it's always nice that someone opens the door to their home, you know?"

Much of this support took place in his own home, where he hosted weekly meetings. Ivan used his social capital to liaise between his family and local organizations—El Congreso, BreakOut! (an organization dedicated to ending the criminalization of LGBTQ youth), and health care institutions like No AIDS Task Force (later, CrescentCare).[33] Ivan also connected his LGBTQ family to jobs in the food service sector, either alongside him in the local taco chain or in his own burgeoning side hustle, which he operated out of his house in Kenner.

Ivan's family meetings intertwined fun and merriment with fundraisers, sharing foods, and connecting folks to medicine and other resources. When one transgender woman was attacked and hit in the head with a glass bottle during a routine visit to a corner store, the family showed up.

"Can you imagine, this girl was not prepared for this expense, you know?" Ivan said with dismay. "Now, how much does she have to pay? And aside from that, it's not so much about the money, because the money comes and goes, but if it was worse? What if they had killed her?" Ivan hosted a bingo night complete with dinner to raise funds for her.

In another incident, at the local taco chain, Ivan's friend was harassed by a customer for being transgender. Ivan explained that the customer said "really ugly things to her, calling her names, to the point that he almost got violent with her." As the situation approached physical violence, the manager kicked the customer out. Ivan was so pleased by the response and took some credit for educating the manager on transgender rights. It was a traumatic and unfortunate incident, yet Ivan was grateful for the support and safe space demonstrated by the employer. He sought to foster that welcoming and affirming space through his own future food establishment and certainly through his pageants.

On December 13, 2015, I attended the second annual "Miss New Orleans Latina Gay" pageant at Casa Tequila, a bar and restaurant in Kenner—another Jefferson Parish suburb. The show featured a dance performance by each of the five contestants, who represented four different nations in the Americas and one from the Philippines. The contestants competed in three areas: swimwear, "traditional" outfit, and evening attire. In between the three rounds, Ivan performed his classics, switching back and forth from Ivan to Ivette, seamlessly changing mid-performance from khakis and a blazer to a full-length gown. The front of the stage was reserved for a panel of judges consisting of local celebrities—artists, health care workers, nonprofit directors, and even an English-speaking oil rigger (the boyfriend of the emcee).

Organizers from El Congreso hosted a table at the pageant, promoting their collaboration with BreakOut! Starting in 2011, El Congreso and BreakOut! leaders Jacinta Gonzalez and Wes Ware connected their members' shared struggles fighting against criminalization and for their rights to space in the city.[34] Part of their unlikely partnership included the campaign "From Vice to ICE," which developed links between immigrants, people of color, low-wage workers, and the LGBTQ community.

"When we started to get close with them on campaigns, it was a little different, something new for me," Santos, one of El Congreso leaders, said of collaborating with BreakOut! "But they have always been important allies. In all of our actions, in all of our struggles, they've been a part of those fights."

The "From Vice to ICE" name reflected the criminalization of these communities: "Vice" because the New Orleans Police Department targeted young Black transgender women, charging them with crimes like "Crime against nature by solicitation" and prostitution; "ICE" because of the ongoing collaborations between the NOPD and ICE in profiling immigrant communities. With a grant from the LBGTQ Racial Justice Fund, the two organizations expanded their work on anti-criminalization initiatives and trained members like Santos on interrelated social justice issues. Despite language barriers and initial hesitations from each group, the "From Vice to ICE" campaign brought members together for monthly meetings to discuss shared struggles and plan actions.

Ivan and his family regularly attended those planning meetings, which also included social events, mixers, makeup/beautification tutorials, HIV prevention/treatment workshops, marches, and "Know Your Rights" trainings. The groups collaborated to locate resources for the undocumented LGBTQ community, especially in relation to the rampant deportations. When transgender immigrants were detained, they united forces to fight against mistreatment and abuses that took place in the detention centers. In the fall of 2015, the organizers came together to secure the release of two trans women who were detained in Louisiana.

Members of BreakOut! and El Congreso also connected their struggles through the demand for identification cards for their members. IDs are needed daily; yet transgender and undocumented communities oftentimes do not have access to adequate forms of documentation. In Louisiana, undocumented immigrants cannot get state-issued licenses, and using international IDs (a passport or driver's license from their country of origin) outs them as foreigners and makes immigrants even more susceptible to questions about immigration status. For transgender communities at that time, Louisiana required a signed physician's statement declaring that the applicant had "undergone a successful gender change/reassignment" and a court order certifying a name change.[35] Transgender and nonbinary people were forced to use state-issued IDs that do not correspond with their gender.

Responding to requests from El Congreso members, Denis and Jacinta used funds to purchase an ID card printer to design and produce El Congreso ID cards in 2009. El Congreso members and their families could get an ID card by paying ten dollars and attending a minimum of three Wednesday night meetings. The ID cards stated their name and birthdate, gave an expiration date to renew, and included a photo on the front of the card. The back of the card read in English that the cardholder was a member of El Congreso and listed two numbers to the Workers' Center, including the legal department. Local law enforcement officials were aware of the El Congreso–issued ID cards, and members successfully used these them during traffic stops or car accidents and as identification to enter federal buildings.

As part of the "From Vice to ICE" collaboration, El Congreso frequently loaned the ID machine to BreakOut! for members to create their own ID cards. The ID machine allowed BreakOut! and El Congreso to provide ID cards for their members that confirmed their identity. When my crew of friends waited in line to get into Casa Tequila, a bouncer checked IDs at the door. I watched as two people presented their El Congreso IDs. Ivan assured me that some of his family members had their gender-affirming IDs, too.

Later that night, after over three hours of performances, Cinthia won the competition. She was crowned Miss New Orleans Latin Gay 2015 by Briyith, a Honduran transgender woman who had won the inaugural crown the previous year. Both are members of Ivan's family. As Ivan placed a ribbon sash around Cinthia and handed her a bouquet of flowers, she stood proudly on the center stage in the suburban strip mall. "Not an organization, but a family," Ivan reminded me. Hosting gay beauty pageants had long been a goal of Ivan's. They brought together his core interests in entertainment, food, decorations, dance, costumes, and community. And he helped make his LGBTQ immigrant community welcome, visible, and celebrated, cultivating that space in a conservative suburban town.

CONCLUSION

"Mamajuana. Or, Pichichi," said Ivan in 2012 when I asked him what he'd like to name his future food establishment. "Mamajuana for my mother. Pichichi is my father's nickname. Or I'd name it El Jarocho. Or El Pasillo. La Bamba," he mused. Four years later, he settled on the name Antojitos Garibaldi, which became his booth at the Westbank Flea Market. The name was in reference to Plaza Garibaldi—the home of mariachi music in Mexico City—and the colorful logo featured a mariachi singer napping against a cactus with serape around his waist, sombrero pulled over his eyes, and guitar propped up next to him.

Since its opening, Antojitos Garibaldi has been a space of employment for the LGBTQ immigrant community. Ivan has employed several of his family members, including both pageant contestant winners, Cinthia and Briyith. When one of Ivan's employees who was also a contestant was detained, Ivan used all his resources to fight to get her out of immigration detention, where she was held in solitary confinement.

Ivan's decision to form his family in response to prevalent anti-LGBTQ sentiments was predictable, but the unexpected aspect lay in the unique ways he and his family navigated suburban life—engaging in food vending and participating in gay pageants. The Casa Tequila and Copacabana owners chose to partner with Ivan even though other bars feared the reactions from the conservative suburbs for hosting an event for LGBTQ community. "Go to New Orleans," other bar owners told him, but Ivan persisted. He lives in Kenner and he works in Jefferson Parish. That's his community and what he knows.

Ivan's work organizing with his LGBTQ family coincided with the partnership between El Congreso and BreakOut!, who sought to build power by joining forces and meeting people where they were. For Jacinta and Wes, the connections between El Congreso and BreakOut! were palpable. For their members, like Santos, it took more intention to locate these intersections. But once they did, it was a huge success. They even designed a toolkit for others to replicate the activities that help seemingly divergent groups better understand and identify their shared struggles.[36]

By building partnerships with Black, Vietnamese, and LGTBQ communities, immigrants shape the processes of suburbanization and make and remake Greater New Orleans on their own terms. And they pay it forward, too. Tracing the four case studies across the Jefferson Parish suburban area—the Gretna day-laborer corner, the Algiers Flea Market, the Westbank Flea Market, and Ivan's pageants—illustrates ways that disenfranchised people have successfully claimed the right to space and enriched their communities by forging unexpected alliances.[37] These examples show how this process is attainable, both in tandem with local governance and irrespective of local governance, and is built on collective action that often unites people from different backgrounds—figures like Betty Grandbouche, who, for over four decades, championed the growth of the Algiers Flea Market, fought off city council and neighborhood legal battles, and welcomed Vietnamese immigrants, yet turned her back on the Central American and Mexican food vendors like Imelda who arrived after Katrina. But Angela Dix welcomed them, built out their booths, and helped with issues like health care, immigration services, and home buying. Tri Cung has cultivated a similar space in the Westbank Flea Market. Through trust and by showing up for each other, the flea market managers fostered community and, in some ways, family.

Many of these unexpected alliances are based in empathy. Tri Cung and his family had their own booth at Betty Grandbouche's Algiers Flea Market. That experience left such a mark that they went on to establish their own open-air market to pay forward the generosity and support they received as new immigrants in the 1980s. For Tri, he and his uncle simply recognized that having food available would complement the other vendors selling household items.

Angela completely shifted gears to adhere to the needs of the immigrant vendors. "I just think everybody wants a chance to be given a chance. I mean, if I was in their country and I needed help, I would want their help too," she said, "What I do is I put myself in other people's shoes and say, 'If this was me, what would I want?'" She has been able to sustain the market by supporting her vendors.

Angela's and Tri's focus on the value of space through their ad hoc form of grassroots economic restructuring in the suburbs looks much different than economic restructuring in the city. Public-private partnerships like the St. Roch Market send millions of public funds into revitalizing important historical buildings, but then they turn over those spaces to developers who focus on exchange value rather than use value. These partnerships tend to benefit a whiter and wealthier community who feign community-oriented ethos and collaborative decision-making processes but have little oversight, transparency, and accountability.

For the Gretna corner, rather than continuing the cat-and-mouse approach with the day laborers, Gretna city officials—after pressure from El Congreso organizers Denis and Jacinta, who brokered that deal—took cues from and worked *with* the day laborers to create an important space by organizing the day laborers and asserting their needs with city officials.

Once they can claim their right to the space, these immigrant communities often recreate their space in the image of back home. Tri Cung's uncle built the hydroponic farm, which reminded him of Vietnam; Juan José likened the flea markets to the "*tianguis*," open-air markets in Mexico; and the foods, of course, reflect the familiarity of home. Carlos kept seeking out Ivan's bowls of spicy *menudo*. Sara's clients keep coming back for her Honduran specialty, *pollo con tajadas*. Juan José, who ran his family-owned restaurant from 2016 until 2019, said, "Honduran people who passed through Mexico and tried the food there would say to me, 'In my Honduras, in Guatemala, there are markets like this. I hear you yell and everything. And the food you have. And the prices. And you treat everyone the same.'"

Vendors like Sara, Venecia, and Ivan, who started out in the informal sector and sold food itinerantly to make ends meet, formalized their businesses by opening a booth in the flea markets. It gave them a way to legitimize their right to space. It also allowed them mobility to build capital to grow into a larger operation like Pho Tau Bay. In 2022, Ivan and Gilberto opened their own brick-and-mortar restaurant, Garibaldi's, in the Kenner suburbs while still maintaining their Westbank Flea Market booth. A sign in front of Garibaldi's restaurant reads, "We support JPSO," the Jefferson Parish Sheriff's Office. Noticing our confusion, Ivan said, "We took a tray of tacos to the sheriff's meeting the other day. We're not fucking around. You got to do what you got to do." The unexpected alliances know no bounds.

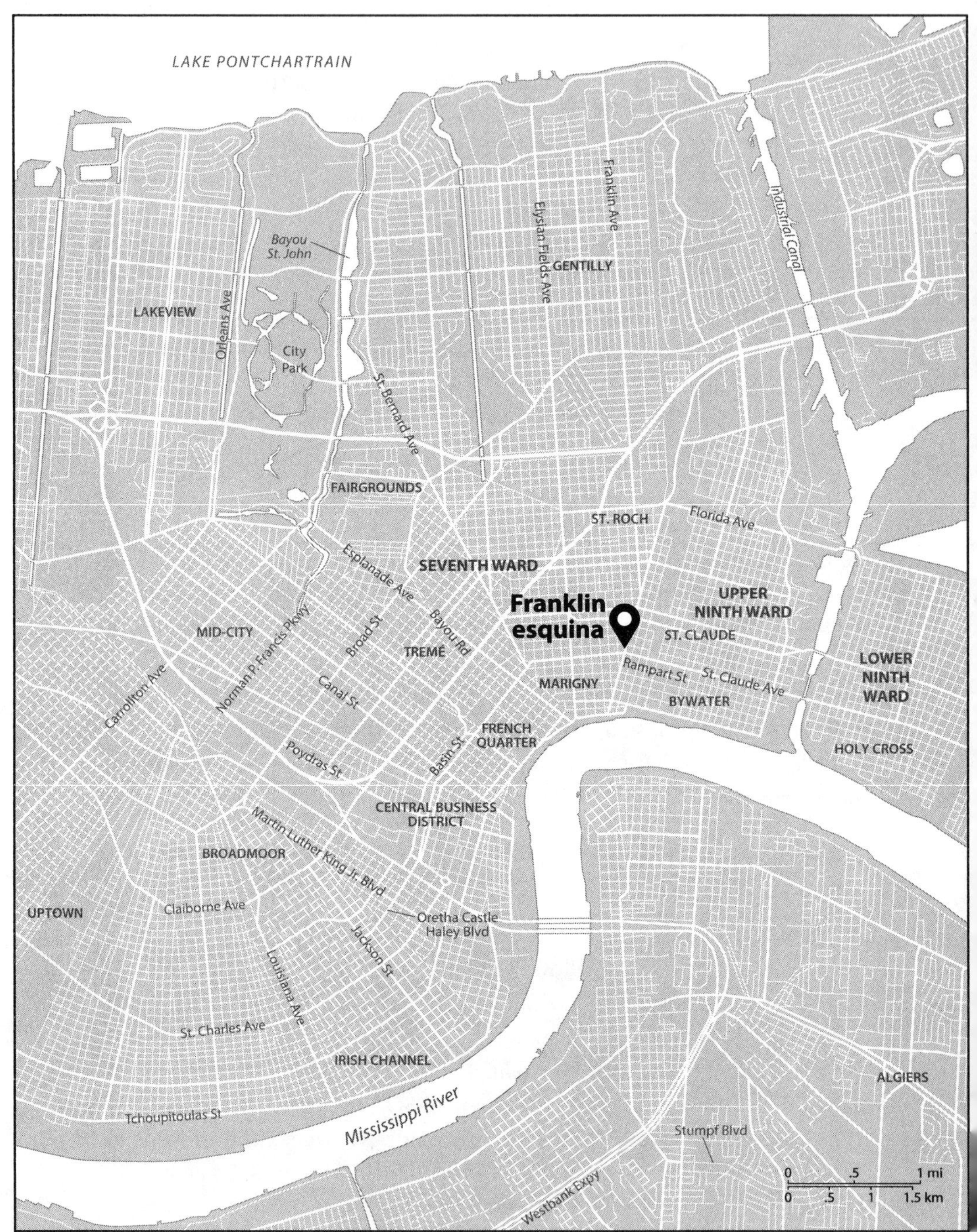

Franklin esquina in New Orleans.

Conclusion
Right to Remain

Is this the New Orleans of Carnival mirth, all torch and castanets, which on Mardi Gras parades Mexico's romance on a float festooned with lilies and carnations, on another the lovable heroes of Lalla Rookh in bejeweled costumes and on still another Prince Charming in orange satin walking a glittering-gowned Sleeping Beauty?

— JOSÉ MARTÍ,
"Mob Violence in New Orleans," 1891

Faubourg Marigny Improvement Association—trying to steal a property from me to stop my business on St. Claude. Not hipster enough? Gentrification.

— WENDELL PIERCE,
on Twitter, in defense of his redevelopment project on St. Claude Avenue, 2015

What is it like to live in a laboratory? To experience the mundanities of finding housing, placing kids in school, getting a job, navigating by car or bus or streetcar—even the most fundamental act of eating food—as part of a grand experiment.

— MATT SAKAKEENY,
"Living in a Laboratory," 2015

Located in the parking lot of a Shell station on the corner of Franklin and St. Claude Avenues, the Franklin esquina operated on a pivotal thoroughfare in New Orleans's Upper Ninth Ward. Unlike the other four core day-laborer corners, the Franklin esquina had no major hardware store nearby; it functioned, instead, as a convenient crossroads for contractors looking for workers. Situated near the Marigny, St. Roch, St. Claude, and Bywater neighborhoods, the corner served as an easy access point to the Lower Ninth Ward by way of the Industrial Canal and emerged as a key hub for worker recruitment in the immediate aftermath of the Katrina disaster. After Katrina, rapid redevelopment began to reshape the Upper Ninth Ward, including the renovation of the controversial St. Claude Market, located just a block away from the day-laborer corner. At the same time, the Franklin esquina increasingly faced a heightened presence of ICE and Border Patrol agents policing the gas station parking lot.

On January 12, 2010, a raid occurred on the Franklin esquina, resulting in the apprehension of El Congreso member Joaquin Navarro, a Honduran immigrant. During the incident, Joaquin initially fled, attempting to evade a pursuing Border Patrol vehicle. A bystander intervened and subdued Joaquin by pinning him to the ground. Another bystander who witnessed the incident called the police and reported that a "black male in a black sweatshirt" was "holding down a Hispanic male wearing a black cap." The police arrived, arrested Joaquin, and handed him over to Border Patrol. El Congreso organizers helped secure his release, but they still had an uphill battle to fight his deportation.[1]

Subsequently, El Congreso formed the Southern 32 in June 2012, uniting Joaquin with thirty-one other immigrants facing deportation due to civil rights and labor abuses.[2] The shift from Denis organizing day laborers at the corners as part of the "Know Your Rights" campaign to the broader, more comprehensive "Right to Remain" campaign meant hundreds more members fighting against a growing deportation machine. To accommodate the membership growth, El Congreso moved its Wednesday meetings from the Tremé office space to the Bywater neighborhood, less than a mile east from the Franklin corner down St. Claude Avenue. El Congreso leaders paid a weekly rental fee for the more spacious locale, situated in a historic chapel sanctuary in the Holy Angels Marianite convent established in 1848.[3] The fee helped support building maintenance amid a dwindling nunnery.[4] Some of the Spanish-speaking nuns even attended the meetings, taking notes as Southern 32 members gave testimonies preceding their respective hearings.

Prior to Joaquin's court date, the Workers' Center legal team and El Congreso members convened to organize a supportive action for his impending hearing. Because Joaquin's incident was a clear case of racial profiling, the legal team filed a FOIA request to obtain the testimony from the officers to prove they had no probable cause.[5] The lawyers were correct—the police report corroborated Joaquin's testimony, yet the Border Patrol account did not mention the bystander's role or the fact that Joaquin was arrested blocks from the esquina.[6] In 2013, Joaquin won his case, and I joined dozens of El Congreso members who met outside the hearing to debrief and celebrate. Joaquin was granted deferred action, meaning he could apply for a work permit, have some protection from deportation, and have the right to remain in New Orleans.

In the years following Joaquin's arrest, and with no hardware store nearby, only a few day laborers remained at the Franklin esquina.[7] In contrast to our visits to the four other day-laborer corners, which easily numbered over a hundred, Denis and I managed to visit the Franklin esquina only twice during our time together due to its eventual decline. Therefore, there were no enticing food dishes from the Franklin corner to share because, by 2011, the absence of day laborers had eliminated the opportunity for such encounters.

In the decade following the Franklin esquina's dissolution, the Upper Ninth Ward continued to undergo a convergence of cultures and uneven power dynamics, revealing complicated transitions within the city after the flood. As debates unfolded concerning how policymakers, often working in tandem with developers, approached these urban redevelopment transformations, dialectical tensions emerged. These tensions involved a range of stakeholders with varying claims to the city, from existing residents and immigrant newcomers to transplant communities and the creative class, all the way up to the privileged elite and politicians.[8]

Navigating these tensions was a complicated task, no doubt; yet the prioritization of outsiders and profit-seekers prevailed to the detriment of the well-being of existing residents. Local communities were forced to contend for their right to space and their right to return, while new immigrant communities strived to secure their right to remain. Questions of visibility were at the heart of these processes: these communities were forced to carve out their own niches, continue to fill vital service industry jobs, and create culture while being rendered invisible and segregated, forced out to the peripheries of the city.[9] In some cases, like the Workers' Center's campaigns, poor and working-class communities of color were able to cultivate political power together amid the towering landscape of profit-driven capitalism.

Thus, the Franklin corner serves as a microcosm of the themes explored in this book and interconnects these powerful narratives, interweaving issues around housing and labor politics, food security, and visibility (or lack thereof) of Central American and Mexican communities. In a city grappling with uneven recovery, these narratives also reflect how preservation of certain buildings and capital accumulation outweighed housing rights and community well-being; nevertheless, as this book reveals, poor and working-class individuals waged an asymmetrical fight for justice through self-sufficiency and by resisting exploitative systems and building multiracial coalitions. The Franklin esquina acts as a lens that brings to light and reflects on some of these power dynamics that transpired across the city, as outlined in *Rebuilding New Orleans*.

RIGHT TO FOOD CULTURE

In the absence of the Franklin day-laborer corner, a few taco joints opened up in the area farther east from the esquina, along the contiguous St. Claude Avenue. One of Magda's lonchera ventures featured in chapter 3 intermittently popped up on St. Claude Avenue before her move to the Seventh Ward. Established loncheras like the fleet of La Coyota trailers—grandfathered in during the food truck policy reform, also described in chapter 3—set up shop in front of a blighted store on St. Claude Avenue selling tacos, burritos, gorditas, and quesadillas to a broader customer base beyond just the usual day laborers.

Aligning with the ongoing gentrification in the Upper Ninth Ward, white-owned taco spots emerged along the busy corridor, too. In 2019, Galaxie Tacos opened in a former 1940s-era Texaco gas station located just under a half mile east from the Franklin esquina.[10] Led by a restaurateur and chef duo, both white men with impressive New Orleans culinary pedigrees, the Galaxie owners drew inspiration from extensive time they spent in Oaxaca and Mexico City.

While it might seem superficially ripe for a harangue about cultural appropriation, the homemade tortillas crafted from imported Oaxacan *maís* (ground in-house) along with the mezcal cocktails and Louisiana catfish reflect the attempt at a genuine approach to Mexican cuisine and local sourcing on the part of the restaurant owners and staff. Hiring a chef originally from Oaxaca as a part-owner in 2023 came a bit late but served as another crack at reinforcing that commitment not just to be another white-run Mexican restaurant.[11] A menu with all food items under ten dollars softened the semblance of gentrification. Moreover, the preservation of a derelict gas station and its conversion into a functioning restaurant with ample outdoor space is also noteworthy. However, the benefits leveraged by the duo, such as access to wealth, influential networks, and connections to designers, remain out of the grasp of most small, locally owned businesses. And the crowd the restaurant brings in (I usually get the *barbacoa* tacos) does not reflect the Mexican community.

At my first visit to Galaxie Tacos in January 2020, I ran into Melissa Araujo, a Honduran chef who was working back-of-house there, learning tricks of the trade, while she embarked on plans for her own high-end Honduran restaurant. She certainly had a vision. The James Beard Foundation Award winner (2015 Best Chef in the South and nominated again in 2024) and former *Chopped* and *Beat Bobby Flay* contestant got her own chops working in high-end restaurants across the city and beyond. In an interview in 2018, she said to me, “I want to be the first Michelin-star restaurant in New Orleans.”[12] Her achievements are extensive and her dreams are big, each buoyed by a touch of hubris.

Born in La Ceiba, Honduras, in 1979 and raised in New Orleans, Melissa’s background blends Sicilian and Honduran roots, all of which influence her culinary training. Melissa’s idea for her own restaurant began in 2013. Outside of her upscale dining jobs, she popped up as Saveur Catering, in places like Algiers Point and bars like Chickie Wah Wah, selling a combination of New Orleans and Central American foods to a predominantly white crowd. Drawing from her professional training and New Orleans influences and building from her Honduran grandmother’s recipes, she called the business “boutique catering” because of its farm-to-table approach and dedication to local businesses with locally sourced foods.

When I interviewed Melissa in 2018, she was, like Rogerio Paiva, the Brazilian pizzeria owner featured in the introduction, employed by FEMA administrators to sell food to federal recovery workers. Specifically, she was working on contract making hundreds of box lunches to send to Houston for disaster relief workers after Hurricane Harvey decimated the region. As Melissa built capital through lucrative gigs like FEMA, she officially formed the Araujo Restaurant group in 2017 to begin her expansion. The Bywater neighborhood in the Upper Ninth Ward would soon be the chosen spot for her forthcoming restaurant, Alma, located in the heart of the neighborhood and less than a mile from the Franklin esquina.

Situated east of the French Quarter along the Mississippi River, the Bywater is a cultural epicenter (read: tourist destination) with a range of high-end restaurants, music venues, and bars that cater to local residents and tourists alike. During an evening stroll down the potholed Dauphine Street in the heart of the Bywater, it's hardly unexpected to encounter a bachelorette party spilling out of an Airbnb, El Congreso members leaving a meeting, musicians Kermit Ruffins and Cory Henry resonating from Vaughan's Bar, or a souped-up pedicab bike leading a procession of costumed pleasure seekers. These could all take place on a weekday.

During Carnival season, the Bywater thrives as Mardi Gras Krewes and punk-anarchist groups take over the streets with walking parades. On Mardi Gras Day, colorful flags and glittered revelers lead St. Anne's and St. Anthony's parades—two pathways of many taking place across the city on Fat Tuesday—on foot through the Bywater with bands like the Storyville Stompers keeping tempo or the Panorama Brass Band playing dirges in the light. It's an ephemeral celebration filled with uncommodifiable pleasure mixed with some sadness, too. Throughout most of the year, Social Aid and Pleasure Clubs claim the streets as second lines strut deep into the Ninth Ward on certain Sundays with street food vendors slinging cold drinks and hot plates to parade-goers. The contrast between the mostly white crowd at the Carnival parades around the Bywater and the majority-Black crowd at the second lines is stark. However, both crowds, often numbering in the thousands, employ similar tactics of commandeering the streets, imbibing all sorts of culture, and marching to the beat of their respective drums.

Given this enchanting local culture combined with the neighborhood's historic architecture, riverfront charm, and overall imaginative atmosphere, the Bywater has increasingly attracted outsiders and the realm of baggage and demographic changes they bring. These racial and class shifts parallel other areas such as Mid-City and Tremé, discussed in chapter 1. Notably, the Black population in the Bywater decreased from 61 percent in 2000 to 17.4 percent in 2020.[13] At the same time, income rates of residents rose by 18.3 percentage points. From 2007 to 2014, the average home value on the river side of St. Claude Avenue in the Upper Ninth Ward (which includes the Bywater and Marigny neighborhoods) increased 44 percent.[14]

The proliferation of short-term rentals aggravated the housing crisis because local communities were forced out to make way for higher speculative returns generated by renting to out-of-towners.[15] Like the demolition

A brass band takes the streets in front of a lonchera. Photo by Fernando López, @sentir.con.ojos.

of 4,500 public housing units in the post-Katrina era, the proliferation of short-term rentals and lack of affordable housing alternatives have had damning effects on the displacement of poor communities in the Bywater neighborhood.

Even the Marianite nuns who supported Southern 32 were forced out in 2014.[16] "Our prayer is that it not be a brothel or an abortion clinic," said Sister Lacour when asked about what would be next for Holy Angels Convent after they put it up for sale.[17] Her Catholic prayers were somewhat answered. In 2022, the "Holy Angels Apartments," an affordable housing apartment complex, opened its doors—at least a public benefit and a bit of a reprieve from a barrage of developers proselytizing about the wonders of high-end luxury apartments.

WHOSE RIGHT TO AN AFRO-CARIBBEAN PARIS?

Emerging as a pioneer of redevelopment in the post-Katrina landscape, Pres Kabacoff, a New Orleans native and president of HRI Properties, has left his whitewashed vision across the city. His portfolio is unapologetically committed to attracting an affluent clientele and includes the Bywater Lofts, located just blocks from Melissa's Honduran restaurant, Alma.

"You can walk across it like a Paris," said Kabacoff. "In Paris, you can go fifty or one hundred blocks and have a fascinating, comfortable, safe experience. New Orleans is our Afro-Caribbean version of that. And if you can fix the center, you can walk from river to lake and have a similar experience."[18] But what does he mean by "fix"? Kabacoff's vision clearly acknowledged the significance of Black and Latin American influences, yet his version of an Afro-Caribbean city reduced New Orleans to a static and embellished identity built off the commodification of Black and Caribbean culture. Simply, his perception treated this "Afro-Caribbean" influence as an aesthetic rather than as people and residents.

The displacement caused by this and similar redevelopment projects undermines the claim of an "Afro-Caribbean" city when Black and immigrant residents are forced out due to demolition of public housing, a lack of affordable housing to replace the demolished public housing, and the constant criminalization outlined throughout this book. Using a criminalization narrative to justify the demolition of the public housing, Kabacoff succeeded in implementing his vision, which included tearing down 821 apartments—the Iberville Housing Development—which were part of a structurally sound public housing development in the city center. The project made way for the Bienville Basin, a mixed-income housing development.[19]

Kabacoff's idea for the demolition of Iberville predated Katrina, yet the storm's aftermath provided a textbook disaster capitalism opportunity to take root. Located less than two miles west of the Franklin esquina, just off the French Quarter in the Tremé–Lafitte neighborhood—an ideal housing location for service industry workers and a speculator's dream—the Iberville Housing Development was slated for demolition in 2013 by federal and state housing authorities through the Hope VI program.

While proponents proclaimed that the mixed-income development would revitalize the neighborhood, critics raised concerns about the displacement of poor families and the loss of the affordable housing units. Kabacoff said bluntly, "We didn't want to have it just look like a cleaned-up public-housing project. The key is to attract market-rate residents."[20] Developers like Kabacoff opted for profit-driven motives rather than affordable housing for the existing residents. The Department of Housing and Urban Development and the Housing Authority of New Orleans supported his vision.

With few options at their disposal—much like the residents of the B. W. Cooper Public Housing Development, the demolition of which was featured in chapter 2—Stand with Dignity members used their lessons learned from the HUD Section 3 policy to fight for labor rights. Joining forces with El Congreso leaders in 2014, they picketed against low wages and poor working conditions at the Iberville worksite with signs like "I am a walking hazard." The members put pressure on the contractors to ensure employment opportunities and to improve working conditions by holding Kabacoff's team accountable to the federal policy. Kabacoff's contractors were implicated in a range of violations, including asbestos exposure, inadequate protective gear, limited career mobility, and low wages. But recognizing that pressure solely on contractors to improve working conditions was insufficient, Stand members sought out Kabacoff.

"We needed to make the right request with living wages and career ladder and needed to talk to the highest-up person as possible. And we decided to request a meeting with Pres Kabacoff," Toya Ex Lewis said. "So we faxed him to respond by a certain date. And he didn't respond."

When Kabacoff failed to acknowledge the request, Stand members escalated the matter by reaching out even higher: to his wife. Sallie Anne Glassman, an artist and voodoo practitioner originally from Maine, claimed in 2003 that she had successfully cured cancer through her voodoo practice.[21] She opened the Island of Salvation Botanica, a store in the New Orleans Healing Center, a refurbished furniture store developed by Kabacoff in 2011. In her store, she conducts readings and sells voodoo supplies, medicinal herbs, incense, gris-gris, oils, candles, art, and books. The space sits diagonally across the street from the Franklin esquina.

"We decided to go visit his wife at her botanical inside the New Orleans Healing Center," Toya said. "We went to the botanical, started off with a question about healing, asked her questions about healing, and then led into, asking her point-blank, does having access to full employment and living wages, does that mean healing? And then we asked her why her husband doesn't do that." Toya continued, "She said he doesn't really read that much. And that's why he didn't get it [the fax]. We asked, 'Can you ask him to respond?' Then she said 'OK.'"

He scheduled the meeting the next week. Toya, Colette, Williana, Miss Faye (Toya's mom and Stand member), and Miss Brenda (a longtime Stand leader) went to Kabacoff's office on Poydras Street.

"I remember he had this big bowl of candy, and everyone stuffed the candy in their pockets," Toya said, laughing. "Then we told the story of how the Davis–Bacon [federal labor law that establishes a requirement to pay the local prevailing wages on public works projects] isn't enough—as low as eight dollars and one cent an hour on residential and ten dollars on commercial sites." She continued, "He said, 'That's following the rules.' And then we asked if he'd work for that. He said, 'Not for a minute.' He didn't laugh or nothing. He was serious."

Following the meeting, they secured some victories, including a wage increase to fourteen dollars per hour. Colette Tippy, the Stand organizer, said, "We did do a lot of enforcement of laws that were on the books to make sure that the Section 3 was being followed. And that the OSHA laws were being followed." Stand ultimately filed an OSHA complaint against a contractor on the site, leading to a walk-through by the agency and a fine. As part of these efforts, Stand was a thorn in Kabacoff's side, but he still got his mixed-income housing that prioritized above-market rates.

These approaches are emblematic of capitalist practices that cater to exchange value defined by developers, corporations, and speculation rather than address the use value—the residents, grassroots concerns, and realities of everyday people. And these practices abounded across the Upper Ninth Ward where the few remaining poor residents faced housing precarity along with the persistent challenge of food security.

Until the supermarket chain Robért reopened on the border of the Upper Ninth Ward in December 2017 after being shuttered by Katrina damage, the Marigny and Bywater neighborhoods lacked a full-service grocery that offered satisfactory produce. The proliferation of countless high-end food establishments contrasted sharply with the limited availability of affordable food options in the area. Near the Franklin corner, a trio of public-private development projects, including the New Orleans Healing Center, led by Kabacoff's development firm HRI Properties, aimed to address these issues through radically different approaches.

RIGHT TO FOOD SECURITY

In 2011, a controversy erupted on the same block as the Franklin esquina when the owner of the Shell station, Troy Henry, a New Orleans–based Black businessman and onetime mayoral candidate, purchased the neighboring camelback shotgun. Using a loophole "priority bid" to bypass the auction sale, the New Orleans Redevelopment Authority sold Henry the blighted house on the single lot on St. Claude Avenue for $19,000 (it appraised for $273,000 at the time).[22] Henry joined forces with actor Wendell Pierce, of *Treme* and *The Wire* fame, through their LLC called Sterling Farms. They aimed to address the food security issue across the state by opening small grocery store chains with fresh produce.[23] And the Franklin corner would be their Upper Ninth Ward project.

Much to the chagrin of the mostly white neighborhood association, the two pitched the idea to demolish the shotgun, extend the Shell station, and build a brick storefront strip mall to host the small grocery store. In response to the pushback, Pierce expressed his frustration on Twitter: "Not hipster enough? Gentrification." The architectural mock-up for Henry and Pierce's small grocery vision was in stark contrast to the refurbished historical buildings on the block. However, it blended in with the newer commercial construction on St. Claude with a light brick facade and small strip mall design.

At the same time in 2011, Kabacoff refurbished the historic Universal Furniture Store building into the New Orleans Healing Center, which housed a gym, a restaurant, small businesses, Glassman's botanical store, and the New Orleans Food Cooperative, a small, member-owned full-service grocery store across the street and adjacent to the Franklin esquina. The Healing Center sits directly across St. Claude Avenue from the St. Roch Market. Located just a block away from the Franklin esquina, the St. Roch Market came to fruition after the city of New Orleans secured $3.7 million in HUD Community Development Block Grant Disaster Recovery funds to renovate the dilapidated fish market. Two years later the city leased the refurbished building to the white management company that created the St. Roch Market. The high overhead cost of operating a booth there and the limited availability of fresh produce in the market rendered it inaccessible for local residents, as outlined in chapter 4.

The three buildings and their developers, each intent on addressing food options in the neighborhood, sparked a debate about what food security should look like. The two white-led developments refurbished existing infrastructures with the help of private-public partnerships in order to sell fresh and prepared foods at higher costs.[24] Meanwhile, Henry and Pierce's project, which also had some public support, faced legal challenges from neighbors and resistance from the Historic District Landmarks Commission (overruled by the City Council, 5–4) as the two sought to demolish the blighted shotgun to make way for their shopping center. Analyzing Henry and Pierce's yet-to-be realized small grocery plans alongside the St. Roch

Market and Healing Center complex provides valuable insights into the complexities of urban development projects and how these developers envision the neighborhoods' needs while considering (or not) the interests of poor and working-class communities and existing residents.

RIGHT TO VISIBILITY?

Failures to aptly address issues like food insecurity combined with high rent and hyper-criminalization forced people out of their neighborhoods, disrupting communities and relegating poverty to less visible areas.[25] These individuals often included the very workers who contributed to rebuilding and maintaining the city, the cultural producers behind the street foods, the tireless employees who kept the restaurant kitchens running, and the musicians who provided the rhythms for the parades. Efforts were made in the Upper Ninth Ward to increase the visibility and representation of these immigrant communities, in particular. These efforts materialized in the form of tributes to these workers, offering welcoming spaces for performances, and making food cultures more legible to wider audiences.

Just a half-mile southeast from the Franklin corner, on the corner of Homer Plessy Avenue and Royal Street, a giant mural of the "Tamale Man" is painted on the facade of a warehouse. The depiction captures a bearded, sombrero-wearing Mexican street food vendor renowned for selling tamales in the French Quarter. In 2021, local artist Brandan "BMike" Odums painted the image on a 35,000-square-foot building near railroad tracks that split the Bywater and Marigny neighborhoods. The space is owned by a white developer, Sean Cummings, who once called the Bywater a "green banana."[26] Like Kabacoff, Cummings left his own legacy of whitewashed redevelopment, characterized by the Rice Loft Apartments and arts warehouses in the Bywater.

Adjacent to the "Tamale Man" mural, Odums also painted a young Black girl with her hands in the air as if to say, "So what?," which can be seen on the front of the warehouse entrance. Directly across from the young girl, another large mural features the busts of eight Black historical figures, ranging from Angela Davis to P. B. S. Pinchback (the first Black governor of Louisiana) and Homer Plessy. Like the street name, the latter is a tribute to Plessy, a Black man who, in an act of civil disobedience, was removed from a railroad car in 1892. The case eventually led to the racist Supreme Court decision that crystallized "separate but equal." While the warehouse murals reflect a cadre of historical figures and neighborhood heroes meant to bring more diverse representation to the visual landscape, it stresses the Black and Brown communities that have been historically marginalized and, in this neighborhood, displaced.

Just under a mile southeast from the "Tamale Man" and deeper into the Bywater, the Latin American workers monument was erected in 2018 along a path in Crescent Park, a riverfront park that spans the Mississippi River through the Bywater neighborhood. The twelve-foot bronze statue with a six-foot-tall marble base depicts one laborer with a hammer climbing a ladder onto a roof, another laborer standing on the side, and a third laborer holding a broom.

Dr. Juan Jorge Gershanik, an Argentinean-born, New Orleans–based neonatal doctor, and his family gifted the statue to the city. Created by the Italian-born sculptor Franco Alessandrini, the base reads, "This monument is a tribute to the Latin American workers who helped to rebuild the city of New Orleans in the aftermath of Hurricane Katrina August 29th, 2005."[27] This monument is an ode to the labor of these workers and one of the few public acknowledgments of the day laborers' contributions to the city. Yet the monument is on a pathway tucked away in a hard-to-reach park on the river side of the walled-off levee.

While paying homage is one avenue to grant visibility, establishments like the Domino, a bar located a block from Galaxie Taco, helped provide visibility by making an inclusive and welcoming space in the Bywater neighborhood for individuals like Ivan. Before 2022, Ivan—the drag show virtuoso and Mexican restaurateur featured in chapter 4—had almost exclusively organized his drag show performances in the more conservative suburbs of Jefferson Parish because it was too expensive to rent space in the more libertine city. Since 2022, he has hosted multiple drag shows in the Domino, which is known for its karaoke, open mic nights, and synth DJ sets targeting the Bywater crowd.

At their "Gran Show de Divas Latinas" event, which took place on March 17, 2023, Ivan and Gilberto's crew sold tacos brought over from their restaurant Garibaldi's before preparing for the show inside. For his performance, Ivan dressed in drag as the Mexican diva Paquita la del Barrio, wearing a tight leopard dress and full-face makeup, dancing alongside his longtime collaborator, Briyith. Because the show started late, much of the Bywater crowd had left; Ivan and the rest of the divas performed for a small group of people from their community in the heart of a highly gentrified neighborhood. After their show, Ivan and Gilberto made their trek back to Kenner later that

Ivan as Ivette (*center*) with crew outside of the Domino. Photo by Fernando López @ sentir.con.ojos.

night, just over fourteen miles across the city. The inclusivity by the Domino's owners and Ivan's work to build collaborations that extend beyond just his usual haunts are efforts to bridge these divides and increase visibility.

Legibility can also foster visibility. It is hard to situate a taco truck within the larger argument of cultural commodification vis-à-vis the New Orleans tourism industry, because not many tourists come to New Orleans looking for tacos and especially not the Honduran baleada. Central American and Mexican immigrant foods aren't quite salient symbols of New Orleans culture like jazz, brass bands, Mardi Gras, or gumbo dishes are; rather, they represent a complex position in the city, hidden yet in plain sight, representing people who serve the construction and food service industries.

"Alma will become a brick-and-mortar," Melissa confidently declared in an interview in 2017, "and it will be a casual place where you can go eat, you know, Honduran food."[28] Despite a long history of migration and exchange between the two places, Honduran food has remained relatively obscure in New Orleans at this time. Given that, throughout her career, most of

Melissa's clients have been white, she has sought to make Honduran dishes more legible to this broader community. While most of the mom-and-pop small restaurants and other Honduran food establishments appeared in the post-Katrina context, few of those spaces that remain had yet to reach an audience beyond the predominantly Central American and Mexican consumers.

At Alma, which means "soul" in Spanish, the inside seating area offers a casual atmosphere with a back-of-house run by Honduran women. The restaurant gives almost a hostel-esque feeling due to mounds of suitcases crammed under tables by tourists as they get their last food fix before leaving the city. Today, the menu at Alma features a baleada with a much higher price tag than a four-dollar baleada one can find at a lonchera due to the use of locally sourced ingredients, a commitment to sustainable sourcing that Melissa has maintained. While visiting Honduras in 2022, I told Denis that I paid sixteen dollars for a baleada at Alma. "Dios mio," he gasped as he covered his mouth with both hands.

Despite the tributes to inclusivity and legibility, visibility in these approaches is somewhat limited in scope given that they do not address the broader systemic issues at hand. While the visibility of cultural representations of these laborers and cultural producers is enhanced, these efforts still leave out the people, thus prompting questions about their underlying purpose and intended audiences. Is visibility enough without meaningful actions, especially in terms of labor laws, housing affordability, and basic civil rights?

CONCLUSION

All these people had visions for the city's future and their role in it and ideas of what should and should not be visible. Melissa, a business owner, wanted to make Honduran food more visible through her upscale restaurant. Kabacoff wanted an Afro-Caribbean Paris but without poor people. Purveyors of the tourism industry wanted Black culture like second lines visible but not the poor Black people who make those parades function. Wendell Pierce wanted something other than gentrification and hipster aesthetic. The Marigny neighborhood association wanted the preservation of certain historic buildings. Sister Lacour, the Marianite nun, wanted anything but a brothel or an abortion clinic in her soon-to-be converted convent. City Council members wanted food trucks visible but not lonchera trailers.

But what about the people most impacted by these visions—the laborers, the existing residents, the cultural producers? In some cases, like in chapter 3, when the lonchera owners chose to remain in the shadows rather than join the Food Truck Coalition, that visibility meant vulnerability. For communities with precarious documentation status, just engaging in political activities could be risky. For some poor and working-class Black people, visibility just meant the right to return to their city with good jobs and housing. For immigrants, that visibility meant the right to remain and be allowed to settle in the city without fear. Their aims were straightforward: the right to a secure place to work, live, and produce culture. Resisting the white spatial imaginary was essential to achieve that goal.

As demonstrated throughout this book, groups like Stand with Dignity and El Congreso are great models for how poor and working-class people came together to foment structural change on a city, state, and federal level. At points when survival hinged on the ability to organize, the Workers' Center fostered a space that was accessible—with childcare, someone speaking the appropriate language, no financial barrier to entry, and free transportation—to build a powerful movement from the grassroots level.

Their work pushed public agencies to improve their relations with the immigrant community and Black communities by ending collaborations between ICE and local police, discontinuing ICE detainer holds, and enhancing local job opportunities through HUD Section 3 policy enforcement. These achievements and many more stem from the Workers' Center organizers listening to grassroots voices to understand their needs and bringing attention to tactics of hyper-policing and racialized practices endemic to the city. However, much work remains to be done. Today, policies remain in place that criminalize and terrorize street food vendors who often rely on their hustle economies to make ends meet. Conservative politicians campaign on harsh immigration policies.

Documenting these power dynamics provides lessons learned for other cities globally while also offering examples of how similar processes of capitalism (and the resistance) take place in Honduras. *Rebuilding New Orleans* can be a blueprint to show how Black and immigrant communities have come together to push back against these white spatial imaginaries, in intentional ways through organizing as well as in organic ways by people coming together through the unexpected alliances that emerged as part of these everyday struggles in the post-disaster city. While the introduction presented a brief overview of prominent Latin American historical figures like Benito

Juárez and José Martí who left their mark on New Orleans, *Rebuilding New Orleans* presents the narratives of the everyday people, heroes in their own way, by documenting their struggle for the right to the city.

Following Denis to five of the day-laborer corners located across the metropolitan area—Gretna, Central City, Mid-City, the Seventh Ward, and the Upper Ninth Ward—provided a nuanced glimpse into areas of New Orleans often left out of the broader discussions about the city. Exploring the stories of food producers as a framework for this book helped to surface and connect issues from a bottom-up perspective. And following Denis and others to Central America shed light on how these immigration narratives link New Orleans with Honduras, ethnographically and on a broader macro level. Last, by bringing in a range of campaigns—"Right to Remain" and "Right to Return" to NOLA Shakedown and the Southern 32—this book moves beyond a diagnostic approach to the post-Katrina systemic failures, instead illustrating the ways in which multiracial organizing occurred and unexpected coalitions emerged.

Many of the examples addressed in *Rebuilding New Orleans* were actionable steps orchestrated by people who joined forces across racial differences, identified shared struggles, and fought together to dismantle uneven and racist systems. This book brings these issues to light and serves as a call to do better, to hold people accountable, and to understand the realities taking place on the ground in order to better address the needs of the people—the cultural producers, street food vendors, day laborers, musicians, chefs, drag divas, and other service industry workers—who make up the backbones and the core of the "Unfathomable City."

Acknowledgments

Lots of people have been integral to ways in which this fieldwork, my various projects and excursions, and ultimately this book have taken shape. Thanks go to my parents, Gene and Susan Fouts, who have supported me unconditionally.

The roots of this book can be traced back to the people who formed the Workers' Center and all the powerful campaigns and relationships that came out of it. First, thanks go to Jacinta Gonzalez for bossing me around and teaching me so many lessons. Special thanks go to Colette Tippy for extending the initial invitation to work with these incredible folks and for continuing to keep me close as a friend. Much appreciation goes to Alfredo Carrera, who was always there to field my last-minute questions and hang for some cold *chelas* and pool. Special thanks is due to Chloe Sigal, who clarified campaigns and timelines and joined me on a memorable trip to Honduras in 2022. I also want to thank Toya Ex Lewis for helping me think through many steps in New Orleans with so much intention and for collaborating on powerful projects like the New Orleans Black-Led Labor History and Project Neutral Grounds. And I am grateful to Fernando López for all the collaborations and photos, for keeping each other in check, and for all the stories we've shared since we had that first yerba maté in 2012.

A deep appreciation goes to the entire Workers' Center team from 2011 to 2017: Alfred Marshall, Santos Canales, Rito Alvarado, Jacob Horwitz, Ilda Sarmiento, Williana Tadlock, Daniel Castellanos, Eusebia Gonzalez, Jolene Elberth, Stephanie Martin, Tiana Noble, Sarah Hailey, Lorena Murga, Sophie Ashley, J. J. Rosenbaum, Jan Collatz, Julie Mao, Mary Yanik, Sima Atri, Anne Recinos, Nikki Thanos, and all the other members and interns who played crucial roles during this important time. What they all did was so powerful and, in many ways, unprecedented.

Ivan Castillo has also been part of this work since the beginning, in 2011. Since then, I've followed him across New Orleans to Baltimore and to so many of his drag shows that I've lost count. I'm grateful for his powerful story and the people in his community, especially Gilberto. Thanks go to Sllim Ydur for inviting me on his radio show, *Gumbo Tapado*, and for sharing his Calypso beats and his story from Honduras to New Orleans. I'd also like to thank Angela Dix, Sandra, Sara, Iris, Floricelda, Venecia, the Romero family, Mirna, David, and all the other food vendors who generously offered up their time, space, and wonderful foods with me, and Denis and his family who shared so much with me—knowledge, family, and a trove of memories in New Orleans and Honduras.

From the start, I received invaluable support and encouragement from folks at the University of New Orleans's urban studies master's program between 2010 and

2012. Special thanks go to Renia Ehrenfeucht, Steve Striffler, David Beriss, Marla Nelson, Rachel Luft, Jeffrey Ehrenreich, Rachel Breunlin, and Pamela Jenkins. Their mentorship played a pivotal role in shaping my trajectory.

At Tulane, I am grateful for the support of Jana Lipman, who took me under her wing and set me on the right path. I'd also like to thank Nick Spitzer, Vicki Mayer, Rebecca Snedeker, Allison Truitt, Jimmy Huck, Edie Wolfe, Bridget Smith, Christine Hernández, Denise Woltering, and other folks at the Stone Center for Latin American Studies, the New Orleans Center for the Gulf South, the Latin American Library, and the Center for Public Service. I also greatly benefited from the postdoctoral fellowship at Lehigh University and value the friendships of Allison Mickel, Jon Irons, Cory Fisher-Hoffman, and Hugo Cerón that I made during that time.

I'd like to acknowledge the folks at the Southern Food and Beverage Museum, particularly Liz Williams, who provided great advice and support and allowed space for so many projects and exhibitions. The Southern Foodways Alliance has also been integral to much of this research, including symposiums, an oral history training, podcasts, and the opportunity to be part of the El Sur Latino project from 2016 to 2017 with Fernando López and the folks at the *pulgas*.

In New Orleans (with a little Kentucky and PY slipped in), so many friendships over such a long period have helped in direct and indirect ways. I found an astrological chart to be the most fitting and, somehow, the least awkward approach to organization. Aries: Gus Hoffman (for generously hosting me, for all the costuming, and for all the bowls of white beans), Jeanne Firth, Helen Freund, Laura Mellem, Natalie Blaustone-Dye, Heather Berley, Melody Chang, Miranda Stramel. Taurus: Alpha Gebre, Doug Donaldson, Lydia Pelot-Hobbs, Kathy Kemp, Ryan Adams, Elena Pinsky, Erica Buher, Elliott Powell, Madeline Peters, Kathleen Curry. Geminis: Will DeVary, Jake Scobey-Thal, Lucy Cordts, Tristan Call, Abbey Hart. Cancer: Will Bercik, Nicole Snyder, Jesy Rae Buhl, Dean Labowitz, Deb Levy, Lauren Cargo. Leo: Harper Kelly, Riley Hewko, Jenn Glick, Leanna First-Arai, Jessa Derania, Maxx Marty, Kate Heller, Maile Speakman, Ben Berman. Virgo: Laura Burns, Mike Madej, Christina LeBlanc, Jackson Smith, Barrie Schwartz, Max Skelton, Haley Kerr. Libra: Baird Campbell, Cars Stewart, Bryn Stole. Scorpio: Deniz Daser, Ana Croegaert, Caroline Schulz, Dave DeCotiis, Sasha Solodukhina (for all the deadlines and for the book cover mockup). Sagittarius: Al Page, Lisle Siegrist, Nina Feldman (who went on a lot of these journeys). Capricorns: Harvey Sanders, Katie Jane Fernelius, Sophie Kosofsky, Maggie McWilliams, Jes Godinez, Meatball, Mika Keegstra, Elizabeth Steeby. Aquarius: Erin McCutcheon, Max Krochmal, Andy Dahl, Simi Kang, Christiana Botic, Emily Mackenzie (for also graciously hosting me, for so much Bella Ciao, and for so many nightcaps), Matt Sledge. Pisces: Vanessa Castañeda, Jack Kelly, Mira Kohl, Allison Caplan,

Liora Diamond, Kelcy Wilburn, Clare Cannon, Lauren Nichols, Michaela Bono. Support manifests in so many forms.

If New Orleans wasn't enough, in Baltimore, I have lots to be thankful for, too. I am grateful to the University of Maryland, Baltimore County, for providing the necessary support and infrastructure to cultivate this community-engaged and social justice–oriented research. I have Nicole King to thank for believing in me, for serving as a model of ethical community-engaged research, and for the friendship we share. I am also grateful for Tamara Bhalla, Michael Casiano, Morgan Dowty, Ashley Minner, Courtney Hobson, Jessica Berman, Rachel Brubaker, Rebecca Uchill, Tania Lizarazo, Thania Muñoz, Keegan Finberg, Charlotte Keniston, Michelle Stefano, Kate Drabinski, Niki Fabricant (for sharing drafts and important edits), Steph Saxton, Christy Thorton, Stuart Schrader, Josh Davis (who gave invaluable feedback on an early proposal), Jess Douglas, Andy Holter, Carly Bales, Glenn Cartaxo, Cameron Hartofelis, Laura Ruth Venable, Clare Kemmerer, Madeleine Pope, Ino Aksentiev, Nick Petr, Ashley Hufnagel, Rosemary Liss, Becca Morrin, Jonna McKone, Nicole Labruto, Kenny Kirby, Jen Kirby, Juliet Linderman, Josh Sisk, Molly Porter, Alex Hayworth, Emily Lerman, and Aisha Alfadhalah for being incredible friends and colleagues. A special thanks is due to Baynard Woods for mentorship and thoughtful and thorough edits on the final draft. And Anneke Dunbar-Gronke gets both a New Orleans and a Baltimore appreciation for clarifying so many legal questions and for lessons on grudges. I am incredibly lucky to have all these people in my life.

I am especially thankful for the Dresher Center for the Humanities at UMBC, the Whiting Foundation, the American Folklife Center, the UMBC Department of American Studies, the College of Arts and Social Sciences at UMBC, the Gulf South Research Fellowship through the New Orleans Center for the Gulf South, the Labor Research and Action Network New Scholars Grant, the Tinker Foundation, the Southern Foodways Alliance, and the Tulane University School of Liberal Arts for funding various stages of this work. Thanks also go to Ruth Gomberg-Muñoz, Brandon Proia, Kate Marshall, Valerie Burton, Julie Bush, and Megan Pugh for draft edits. I appreciate the support from the University of North Carolina Press, especially Cate Hodorowicz.

I am honored to tell the rich and powerful stories featured in this book.

Notes

Introduction

1 Murga, "Organizing and Rebuilding."

2 "Who Lives in New Orleans and Metro Parishes Now?"

3 I did "accompaniment" methodology while volunteering with the Workers' Center. Accompaniment originates from liberation theology and activist traditions and has evolved into a methodology of reciprocal relationships and shared experiences between researchers and marginalized communities. Scholars such as Paul Farmer, Glenn Adams, Staughton Lynd, Barbara Tomlinson, George Lipsitz, and Mary Watkins highlight that accompaniment involves justice-oriented engagement, mutual respect, and reflexivity while addressing the structural violence, power dynamics, and risks of perpetuating inequalities inherent in such work. I credit Dr. Rachel Luft for introducing me to the Workers' Center. It wasn't an easy entry process. My Workers' Center interview took place in February 2011 with Stand with Dignity organizer Colette Tippy in the small kitchen located in the back of the camelback shotgun office. As we sat at the cluttered kitchen table, Colette—with my résumé in hand—grilled me about my research. After passing the first phase with Colette, she sent me upstairs to face Jacinta Gonzalez, the lead El Congreso organizer and Denis's colleague. She asked some basic questions, like did I have a reliable car (yes) and what were my reasons for wanting to volunteer with El Congreso? She had me translate a single-page letter, which was the first document she could find. I did it quickly and satisfactorily. Later I'd learn that I actually had it easy—when National Guestworker Alliance organizer Jacob Horwitz applied to be a volunteer, he had to translate an entire chapter from W. E. B. Du Bois's *Black Reconstruction* from English into Spanish.

4 Barrios, *Governing Affect*, 180. Barrios's ethnographic work (which also expands to Honduras) is a powerful critique of neoliberal post-disaster reconstruction approaches, emphasizing the intersection of policy, politics, and human emotion to address issues of difference, voice, and inequity. Todd Price, "Taco Trucks and the Hispanic Influx," *Times-Picayune* (New Orleans), June 30, 2007; Andy Grimm, "Hispanic Immigration Post-Katrina Finding Permanent Roots in Metro New Orleans," NOLA.com, August 28, 2015, www.nola.com/news/hispanic-immigration-post-katrina-finding-permanent-roots-in-metro-new-orleans/article_ddb9794b-8bd7-5be8-8d55-6669024d3cb3.html.

5 Plyer, "Facts for Features." From 2000 to 2020, New Orleans's Black population dropped from 69 to 57 percent, while the white population climbed from

27 to 31 percent in the same period. This stark shift is most palpable in the historically Black Tremé neighborhood, which abuts the French Quarter, is the neighborhood that housed the Workers' Center, and is where I called home for four years. In the Tremé, the Black population dropped from 92.4 percent in 2000 to 56 percent in 2017; meanwhile, the white population skyrocketed from 4.9 to 35.6 percent, and the "Hispanic" population grew slightly from 1.5 to 5.1 percent.

6 Daser and Fouts, "Great Unbuilding." See also Stone's important dissertation work, "New Louisiana Purchase."

7 Daser, "Citizens of the City," 148–54.

8 Brenner and Marcuse, *Cities for People*; Klein, *Shock Doctrine*, 6; Lipsitz, *How Racism Takes Place*; Thomas, *Desire and Disaster*.

9 Thomas, *Desire and Disaster in New Orleans*.

10 Graeber, *Utopia of Rules*; Lipsitz, *How Racism Takes Place*; Thomas, *Desire and Disaster*.

11 Purcell, "Possible Worlds."

12 Lipsitz, *How Racism Takes Place*, 25–50. For more on spatial hierarchies, see McKittrick, *Demonic Grounds*.

13 Gruesz, "Gulf of Mexico System." For more on how food shapes perspectives of identity and place through a local and global lens set in post-Katrina New Orleans, see the powerful essay by Beriss, "Red Beans and Rebuilding."

14 Darensbourg, "Hunting Memories of the Grass Things"; Laine Kaplan-Levinson, "New Orleans 300: Bulbancha," *TriPod: New Orleans at 300* (blog), accessed February 24, 2024, https://tripodnola.org/episodes/new-orleans-300-bulbancha-3000.

15 Woods, *Development Drowned and Reborn*; Usner, *Indians, Settlers, and Slaves*, 63; US Department of the Interior, Bureau of Indian Affairs, memorandum regarding Tunica-Biloxi Indian Tribe, 5.

16 J. Johnson, *Wicked Flesh*; Usner, "From African Captivity to American Slavery," 25; Vidal, *Caribbean New Orleans*, 43–93.

17 "El Misisipi (New-Orleans [La.]) 1808–1810," accessed September 28, 2024, www.loc.gov/item/sn83026406.

18 Antonio de Sedella Collection, Howard-Tilton Memorial Library, Tulane University, New Orleans.

19 Gruesz, *Ambassadors of Culture*; Hamnett, *Juarez*; Smart, *Viva Juárez!*

20 Muñoz Bravo, "'Largo y sinuoso camino'"; Lipsitz, *Possessive Investment in Whiteness*, 239.

21 Miller, Marilyn G. "'Allá En Tierras Del Sur.'"

22 Sluyter et al., *Hispanic and Latino New Orleans*; Weise, *Corazón de Dixie*, 18–20.

23 Koeppel, *Banana*, 145.

24 MacCameron, *Bananas, Labor, and Politics*, 10.

25 After amassing sizable debt, the Honduran government acquiesced to the US State Department's "Knox Plan," which took over Honduras's commercial development. Charles Mercer, "Rise of United Fruit Told; Zemurray Plays Big Part," *Times-Picayune* (New Orleans), August 15, 1954; Chapman, *Bananas*, 71.

26 Mercer, "Rise of United Fruit Told."

27 Italian immigrants from the Piedmont region were among the first documented cases of striking workers in Costa Rica. Jamaican workers resisted the labor abuses of Minor Keith—an influential American businessman and key figure in the banana trade and railroad infrastructure in Central America in the late nineteenth and early twentieth centuries—by forging their own resistance movements through shadow institutions like churches and lodges that helped cultivate labor unions. Bourgois, *Ethnicity at Work*; Chomsky, *West Indian Workers*; Chomsky, "Afro-Jamaican Traditions and Labor Organizing," 837.

28 In June 1913, New Orleans waterfront workers struck against United Fruit after the company slashed wages and rejected their union. United Fruit's response included hiring strikebreakers, escalating tensions. On June 11, violence erupted as police, backed by United Fruit officials, blocked strikers from boarding the *Heredia*, a steamship bound for Central America. Six strikers were shot, and a worker, Robert Neuman, was killed. The American Federation of Labor and the Industrial Workers of the World–affiliated Marine Transport Workers supported the strike. *The Lumberjack*, a Louisiana-based IWW newspaper, condemned United Fruit as the "shameless Fruit Trusts." Editor Covington Hall, an IWW organizer, aimed to expose labor disputes, emphasizing the company's disregard for human life. The aftermath saw forty-three jailed strikers released due to insufficient evidence. The incident, covered extensively by *The Lumberjack*, revealed the volatile relationship between labor and powerful corporations in the early twentieth century. W. J. Parks, "United Fruit Co. Riot," *The Lumberjack* (Alexandria, LA), June 19, 1913, Chronicling America: Historic American Newspapers, Library of Congress (online source of the later *Lumberjack* citations as well); Reed, "Lumberjacks and Longshoremen," 54–59; "The Situation on the Riverfront," *The Lumberjack* (Alexandria, LA), June 12, 1913; "Acto Triste Hemoso [*sic*]," *The Lumberjack* (Alexandria, LA), June 19, 1913; "About *The Lumberjack*," Chronicling America: Historic American Newspapers, Library of Congress, https://chroniclingamerica.loc.gov/lccn/sn88064459/; Chapman, *Bananas*.

29 Bourgois, *Ethnicity at Work*.

30 As part of a noncompete clause, Zemurray first retired from the banana industry to Tangipahoa Parish just north of New Orleans on a former rice plantation whose owner, Alfred Tenner, once enslaved 100 people. "Samuel Zemurray, 84,

Is Dead; Headed United Fruit Company," *New York Times*, December 2, 1961; Aslakson, "Immigrant Lawyers and Slavery," 51.

31 Zemurray moved from retired leisure on his plantation home in Louisiana's rural Tangipahoa Parish to 2 Audubon Place, a mansion of Georgian and Greek Rival architecture, located in a gated community just off St. Charles Avenue in Uptown New Orleans. "Business and Finance: United Fruit Obeys," *Time*, January 23, 1933; Chapman, *Bananas*, 102. In 1975, the Zemurray family donated the house to Tulane University, where it serves as the president's mansion.

32 *La Voz Latina* called it the "premier" city of banana imports: "La divisa Zemurray aquilata valores 'Unifruco'; Acaso trasladarse la matriz a Nueva Orleans," *La Voz Latina* (New Orleans), January 1938. United Fruit officials had a ten-story Spanish Renaissance–style structure built in 1920 in the downtown Central Business District. The building, which was sold by United Fruit in 1965, still remains a vestige of the early fruit trade with the words "United Fruit Company 1920" rounded off with ornate fruit baskets above the entryway. Mike Scott, "United Fruit Co. Building, Once the Height of Modernity, Awaits Its Next Chapter as It Turns 100," NOLA.com, accessed August 4, 2021, www.nola.com/entertainment_life/article_04b2bff0-e269-11eb-8b44-8b75372f778d.html; MacCameron, *Bananas, Labor, and Politics*, 35, 43; Chapman, *Bananas*, 70–73, 100–101; Cohen, *Fish That Ate the Whale*, 4–7, 79–115; Koeppel, *Banana*, 74. "Gateway to the Americas: Pan-American Life in New Orleans, 1946–1970," accessed September 28, 2024, https://exhibits.tulane.edu/exhibit/pan-american-life-in-new-orleans/pan-american-life-in-new-orleans-timeline/gateway-to-the-americas-1946-1970. See also Campanella, *Geographies of New Orleans*, 193–203; and Lipsitz, *Possessive Investment in Whiteness*, 239.

33 Meredith Bethune, "The Sweet Success of Bananas Foster Has an Unsavory Past," NPR, September 30, 2016, www.npr.org/sections/thesalt/2016/09/30/493157144/the-sweet-success-of-bananas-foster-has-an-unsavory-past.

34 Campanella, *Geographies of New Orleans*, 193–203.

35 Donato et al., "Immigration, Reconstruction, and Settlement."

36 Sluyter, "(Post-)K New Orleans and the Hispanic Atlantic"; Euraque, "'Honduran Memories,'" 9; Trujillo-Pagán, "Recovering Latinos' Place," 194. They took the name "Lempira" from the national currency of Honduras named after the great Lenca chieftain who helped unify tribes fighting against Spanish conquest in the region during the sixteenth century.

37 Joel Kotkin, "New Orleans, Struggling to Revive Its Once Dominating Port," *Washington Post*, August 12, 1989.

38 Canak and Miller, "Gumbo Politics"; Gotham, "Marketing Mardi Gras," 1740; Pelot-Hobbs, *Prison Capital*, 7–8; E. Fussell, "Constructing New Orleans."

39 E. Fussell, "Constructing New Orleans," 848.

40 Euraque, "'Honduran Memories,'" 16–18.

41 Global trade policies like NAFTA in the late 1990s contributed to this growth with uneven exports, environmental degradation, outsourcing, and rampant growth of multinational corporations contributing to job displacement and economic instability in Mexico. The comprehensive immigration reform, passed by Congress in 1996 and called Illegal Immigration Reform and Immigrant Responsibility Act, codified illegality into the federal nomenclature and created harsh penalties like expedited deportation removals and beefed-up immigration enforcement that further prevented mobility of immigrants into and out of the United States. The Patriot Act, which was passed in 2001, exacerbated this enforcement and fearmongering. As a result, the number of undocumented immigrants—mostly Mexican—in the United States tripled between 1994 and 2007. Gálvez, *Eating NAFTA*; Verea, "Immigration Trends After 20 Years of NAFTA"; Striffler, *Chicken*, 134–37.

42 Pelot-Hobbs, *Prison Capital*, 72. Before Hurricane Katrina in 2005, other immigrant communities resided in the city, including Vietnamese immigrants, who had a significant presence in certain neighborhoods, particularly in the New Orleans East neighborhood Village de l'Est. The Vietnamese community in New Orleans began to grow in the aftermath of the Vietnam War, with many refugees settling in the United States. By the 1980s and 1990s, New Orleans had become home to a thriving Vietnamese population. Carl L. Bankston III, "Vietnamese in Louisiana," *64 Parishes*, accessed February 23, 2024, https://64parishes.org/entry/vietnamese-in-louisiana; Simi Kang, "Feeding Versailles," *Hyphen*, January 25, 2017, https://hyphenmagazine.com/blog/2017/01/feeding-versailles.

43 Sluyter et al., *Hispanic and Latino New Orleans*.

44 Cacho, *Social Death*, 123. I hadn't considered the CAFTA link until I attended in Montreal the November 2023 American Studies Association conference panel "Latinx Migration and Transnational Solidarities," chaired by Lisa Cacho, particularly the paper "Genealogies of the 'Northern Triangle': Economics, Migration, and Anti–Central American Sentiment," by Joselin Castillo.

45 "Coffee Production Worldwide in 2020, by Leading Country," Statista, accessed February 24, 2024, www.statista.com/statistics/277137/world-coffee-production-by-leading-countries.

46 Chris Price, "Brew Orleans," *Biz New Orleans* (blog), March 31, 2017, www.bizneworleans.com/brew-orleans/; Daniel Workman, "Honduras Top 10 Exports," World's Top Exports, accessed February 24, 2024, www.worldstopexports.com/honduras-top-10-exports.

47 In 2013 I conducted preliminary fieldwork across Honduras through a fellowship with the Tinker Foundation and support from the Stone Center for Latin American Studies at Tulane. I conducted another month of fieldwork in 2015

with a grant from Tulane's School of Liberal Arts Summer Merit Fellowship. In 2022, I returned to Honduras to visit Denis with Chloe Sigal (a former El Congreso organizer) through the Global South Fellowship grant, which is part of the New Orleans Center for the Gulf South at Tulane University.

48 I use a pseudonym for the restaurant.

49 For an in-depth look at self-reliance in the face of structural food inequalities and racial capitalism, see Reese, *Black Food Geographies*.

Chapter 1

1 In place of his real name, I have used a pseudonym.

2 Plyer, "Facts for Features: Katrina Impact."

3 Daser, "Citizens of the City," 148–54; Gorman, "Latino Migrant Labor Strife"; Dale, "Katrina Relief"; Trujillo-Pagán, "Neoliberal Disasters and Racialisation."

4 Some estimates say 30,000 while others say 100,000. See Taylor, "New Orleans Since the Storm"; and Fletcher et al., *Rebuilding after Katrina*.

5 One statistic showed that eight out of ten immigrant workers experienced wage theft (the nonpayment or underpayment of promised wages by an employer) after Katrina—a clear result of this deregulation. Trujillo-Pagán, "Neoliberal Disasters and Racialisation"; Michelle Chen, "Four Years after Katrina, Workers Still Exploited in the Big Easy," *In These Times*, August 31, 2009; Browne-Dianis et al., "And Injustice for All," 29.

6 For street vendors like Mateo, law enforcement used antiquated food truck policy: a city ordinance until 2014 forced food trucks and trailers to move every thirty minutes as a method to threaten food vendors who parked near esquinas (neighboring Jefferson Parish banned taco trucks outright). See chapter 3 and Fouts, "Re-regulating *Loncheras*."

7 Cuervo, Leopold, and Baron, "Promoting Community Preparedness and Resilience," 161; E. Fussell, "Hurricane Chasers in New Orleans"; Hayden, "Street Food as Infrastructure."

8 Mukhija and Loukaitou-Sideris, *Informal American City*. Often considered endemic to the Global South, informal economies have flourished in the neoliberalism age of privatization and deregulation.

9 Purcell, "Possible Worlds," 142.

10 Fine, *Worker Centers*, 3. For an in-depth ethnography of Mississippi's chicken-processing plants, immigration, multiracial solidarities, worker centers, and workplace justice, see Stuesse, *Scratching Out a Living*.

11 Fine, *Worker Centers*.

12 Flaherty, *Floodlines*. For a comprehensive overview of policymaking around Katrina's history, including the flawed urban development, racial disparities, and the impacts of Louisiana's oil industry, see Horowitz, *Katrina*, 5–8.

13 Some favorites: "We Know This Place," by Sunni Patterson; Prince's "S.S.T.," which stands for "sea surface temperature," a measurement for hurricanes, and "Brand New Orleans," both charity singles released in September 2005; *Yellow House* by Sarah M. Broom; "Requiem" by Yusef Komunyakaa; and *Floodlines* by Jordan Flaherty.

14 Newkirk, *Floodlines* podcast.

15 German Lopez, "7 Facts about Hurricane Katrina That Show Just How Incompetent the Government Response Was," Vox, August 23, 2015, www.vox.com/2015/8/23/9191907/hurricane-katrina.

16 Laura Sullivan, "How New Orleans' Evacuation Plan Fell Apart," NPR, September 23, 2005, www.npr.org/templates/story/story.php?storyId=4860776.

17 Tierney, Bevc, and Kuligowski, "Metaphors Matter."

18 Estimates suggest direct and indirect fatalities. FEMA estimates are much lower than other sources. "2005 Hurricane Katrina: Facts, FAQs, and How to Help," World Vision, November 25, 2019, www.worldvision.org/disaster-relief-news-stories/2005-hurricane-katrina-facts.

19 Fletcher et al., "Latino Workers and Human Rights," 111.

20 "Fast Facts: Hurricane Costs."

21 Some 51 percent of contracts were issued as limited or no-bid in September 2005 and 93 percent issued in October 2005. "Study: Millions Wasted in Katrina Contracts," NBC News, August 24, 2006, www.nbcnews.com/id/wbna14502390.

22 Taylor, "New Orleans since the Storm."

23 For a comprehensive account of Louisiana's shift to mass incarceration from 1970 to 2020 and the emergence of grassroots movements challenging the conditions and power structures of mass criminalization and racial capitalism, see Pelot-Hobbs, *Prison Capital*; and Bryn Stole, "As Number of Immigrants behind Bars Soars under Trump, Louisiana Becomes Detention Hub," *Times-Picayune* (New Orleans), October 19, 2019, www.nola.com/news/article_197ff094-f1f5-11e9-ad15-f7503d2a8b7a.html.

24 "Who's Cleaning Up New Orleans?," CBS News, October 7, 2005, www.cbsnews.com/news/whos-cleaning-up-new-orleans.

25 Fletcher et al., "Latino Workers and Human Rights," 183.

26 Fletcher et al., "Latino Workers and Human Rights," 120.

27 E. Fussell, "Welcoming the Newcomers."

28 Davis, "Who Killed New Orleans?"

29 Katy Reckdahl, "Dyan French Cole, 'Simply Mama D,' Dies at 72: 'She Was the Rock of New Orleans,'" *Times-Picayune* (New Orleans), May 20, 2017; Trymaine D. Lee, "Momma's Mission," *Times-Picayune* (New Orleans), September 18, 2005, accessed through the website A Katrina Reader: Readings by and for

Anti-Racist Educators and Organizers, http://katrinareader.cwsworkshop.org/mommas-mission.html.

30 Browne-Dianis et al., "And Injustice for All," 56.

31 Fouts, "Who Will Rebuild Houston?"

32 Bryan Llenas, "10 Years after Katrina: Day Laborers Seek Acceptance, Hope for Better Future," Fox News, December 5, 2016, www.foxnews.com/world/10-years-after-katrina-day-laborers-seek-acceptance-hope-for-better-future.

33 Fletcher et al., "Latino Workers and Human Rights."

34 Browne-Dianis et al., "And Injustice for All," 29–30. The exploitative labor practice of not paying became a pattern that extended long after the first year of rebuilding. Fieldwork done by Warren Waren in 2008 reported that 74 percent of workers reported wage theft cases that year. Waren's report, published in 2014, directly connected these labor abuses to deregulation of labor markets, arguing that wage theft was "discernibly worse in labor markets which systematically undermine worker protections in favor of benefits for employers." See Waren, "Wage Theft among Latino Day Laborers," 748.

35 Murga, "Organizing and Rebuilding."

36 Murga, "Racialization of Day Labor Work," 61.

37 It was eventually removed in May 2017.

38 Croegaert, "Architectures of Pain," 580.

39 Gorman, "Latino Migrant Labor Strife," 19.

40 Sam Quinones, "Drifting In on Katrina's Wind, Laborers Alter the Streetscape," *Los Angeles Times*, May 1, 2006, www.latimes.com/archives/la-xpm-2006-may-01-na-neworleans1-story.html.

41 Gorman, "Latino Migrant Labor Strife," 19.

42 James Varney, "40 Jailed in Raids on Immigrants: But Legal Groups Say City Needs Workers," *Times-Picayune* (New Orleans), March 18, 2006, accessed through Brown Library Repository, https://repository.library.brown.edu/studio/item/bdr:65581/; also referenced in Gorman, "Latino Migrant Labor Strife."

43 Gorman, "Latino Migrant Labor Strife." In some cases, NOPD officers arrived with flyers in English warning against loitering and threatening to return the next day with a police vehicle. In other cases, they showed up without warning. Raids moved from the Lee/Harmony Circle hiring area to neighborhoods and motels where the workers lived.

44 Gorman, "Latino Migrant Labor Strife," 21–22.

45 Murphy, "Broken Promises," 16.

46 In an interview in *Salon* magazine, one worker is quoted saying, "We're paying $60 a night to this guy Eddie for a room with no AC, no lights, no electricity, no water and a bed that stinks." He heard about the Katrina work at a job fair in Fresno, California. Roberto Lovato, "Rebuilding the Big Easy," *Salon*, October 20, 2005, www.salon.com/2005/10/19/latino_new_orleans.

47 The report by Fletcher et al. found that in 27 percent of the cases, employers even deducted higher rates of expenses from salaries from undocumented workers, including "housing (43 percent), transportation (43 percent), and food (25 percent)." Fletcher et al., "Latino Workers and Human Rights."

48 Firth, *Feeding New Orleans*, 112–14; Federal Writers' Project, *New Orleans City Guide*, 297.

49 The only other people to have legally camped in the space were the occasional Boy Scout troops and Union soldiers during the Civil War. Murphy, "Broken Promises," 25.

50 Browne-Dianis et al., "And Injustice for All," 56.

51 Browne-Dianis et al., "And Injustice for All," 56.

52 Richard A. Webster, "Unhappy Campers: Eviction Notices Aggravate Laborers Living at City Park," *New Orleans City Business*, February 6, 2006.

53 Browne-Dianis et al., "And Injustice for All," 56.

54 Webster, "Unhappy Campers"; Browne-Dianis et al., "And Injustice for All."

55 Webster, "Unhappy Campers." The report "And Injustice for All" by Browne-Dianis et al. contains interviews and features in-depth accounts of the dire conditions at "Tent City." In the report, 165 students in conjunction with the Advancement Project, the National Immigration Law Center, and the New Orleans Worker Justice Coalition (which became the New Orleans Workers' Center for Racial Justice) interviewed 700 workers in the post-Katrina milieu to document the humanitarian crisis and channel support for the workers.

56 Murphy, "Broken Promises," 25; Webster, "Unhappy Campers"; "Peoples Hurricane Relief Fund and Oversight Coalition."

57 Murphy, "Broken Promises," 25.

58 Murphy, "Broken Promises," 25.

59 Shapiro, "Attuning to the Chemosphere"; Heather Smith, "People Are Still Living in FEMA's Toxic Katrina Trailers—and They Likely Have No Idea," Grist, August 27, 2015, https://grist.org/politics/people-are-still-living-in-femas-toxic-katrina-trailers-and-they-likely-have-no-idea.

60 "Formaldehyde Exposure in Homes."

61 The FEMA trailers carried "elevated levels of formaldehyde in their interior atmosphere," said Nick Shapiro, who traced the FEMA trailers across the country after they had been resold by FEMA (despite their documented toxicity). Shapiro, "Attuning to the Chemosphere," 389. The FEMA trailers sold for just 7 percent return of the initial expenses. Smith, "People Are Still Living in FEMA's Toxic Katrina Trailers."

62 Eric Lipton and Leslie Eaton, "Housing for Storm's Evacuees Lagging Far Behind U.S. Goals," *New York Times*, September 30, 2005, www.nytimes.com/2005/09/30/us/nationalspecial/housing-for-storms-evacuees-lagging-far-behind-us-goals.html.

63 Forrest McBride, "How Is the Red Cross Helping Those Affected by Flooding in Louisiana?," KLFY.com (Lafayette, Louisiana), August 23, 2016, www.klfy.com/local/how-is-the-red-cross-helping-those-affected-by-flooding-in-louisiana/; for an in-depth critique of philanthropic efforts in post-Katrina New Orleans, see Firth, *Feeding New Orleans*.

64 E. Fussell, "Welcoming the Newcomers," 140. This was a problem that continued to transpire in later disasters (such as floods in Baton Rouge) when Red Cross workers denied undocumented workers foods due to their presumed documentation status.

65 Lee, "Momma's Mission," accessed through the website A Katrina Reader: Readings by and for Anti-Racist Educators and Organizers, http://katrinareader.cwsworkshop.org/mommas-mission.html.

66 Food Not Bombs website, http://foodnotbombs.net/new_site/; Common Ground Relief website, www.commongroundrelief.org/about-us.

67 Gibson, *Post-Katrina Brazucas*, 205.

68 See "about" section in Favela Chic Nola, http://favelachicnola.com/our-favela-chic (site discontinued); and Anna McKinnon, "Ruben's Taco Truck Attracts Loyal Local Following," *Nolavie*, May 6, 2013, http://nolavie.com/Rubens-taco-truck-attracts-loyal-local-following-67640.

69 Fouts, "Re-regulating *Loncheras*."

70 Fouts, "Re-regulating *Loncheras*."

71 For example, Common Ground Relief was infiltrated by a federal informant, which, according to Flaherty, "served as a reminder that even legally operating grassroots groups successfully challenging entrenched power can become targets." Flaherty, *Floodlines*, xiv, 104; Brendan McCarthy, "Common Ground Official Was a Federal Informant, Lawsuit Says," *Times-Picayune* (New Orleans), November 7, 2011, www.nola.com/news/politics/article_3f5f2fce-c218-53ea-a4ec-8ba6aa4e16bd.html.

72 "NOWCRJ Mission."

73 Flaherty, *Floodlines*, 97. Curtis, in favor of the Ella Baker–style consensus grassroots (self-funded) model, moved to Latin America to build the International School of Bottom-Up Organizing.

74 Alliance of Guestworkers for Dignity changed its name to the National Guestworker Alliance and is now an independent organization.

75 O'Neal, "Guidelines for Story Circles."

76 I developed an approved abridged version of the *Mr. Moneybags* play in three sets as originally told by Toya Ex Lewis in January 2020.

77 Toya Ex Lewis also says, "I was sitting on the porch one day reading a newspaper and my neighbor [an elderly Black man], well it looked like he was about to lose his job because these Latinx workers were coming in and lowering the wages. So I came in with that understanding and that narrative from my

community, right? Which is by design. . . . So it was a learning curve, and it was moments like that [the Mr. *Moneybags* skit] that I took the opportunity to learn about how deeply connected we should be, how deeply connected our struggles are."

78 During my time with El Congreso, there was one Paraguayan member and one Colombian member, whom we called Jorge "Colombia."

79 Saket Soni, "Louisiana Grower Sued for Forced Labor," *People's Tribune*, www.peoplestribune.org/PT.2008.03/PT.2008.03.10.html (site discontinued).

80 Tiano, Murphy-Aguilar, and Bigej, *Borderline Slavery*, 209–11.

81 Soni, "Louisiana Grower Sued for Forced Labor." Based on the 2021 Supreme Court decision *Cedar Point Nursery v. Hassid*, this type of direct action would not be allowed; see "Cedar Point Nursery v. Hassid" on SCOTUSblog.

82 Soni, "Louisiana Grower Sued for Forced Labor."

83 "Allegation of Farm Worker Abuse Investigated," NBC News, December 10, 2008, www.nbcnews.com/id/wbna28165454.

84 In place of her real name, I have used a pseudonym.

85 "Taqueria El Chaparral New Orleans LA Reviews," Gayot, accessed February 24, 2024, www.gayot.com/restaurants/taqueria-el-chaparral-new-orleans-la-70125_18no070401.html.

86 Lorin Gaudin and Todd Price, "Best in Dining," *New Orleans Magazine*, November 28, 2006, www.myneworleans.com/best-in-dining.

87 The Wage Claim Clinic initially formed as a collaboration between the Catholic Charities Archdiocese of New Orleans and the New Orleans Pro Bono Project. For more information, see "The Wage Claim Clinic: The Workplace Justice Project," Workplace Justice Project, accessed February 24, 2024, www.wjpnola.org/the-wage-claim-clinic.

88 Gonzalez-Barrera and Krogstad, "U.S. Deportations of Immigrants Reach Record High in 2013."

89 By 2009 and in the context of the Great Recession, statewide anti-immigration policies escalated, the footprint of the Department of Homeland Security expanded, and deportations skyrocketed.

90 Firth, *Feeding New Orleans*.

91 "Hurricane Katrina Evacuees Experience," C-SPAN, December 6, 2005, at 1:04:49, www.c-span.org/video/?190199-1/gulf-coast-evacuees-hurricane-katrina&event=190199&playEvent#.

92 Also cited in Dyan "Mama D" French Cole's beautiful obituary written by Katy Reckdahl, "Dyan French Cole, 'Simply Mama D,' Dies at 72."

Chapter 2

1 Katherine Sayre, "Home Depot in Mid-City New Orleans to Close in November," NOLA.com, August 14, 2013, www.nola.com/news/business/home

-depot-in-mid-city-new-orleans-to-close-in-november/article_08c2dd30-ac03-5aac-ad76-387d93ccdc8d.html.

2 The term "Hispanic" is the designation used in census demographics, but it is limiting as a reference for a complex region and people. See "Mid-City Statistical Area" and "Planning District 4," both from the Data Center website.

3 Lipsitz, *How Racism Takes Place*, 236–37. After Katrina, New Orleans City Council members developed a "Recovery Plan" in which they split the city into thirteen planning districts based on past models created by the City Planning Commission. Planning District 4, which is dubbed as the Mid-City Planning District, includes the ten neighborhoods Tremé, Iberville, Seventh Ward, Fairgrounds, St. Bernard, Bayou St. John, Mid-City, Tulane/Gravier, B. W. Cooper, and Gert Town. Three of these geographically specific areas—Mid-City, B. W. Cooper, and Tremé—are featured in this chapter. Thus, "Mid-City" serves as the name of both the planning district *and* the neighborhood that are foregrounded in this chapter. See "Planning District 4."

4 In place of their real names, I have used pseudonyms.

5 In place of his real name, I have used a pseudonym.

6 Loperena, "Settler Violence?," 801.

7 Klein, *Shock Doctrine*; Loperena, "Honduras Is Open for Business."

8 Loperena, "Settler Violence?," 804; Loperena, "Honduras Is Open for Business."

9 Chatterjee, *Displacement, Revolution*, 5.

10 Burgi-Palomino, *Nowhere to Call Home*. Burgi-Palomino of the Latin America Working Group argues that while gangs do drive internal displacement, *mano dura* policies—hardline security policies implemented in 2002—displace people and destabilize regions.

11 They closed again in 2020 due to the pandemic.

12 Along with the warnings for these nightly disturbances, the restaurant has also come under scrutiny for infrastructural deficiencies. In one case, the restaurant was involved in a lawsuit in November 2014 in which an air conditioner unit fell out of the wall and onto a customer's head, causing "severe injuries." The plaintiff sued for damages for pain and suffering, medical expenses, and loss in wages. The two sides settled for an undisclosed amount, and according to Caty, no other major incidents occurred at the restaurant except for the occasional noise complaint, which she and her family are able to resolve.

13 Harvey, "Right to the City," 39.

14 Ott, "Closure of New Orleans' Charity Hospital."

15 Roberta Brandes Gratz, "Why Was New Orleans's Charity Hospital Allowed to Die?," *The Nation*, April 27, 2011, www.thenation.com/article/archive/why-was-new-orleanss-charity-hospital-allowed-die.

16 Gratz, "Why Was New Orleans's Charity Hospital Allowed to Die?"

17 Kate Moran, "LSU and VA to Build Joint Medical Campus in Downtown New Orleans; VA Expected to Open by 2013," NOLA.com, November 26, 2008, www.nola.com/news/lsu-and-va-to-build-joint-medical-campus-in-downtown-new-orleans-va-expected-to/article_721dfa0b-c5cf-5dd1-8b7f-cbf9e4ec7a69.html.

18 Susan Buchanan, "Hospital Building Accelerates in New Orleans after Homes Were Moved," HuffPost, August 9, 2012, www.huffpost.com/entry/hospital-building-acceler_b_1748384.

19 Buchanan, "Hospital Building Accelerates in New Orleans after Homes Were Moved."

20 Chad Calder, "New University Medical Center, Upcoming Veterans' Affairs Complex Ignite New Orleans Housing, Commercial Boom," *New Orleans Advocate*, September 7, 2015, www.theneworleansadvocate.com/news/13350097-148/new-hospitals-spurring-residential-commercial. In just three years, neighborhood disparities showed that the price per square foot of residential housing increased from $90 in 2012 to $199 in 2015.

21 Della Haselle, "Tulane Avenue Neighbors Barking over Lack of Neutral Ground Trees as Project Nears Completion," NOLA.com, July 30, 2016, www.nola.com/news/politics/tulane-avenue-neighbors-barking-over-lack-of-neutral-ground-trees-as-project-nears-completion/article_44b84499-7757-571b-ba61-b51f3bef2aaf.html.

22 I used 2019 to avoid the outlier of 2020 housing prices. "2604 Palmyra St, New Orleans, LA 70119," Realtor.com, accessed February 24, 2024, www.realtor.com/realestateandhomes-detail/2604-Palmyra-St_New-Orleans_LA_70119_M81951-98297.

23 "Neighborhood Statistical Area Data Profiles," Data Center, accessed February 20, 2024, www.datacenterresearch.org/data-resources/neighborhood-data.

24 Ramon Antonio Vargas, "Half of City's Homicides, Shootings Occur in New Orleans East, in and near 9th Ward: MCC Study," NOLA.com, January 22, 2021, www.nola.com/news/crime_police/half-of-citys-homicides-shootings-occur-in-new-orleans-east-in-and-near-9th-ward/article_e58c30bc-5cfc-11eb-9d8a-cf152bca0fda.html.

25 The Mid-City block's notoriety is so pronounced that it inspired a rap song by MidCityAB and even served as the inspiration for a potent daiquiri flavor. It also served as inspiration for a 2024 art exhibition at Antenna Art Gallery called "Dear Tulane & Broad" by Melody Chang. "Dear Tulane & Broad," Antenna, accessed September 29, 2024, www.antenna.works/dear-tulane-and-broad.

26 Richard Webster, "Even as New Mid-City Hospitals Rise, Tulane Avenue's Past Hinders Its Renaissance," *Times-Picayune* (New Orleans), August 10, 2013.

27 "2424 Tulane—Apartments in New Orleans, LA," Apartments.com, accessed February 20, 2024, www.apartments.com/2424-tulane-new-orleans-la/b8f1bc8.
28 Dávila, *Culture Works*, 11.
29 Ian McNulty, "Around Huge New Hospitals, Small Eateries Create an Anything-Goes Food Frontier," NOLA.com, January 16, 2017, www.nola.com/entertainment_life/eat-drink/around-huge-new-hospitals-small-eateries-create-an-anything-goes-food-frontier/article_6cc7d1cf-def3-5152-b7a4-2ded289983ba.html.
30 Marie Fazio, "Is a New Grocery Store Finally Coming to a West Bank Food Desert?," NOLA.com, October 12, 2023, www.nola.com/news/jefferson_parish/ideal-market-to-open-store-for-avondale-waggaman/article_d107534c-6780-11ee-a661-dbc9e8edd108.html.
31 Chatterjee, *Displacement, Revolution*, 5.
32 Mayer, *Almost Hollywood*.
33 Lipsitz, *How Racism Takes Place*, 236–37.
34 Green, Kouassi, and Mambo, "Housing, Race, and Recovery."
35 El Congreso's rapid expansion post-2012 necessitated four subsequent relocations due to its substantial growth.
36 I followed the lead of countless other volunteers, most notably Tiana Noble, Lorena Murga, Sophie Ashley, and Sarah "Tennessee" Hailey.
37 "Table 39. Aliens Removed or Returned."
38 "Immigration and Customs Enforcement Removals"; "Immigration and Customs Enforcement Removals," accessed September 29, 2024, https://trac.syr.edu/phptools/immigration/remove.
39 Named for Yvonne Marrero, a community organizer from B. W. Cooper who died during Katrina.
40 "Calliope Housing Project, Building No. 3, 1201–31 South Dorgenois Street, New Orleans, Orleans Parish, LA," image, Library of Congress, accessed February 24, 2024, www.loc.gov/item/la0650.
41 The public hearing overflowed with people; opponents to the demolition who congregated outside were pepper-sprayed and tased. Sinha and Browne-Dianis, "Exiling the Poor," 481, 485; Gwen Filosa, "Live Updates on Demolition Vote from Council Chambers," NOLA.com, December 9, 2007, www.nola.com/news/article_27a3d35a-eec2-5f58-a7f2-5a77e026fe17.html.
42 Woods, "Les Misérables of New Orleans."
43 Sinha and Browne-Dianis, "Exiling the Poor."
44 Lipsitz, *How Racism Takes Place*, 225.
45 Sinha and Browne-Dianis, "Exiling the Poor"; and Quigley and Godchaux, "Locked Out and Torn Down."

46 Woods, "Les Misérables of New Orleans," 770.

47 Stand would also take on a "Ban the Box" campaign that eventually passed the Louisiana state legislature in 2017 for state and city hires.

48 US Department of Housing and Urban Development, "Section 3 of the Housing and Development Act of 1968."

49 Katy Reckdahl, "B. W. Cooper Residents Help Rebuild Development," *Times-Picayune* (New Orleans), August 1, 2011, www.nola.com/news/crime_police/article_999631d0-4d29-5791-91ee-e49d05dbf16a.html.

50 Reckdahl, "B. W. Cooper Residents Help Rebuild Development."

51 Richard Campanella, "New Orleans Prisons," 64 *Parishes*, March 1, 2020, https://64parishes.org/new-orleans-prisons.

52 Pelot-Hobbs, *Prison Capital*, 108–9, 143–67.

53 "New Orleans: Prisoners Abandoned to Floodwaters."

54 Despite written complaints filed by Plaintiffs Mario Cacho and Antonio Ocampo. See *Cacho v. Gusman*, Civil Action No. 11-225-SS, accessed September 29, 2024, https://casetext.com/case/cacho-v-gusman.

55 "Undocumented Immigrants in New Orleans Make Progress with Sheriff Gusman, Hope NOPD Will Follow Suit," WWNO, October 14, 2013, www.wwno.org/show/all-things-new-orleans/2013-10-14/undocumented-immigrants-in-new-orleans-make-progress-with-sheriff-gusman-hope-nopd-will-follow-suit.

56 See the testimony and the report linked in "New Report: The Criminal Alien Removal Initiative in New Orleans."

57 Fernando López visited El Congreso the previous year with the Undocubus caravan, a group of forty individuals who caravanned from Arizona to North Carolina as part of the "No Papers, No Fear" campaign aimed to bring attention to the rising deportations at the Democratic National Convention in Charlotte in 2012. I met Fernando when the bus broke down in Kenner and Jacinta sent me out to help ameliorate the situation without giving me much direction on how to do that in the sweltering August heat. I brought them *terere*, a form of cold yerba maté, to help combat the heat. Fernando and I would continue to work together on numerous documentary projects after he left the Workers' Center in 2017.

58 The biometric technology was developed for use originally in US military operations in Afghanistan and Iraq.

59 Zoë Carpenter, "How the Government Created 'Stop-and-Frisk for Latinos,'" *The Nation*, September 3, 2014, www.thenation.com/article/archive/how-government-created-stop-and-frisk-latinos. Carpenter's reporting also revealed that CARI raids were designed to help ICE reach a quota.

60 I'm forever grateful for Jennifer Saracino teaching my Tulane class that day so I could be a part of that action.

61 The ICE field office is located on the third floor of the privately owned Hyatt House building, a twenty-four-story tower.
62 "New Report: The Criminal Alien Removal Initiative in New Orleans."
63 "NOPD Consent Decree Monitor, New Orleans, Louisiana."
64 Thanks to Blaine Cerney for tipping me off about United Fruit and for letting me do laundry while in Tegucigalpa.
65 Harpelle, "White Zones," 307–9.
66 Zemurray continued to be a complicated and polemical figure throughout his tenure. Philanthropically, Zemurray donated large amounts of money to universities, New Deal campaigns, and the left-wing media. At the same time, he plotted with the CIA to overthrow democratically elected officials, including Jacobo Arbenz of Guatemala, to protect his own land interests. Emily Biuso, "Banana Kings: The History of Banana Cultivation Is Rife with Labor and Environmental Abuse, Corporate Skullduggery and Genetic Experiments Gone Awry," *The Nation*, accessed February 28, 2008, www.thenation.com/article/banana-kings/; Chapman, *Bananas*.
67 Harpelle, "White Zones," 307.
68 Lesage and Feintrenie, *Are Sustainable Pathways Possible for Oil Palm Development in Latin America?*
69 Kerssen, *Grabbing Power*, 121.
70 Ritchie, *Palm Oil*.
71 Catherine Tucker, "Coffee Production and Communal Forests in Honduras: Adaptation and Resilience in a Context of Change," Paper Presentation Conference: International Association for the Study of the Commons, Cheltenham, United Kingdom, July 2008, 4–5. Thanks to Elliott Powell for helping me locate these resources and for thinking with me through this research question.
72 This was further done in retaliation against the strong union organizing at the banana factories. Frank, *Bananeras*, 31.
73 Ritchie, *Palm Oil*.
74 Bloxom, "Fueling the Appetite for Water," 26–27.
75 Kerssen, *Grabbing Power*, 23. Like Kerssen, much of Loperena's work centers on the Aguán Valley region, located about 150 miles east of Tela. The Aguán Valley has been the site of peasant-led resistance to this neoliberal development and the site of much violence through the retaliation from the landowners; 123 environmental activists have been killed in Honduras since 2009. Loperena, "Settler Violence?," 806.
76 Spring, "Marriage of Drug Money and Neoliberal Development." US Attorney's Office, "Former Honduran Congressman Tony Hernández Sentenced to Life in Prison and Ordered to Forfeit $138.5 Million for Distributing 185 Tons of Cocaine and Related Firearms and False Statements Offenses," US

Department of Justice, March 30, 2021, www.justice.gov/usao-sdny/pr/former-honduran-congressman-tony-hern-ndez-sentenced-life-prison-and-ordered-forfeit.

77 Méndez, "Silent Violence;" Colin Moynihan, "Ex-Honduras President Found Guilty in Drug Trafficking Trial," *New York Times*, March 8, 2024, www.nytimes.com/2024/03/08/nyregion/juan-orlando-hernandez-honduras-guilty-verdict.html.

78 Bloxom, "Fueling the Appetite for Water," 30.

79 In 2014, Grupo Jaremar signed a loan agreement with the Overseas Private Investment Corporation for over $20 million to fund new capital expenditures in Honduras for palm oil production. The corporation used violence and job creation as justifications for the expansion of its land, positing in its report that "Honduras has been plagued by the crime and the drug trade in recent years, and is one of the Western Hemisphere's poorest countries. Through this loan, the company will be able to provide employment opportunities and continue to benefit the local community through the support of philanthropic programs." "Public Project Profile," Overseas Private Investment Corporation, last modified January 7, 2017, www.opic.gov/sites/default/files/files/jaremare-info-summary-fy14.pdf (site discontinued).

80 "Thriving Lagoon."

81 Jelsson Flores, "Evacúan a 266 personas en Tela por lluvias," *La Prensa* (San Pedro Sula, Honduras), November 29, 2013, www.laprensa.hn/honduras/evacuan-a-266-personas-en-tela-por-lluvias-HBLP428917.

82 The parallels are eerily like Louisiana's wetland destruction due to deregulated corporate interests through Louisiana's natural gas and oil industry.

83 For a great book on safeguarding intangible cultural heritage that proposes practical approaches beyond UNESCO, see Stefano, *Practical Considerations*. See also "World Directory of Minorities: Afro-Hondurans."

84 "World Directory of Minorities: Afro-Hondurans"; "Indura Beach and Golf Resort Tela," Honduras.com, last modified January 4, 2017, www.honduras.com/indura-beach-golf-resort-tela-honduras (site discontinued).

85 Ramor Ryan, "The Last Rebels of the Caribbean: Garifuna Fighting for Their Lives in Honduras," Upside Down World, accessed March 27, 2008, http://upsidedownworld.org/main/content/view/1195/46.

86 Rodriguez, "Garifuna Resistance against Mega-Tourism."

87 Rodriguez, "Garifuna Resistance against Mega-Tourism." Rodriguez shows that a report done by the Organization of American States conducted in 2008 projected Indura would cause significant damage to the Laguna de los Micos and other areas of the Jeannette Kawas National Park.

88 Marlon Bishop, "Garifuna Exodus," *Latino USA*, accessed November 1, 2017, https://www.latinousa.org/2015/01/23/garifuna-exodus/.

89 Chaney, "Malleable Identities," 28.
90 Méndez, "Silent Violence," 440.
91 Méndez, "Silent Violence," 438.
92 "Statement of the OAS General Secretariat on the Conclusion of the MACCIH."
93 Jeff Ernst, "Locals Are Unhappy with 'Hong Kong of the Caribbean' on Honduran Island," Vice, December 2, 2020, www.vice.com/en/article/k7a7ae/foreign-investors-are-building-a-hong-kong-of-the-caribbean-on-a-remote-honduran-island.
94 Geglia, "Honduras."
95 Spring, "Marriage of Drug Money," 403.
96 Ramor, "Last Rebels of the Caribbean."
97 Ramor, "Last Rebels of the Caribbean."
98 Freeston, *Resistencia*.
99 "Goldman Environmental Foundation Mourns the Loss of Berta Cáceres," Goldman Environmental Prize, March 4, 2016, www.goldmanprize.org/blog/mourns-berta-caceres.
100 Nina Lakhani, "Berta Cáceres Assassination: Ex-Head of Dam Company Found Guilty," *The Guardian*, July 5, 2021, www.theguardian.com/world/2021/jul/05/berta-caceres-assassination-roberto-david-castillo-found-guilty. In October 2016, just seven months after Cáceres's brutal murder, I collaborated with New Orleans–based organizations like El Congreso, the Garifuna Collective, Amigos de la America, *Jambalaya News*, and Tulane University to host Olivia Zuñiga Cáceres, the daughter of Berta Cáceres, who was touring the Americas to bring attention to the state-sponsored violence plaguing Honduras.
101 Méndez, "Silent Violence," 440.
102 David Agren, "Honduras Confirms Murder of Another Member of Berta Cáceres' Activist Group," *The Guardian*, July 7, 2016, www.theguardian.com/world/2016/jul/07/honduras-murder-lesbia-janeth-urquia-berta-caceres.
103 Garth and Reese, *Black Food Matters*, 3.
104 Purcell, "Possible Worlds," 142.
105 Ehrenfeucht and Nelson, "Young Professionals."
106 Brogan, McGuinness, and Alvarez, *Field Report No. 19*.
107 In place of her real name, I have used a pseudonym.

Chapter 3

1 La Cooquette, "Authentic Honduran Baleada Recipe," *La Cooquette* (blog), September 13, 2021, https://lacooquette.com/honduran-baleada.
2 Honduran cheese is a fresh, salty cheese comparable to feta or cotija.
3 Dávila, *Culture Works*, 11; Sakakeeny, *Roll with It*; Alex Woodward, "The Musicians, the Permits and the City," *The Gambit* (New Orleans), October 9, 2012.
4 Yúdice, *Expediency of Culture*, 18, 9–39.
5 Dávila, *Culture Works*, 11–17.

6 Graeber, *Utopia of Rules*; Rosales, *Fruteros*.
7 Dávila, *Culture Works*.
8 Given the lack of enforcement of labor laws and the increasingly blurred lines between informal and formal sectors, I'd imagine lots of restaurants fit this category, too.
9 "Second Amended and Restated Consent Decree," US District Court Eastern District of Louisiana, accessed September 30, 2024, https://nola.gov/nola/media/NOPD/Consent%20Decree/778-Second-Amended-and-Restated-Consent-Decree.pdf, 50–51. The consent decree states,

> Within 365 days of the Effective Date, NOPD agrees to develop and implement a plan to provide all individuals within the City essential police services regardless of immigration status, to build and preserve trust among community members, and to prevent and solve crime more effectively. As part of this plan: a) Officers shall not take law enforcement action based on actual or perceived immigration status, including the initiation of stops or other field contacts; b) Officers shall not question victims of, or witnesses to, crime regarding their immigration status. Nothing in this provision shall prohibit NOPD from assisting nonimmigrant victims/witnesses in obtaining U-Visa / T-Visas, where appropriate; c) Officers shall not enforce La. R.S.14:100.13, which the Court of Appeals of Louisiana, Fourth Circuit, has found to unlawfully preempt federal regulations; and d) NOPD shall seek the assistance of community advocates in widely disseminating to the public, in English and in Spanish, NOPD's written policy incorporating these requirements.

10 Julia Preston, "U.S. Deports Record Number of Foreigners in 2011," *New York Times*, September 7, 2012, www.nytimes.com/2012/09/08/us/us-deports-record-number-of-foreigners-in-2011.html.
11 K. Johnson, "Beginning of the End," 160.
12 In 2012, police in Sacramento arrested Juana Reyes, an undocumented woman selling tamales in a Walmart parking lot. Rather than receiving a fine for operating without a license, she was racially profiled, arrested, and placed in a police car along with her two young children. Through the Secure Communities program, she was transferred to ICE to commence her deportation process. Her young children were put in foster care. In response, a national petition, "Don't Deport the Tamale Lady," helped create a public persona and garnered attention from community members, immigration advocates, and local authorities, eventually leading to her release. The tamale lady's arrest and threat of deportation illustrates the precarious nature of these unlicensed businesses, yet many undocumented individuals rely on these types of jobs to bring in money. To them, the risk is worth the flexibility and value of the job.

Ruben Naverette Jr., "Don't Deport the Tamale Lady," CNN, August 2, 2012, www.cnn.com/2012/08/01/opinion/navarrette-deportation-sacramento.

13 Ramon Antonio Vargas and Matt Sledge, "Popular Hispanic, Vietnamese Outreach Program Casualty of New Orleans Police's Effort for More Cops on Streets," *The Advocate* (Baton Rouge, LA), February 1, 2016, www.nola.com/news/popular-hispanic-vietnamese-outreach-program-casualty-of-new-orleans-polices-effort-for-more-cops-on/article_0d5d6798-c3aa-53d1-ad65-fe7db07b90c7.html.

14 "El Protector Program," Nashville.gov, accessed March 15, 2023, www.nashville.gov/departments/police/investigative-services/major-crimes/community-outreach-and-partnerships/el-protector-program.

15 For more information, see the Backstreet Cultural Museum website, accessed March 15, 2023, www.backstreetmuseum.org; Keber, *Buckjumping*; Regis, "Blackness and the Politics of Memory"; and Ehrenfeucht and Croegaert, "Learning from New Orleans," 118.

16 Regis, "Blackness and the Politics of Memory," 757.

17 Centeno and Portes, "Informal Economy," 43. If a person has a felony record, they're locked out of most formal sector jobs. Being undocumented oftentimes means the only jobs that are accessible are in the informal sector. Dávila, *Culture Works*, 50; Zlolniski, *Janitors, Street Vendors, and Activists*, 73.

18 Fouts, "Re-regulating *Loncheras*."

19 Ehrenfeucht and Croegaert, "Learning from New Orleans," 112.

20 Ehrenfeucht and Croegaert, "Learning from New Orleans," 124.

21 Tourists also attend second lines.

22 When questions of taxation of these vendors arise, especially as a method of growing the tax base for the city, vendors can self-report earnings when reporting taxes; moreover, this potential tax base is low-hanging fruit and pennies compared to the tax breaks given to corporations and developers who eschew any sort of public commitment while pursuing maximal profit, oftentimes at the expense and risk of the public sector.

23 "Ordinance Unenforced, but Taco Trucks Keep Moving On," *Times-Picayune* (New Orleans), July 24, 2007, http://blog.nola.com/times-picayune/2007/07/ordinance_unenforced_but_taco.html.

24 John C. Hill, "Once-Diverse City Is Now Segregated," *Times-Picayune* (New Orleans), November 18, 1993, www.nola.com/news/politics/once-diverse-city-is-now-segregated/article_922b97bc-8567-5b03-a263-eced3c142a2e.html; Sluyter, "(Post-)K New Orleans and the Hispanic Atlantic"; Euraque, "'Honduran Memories'"; Trujillo-Pagán, "Recovering Latinos' Place," 194.

25 Louisiana state law allows open containers in public, yet in vehicles, the alcohol container must have a lid, the straw tip must remain covered, and no contents of the container can be removed. Sydney Oppenheim, "Only

Nola: The Drive-Thru Daiquiri," *NolaVie*, January 31, 2022, www.vianolavie.org/2022/01/31/alternative-journalism-fall-2020-consider-the-drive-thru-daiquiri. New Orleans drive-thru daquiri culture also faced its own uphill battle against law enforcement when the first drive-thru daquiri opened in 1981 in Lafayette, then in 1983 with Glynn's Daquiri Place in LaPlace, just outside New Orleans. The vendors eventually won: James Karst, "The History of the Drive-Thru Daiquiri Shop," *Times-Picayune* (New Orleans), March 4, 2016, www.nola.com/entertainment_life/eat-drink/the-history-of-the-drive-thru-daiquiri-shop/article_9b2b6733-6d98-5e9d-9652-4a8b9f20d811.html.

26 Ruiz, "Citizen Restaurant," 8–9; Miguel Bustillo, "Hold the Tacos, New Orleans Says," *Los Angeles Times*, July 14, 2007, www.latimes.com/archives/la-xpm-2007-jul-14-na-tacotrucks14-story.html.

27 Bustillo, "Hold the Tacos, New Orleans Says."

28 I worked on an empanada food truck off and on for a one-year period. We mostly stationed the truck at an uptown farmers' market and at the back of the track at the fairgrounds. We served a range of empanadas.

29 Martin, "Food Fight!," 1867–68.

30 In January 2011, undercover ICE agents attempted a sting operation and posed as a painting company to solicit day laborers. Three day laborers responded to the pickup; however, after driving two blocks from the *esquina*, the three workers—one of whom was Jose Gomez, an El Congreso member—were arrested. According to *The Lens*, the agents "pulled Gomez's jacket over his head, forced him to the ground, and pushed and kicked him repeatedly. When the beating stopped, they handcuffed Gomez and took him to the ICE office." The official ICE report framed the abuse of Gomez as self-defense and said that the agents pulled him over because he resembled a wanted fugitive, for which they never provided evidence. Michael Avery, "Case against New Orleans Laborer Shows a Secretive ICE, Lacking Accountability," *The Lens* (blog), July 2, 2015, https://thelensnola.org/2015/07/02/case-against-new-orleans-laborer-shows-a-secretive-ice-lacking-accountability; Katy Reckdahl, "Immigrant Laborers in New Orleans Testing Obama Administration's New Policy," NOLA.com, June 25, 2012, www.nola.com/news/politics/immigrant-laborers-in-new-orleans-testing-obama-administrations-new-policy/article_f82bbfb9-e1f6-5039-8f22-7daac16e1888.html.

31 Fouts, "Re-regulating *Loncheras*."

32 Kate Taylor, "Meet the Food Trucks Who Helped Change the Laws to Put Food Trucks on the Street," Very Local, October 3, 2022, www.verylocal.com/food-truck-laws-new-orleans-2/23537/; Micheline Maynard, "Why It's So Hard to Be a Food Truck in New Orleans," Bloomberg.com, June 12, 2012, www.bloomberg.com/news/articles/2012-06-12/why-it-s-so-hard-to-be-a-food-truck-in-new-orleans.

33 Richard Rainey, "Mayor Landrieu Vetoes New Orleans Food Truck Law, Says It Would Not Stand Up in Court," *Times-Picayune* (New Orleans), May 1, 2013; "City Council July 25, 2013 Regular Meeting Summary."

34 Jules Bentley, "Fork in the Road: Who's Behind the Push for New Orleans Food Trucks?," *Antigravity* (magazine), March 9, 2013, https://antigravitymagazine.com/feature/new-orleans-food-trucks.

35 Taylor, "Meet the Food Trucks Who Helped Change the Laws to Put Food Trucks on the Street."

36 "About Us," New Orleans Food Trucks website, accessed February 20, 2024, www.nolafoodtrucks.com/about.

37 Gwendolyn Knapp, "Mayor Landrieu Vetoes the Food Truck Law . . . Sigh," Eater New Orleans, May 2, 2013, https://nola.eater.com/2013/5/2/6440943/mayor-landrieu-vetoes-the-food-truck-law-sigh.

38 Until 2023, the only exception to French Quarter vendors has been the iconic Lucky Dogs franchise, which was grandfathered in on a 1972 ordinance. In 1972, the New Orleans City Council unanimously adopted an ordinance addressing the expansion of street vendors in the French Quarter to protect and preserve the area's historic charm, character, and economic vitality. The US Supreme Court unanimously upheld that ordinance in 1976. In its opinion, the court noted that the council reasonably decided that Lucky Dogs (and another longtime street vendor) had "become part of the distinctive character and charm that distinguishes the Vieux Carre." *City of New Orleans v. Dukes*, 427 US 297 (1976), https://supreme.justia.com/cases/federal/us/427/297. Fast-forward to 2023, when a pivotal shift occurred as the city council, with a unanimous 5–0 vote, opted to revise the existing policy. Subsequently, the owner of Lucky Dogs voluntarily surrendered seven permits, which became part of a lottery system. Sophie Kasakove, "French Quarter Monopoly for Lucky Dogs Ends as New Orleans Makes Way for New Food Vendors," NOLA.com, November 16, 2023, www.nola.com/news/politics/new-food-vendors-approved-for-new-orleans-french-quarter/article_4b3c7874-849e-11ee-af41-23c3cd729efc.html; Lee Zurik and Dannah Sauer, "Decades-Old Ordinance Gives Food Cart Monopoly in French Quarter," Fox8 Live, February 15, 2023, www.fox8live.com/2023/02/15/zurik-decades-old-ordinance-gives-food-cart-monopoly-french-quarter.

39 Bruce Eggler, "City Hall 'One-Stop Shop' for Licensing and Permits Is Ready to Open," NOLA.com, March 1, 2013, www.nola.com/news/politics/city-hall-one-stop-shop-for-licensing-and-permits-is-ready-to-open/article_266287c4-d174-5f98-b0ca-caf007539cb3.html.

40 In place of her real name, I have used a pseudonym.

41 Jens Manuel Krogstad, Ana Gonzalez-Barrera, and Mark Hugo Lopez, "Children 12 and Under Are Fastest Growing Group of Unaccompanied Minors at U.S. Border," Pew Research Center, July 22, 2014, www.pewresearch.org

/short-reads/2014/07/22/children-12-and-under-are-fastest-growing-group-of-unaccompanied-minors-at-u-s-border.

42 In place of his real name, I have used a pseudonym.

43 In place of their real names, I have used pseudonyms.

44 Cindy Carcamo, "Nearly 1 in 4 Students in This L.A. High School Migrated from Central America—Many without Their Parents," *Los Angeles Times*, July 15, 2016, www.latimes.com/local/lanow/la-me-belmont-high-school-20160710-snap-story.html.

45 Palmer, "Belle New Orleans," 189; J'Brionne Helaire, "Formerly Enslaved, Rose Nicaud Helped Pioneer Culinary Entrepreneurship," Verite News, February 14, 2023, http://veritenews.org/2023/02/14/rose-nicaud-helped-pioneer-culinary-entrepreneurship.

46 Helaire, "Formerly Enslaved, Rose Nicaud Helped Pioneer Culinary Entrepreneurship."

47 Story featured in the short documentary *Project Neutral Grounds*, directed by Fernando López.

48 The name NOLA Shakedown was coined by Stand leader Roy B., who crafted the "layered meanings of shakedown to describe the joy, grief, confinement, and freedom of people impacted by the issue. The system must change from one that shakes us down to one that builds us up." See "Read Our Report."

49 "Read Our Report."

50 Judge Charbonnet ran a mayoral campaign that year. Richard Webster, "$23,000 in Traffic Fines Reduced to $9 for Man as Pilot Program Takes on New Orleans' Court System," NOLA.com, March 29, 2017, www.nola.com/crime/index.ssf/2017/03/23000_in_traffic_fines_reduced.html.

51 Nina Feldman, "Warrant Clinic May Have Saved City of New Orleans $1 Million-Plus," Next City, October 6, 2017, https://nextcity.org/urbanist-news/warrant-clinic-saved-million-new-orleans.

52 Webster, "$23,000 in Traffic Fines Reduced to $9."

53 Webster, "$23,000 in Traffic Fines Reduced to $9."

54 Laisne, Wool, and Henrichson, *Past Due*.

55 Matt Sledge and Bryn Stole, "Supreme Court Panel Urges Revamp of Louisiana's 'User Pay' Criminal Justice System, but Implementing It Will Be Hard," *Times-Picayune* (New Orleans), April 28, 2019.

56 Charles Maldonado, "NOPD Accused of Racially Profiling Latinos, Aiding Federal Immigration Agents," *The Lens* (blog), September 10, 2014, https://thelensnola.org/2014/09/10/nopd-accused-of-racially-profiling-latinos-aiding-federal-immigration-agents.

57 Maldonado, "NOPD Accused of Racially Profiling Latinos."

58 Project Hustle website, accessed February 20, 2024, www.southernprojecthustle.org.

59 Bentley, "Fork in the Road."
60 Hondagneu-Sotelo, *Doméstica*.

Chapter 4

1 "Who Lives in New Orleans and Metro Parishes Now?"
2 One of my jobs was to collect the monthly dollar from each of the day laborers to pay for the use of the portable toilet, which we'd deliver as payment to the mayor's office.
3 Dennis Persica, "Gretna Hopes Designated Area Is Key to Day-Laborer Issues," NOLA.com, January 31, 2011, www.nola.com/news/politics/article_eff4c06e-56cf-5414-9eb3-28b2936e668a.html.
4 In 2013, Sara was arrested along with eighteen other Workers' Center affiliates as part of a civil disobedience act against ICE in response to the unconstitutional Criminal Alien Removal Initiative raids. Part of her reason for participating in the civil disobedience was to be in solidarity with her neighbors, who were detained by ICE while cooking in their home. "It's time for us to come out of the shadows. The people united will never be defeated. We need to support each other; a single person can't do it all alone."
5 Jabareen, "Right to Space Production," 8.
6 Jabareen, "Right to Space Production," 6–31.
7 Lipsitz, *Possessive Investment in Whiteness*.
8 John C. Hill, "Once-Diverse City Is Now Segregated," *Times-Picayune* (New Orleans), November 18, 1993, www.nola.com/news/politics/once-diverse-city-is-now-segregated/article_922b97bc-8567-5b03-a263-eced3c142a2e.html; Euraque, "'Honduran Memories,'" 9; Trujillo-Pagán, "Recovering Latinos' Place," 194.
9 Ramon Antonio Vargas and Jeff Adelson, "'We're Somewhere Familiar': Jefferson's Hispanic Population Drives Louisiana's Growth," NOLA.com, January 2, 2022, www.nola.com/news/were-somewhere-familiar-jeffersons-hispanic-population-drives-louisianas-growth/article_2304af7c-5f87-11ec-b2a4-cf1feb4fddf8.html.
10 Nijman, *Life of North American Suburbs*, 2–5.
11 Richard Webster, "'They Saw Me and Thought the Worst,'" ProPublica, September 24, 2021, www.propublica.org/article/across-the-parish-line. In 1989, the conservative suburbs in Metairie's District 81 elected the Ku Klux Klan Grand Wizard, David Duke, as their state representative. David Maraniss, "Ex-Klansman Wins Election in Louisiana," *Washington Post*, February 19, 1989, www.washingtonpost.com/archive/politics/1989/02/19/ex-klansman-wins-election-in-louisiana/490b69ae-9042-40ca-990a-14c20c403f82.
12 Ian McNulty, "On New Orleans' West Bank, an Open-Air Market Becomes a Hub for Latin American Food," *The Advocate* (Baton Rouge, LA), May 7, 2019.

13 Named for the Nahuatl word *tiyānquiztli*, used by the Aztec people.

14 Helen Freund, "'Las Pulgas' on the West Bank: Open-Air Markets Highlight Mexican and Central American Cuisine," NOLA.com, August 6, 2018, www.nola.com/gambit/food_drink/las-pulgas-on-the-west-bank-open-air-markets-highlight-mexican-and-central-american-cuisine/article_dc69af6a-9052-5259-bbae-ce878dbd9e5c.html.

15 Maria Clark, "Hidden Gem Brings Liveliness of Latin America to Louisiana," *USA Today*, November 20, 2019.

16 M. Fussell, "Airbnb Go Home," 10.

17 The contract began in April 2015. The fees included utilities, insurance, marketing, and janitors. Based on rental fees, that's $462,000 in gain, which doesn't include profits earned from the developer-owned bar. Nina Feldman, "Designing the Food Market of the Future," Next City, March 16, 2015, https://nextcity.org/features/public-markets-food-halls-food-desert; Boyce Upholt, "Beneath the Instagrammable Veneer of the Food Hall Lies a Perfect Capitalistic Machine," *Heated* (blog), December 26, 2019, https://heated.medium.com/the-troubling-economics-of-food-halls-b301f6563188.

18 Matt Sakakeeny, "Living in a Laboratory: New Orleans Today," *Books and Ideas*, accessed September 30, 2024, https://booksandideas.net/IMG/pdf/20150910_new_orleans.pdf.

19 McNulty, Ian. "St. Roch Market Has a New Operator, Pledging Change to Save New Orleans' Last Food Hall," NOLA.com, September 15, 2023, www.nola.com/entertainment_life/eat-drink/st-roch-market-gets-new-operator-to-keep-food-hall-open/article_cb6fb2ae-523f-11ee-aa2a-0b85400fbda5.html.

20 Nina Feldman, "A Radical Design Movement Is Growing in New Orleans," Next City, October 12, 2015, https://nextcity.org/features/urban-design-activism-socially-engaged-art-design-as-protest.

21 At the time of this writing, the weekly food vendor fee at Dix Jazz Market is a flat rate of $100 with few amenities. At Westbank Flea Market it costs $150 per week, and the space offers more amenities.

22 Shelley N. C. Holle, "Will West Bank Wonders Never Cease?," *Times-Picayune* (New Orleans), October 31, 1997.

23 Susan Finch and Joe Darby, "Algiers Homeowners Sue to Stop the Flea Market," *Times-Picayune* (New Orleans), June 8, 1985.

24 Joe Darby, "N. O. Officials Are Biting Down on Busy Flea Market in Algiers," *Times-Picayune* (New Orleans), April 13, 1985.

25 Pho Tau Bay Restaurant website, accessed April 9, 2023, www.photaubayrestaurant.com.

26 "Vietnam on the Bayou: In 1975, New Orleans Laid Out the Welcome Mat," *Times-Picayune* (New Orleans), April 30, 2017.

27 Michael Welch, "The Hidden New Orleans Flea Market No One Wants You to Know About," Vice, February 18, 2014, www.vice.com/en/article/wd4npy/the-hidden-new-orleans-flea-market-no-one-wants-you-to-know-about.

28 Nina Feldman and Sarah Fouts, "Hidden in Plain Sight: Las Pulgas of New Orleans," *Gravy*, January 11, 2018, www.southernfoodways.org/gravy/hidden-in-plain-sight-las-pulgas-of-new-orleans.

29 "Raid on Algiers Flea Market Nets $256,000 in Illegal Goods," WWLTV, December 14, 2010, www.wwltv.com/article/news/local/raid-on-algiers-flea-market-nets-256000-in-illegal-goods/289-347535285.

30 Feldman and Fouts, "Hidden in Plain Sight."

31 Ian McNulty, "Pho Festival on the West Bank Brings Vietnamese Food Far beyond the Basics," NOLA.com, June 4, 2018, www.nola.com/entertainment_life/eat-drink/pho-festival-on-the-west-bank-brings-vietnamese-food-far-beyond-the-basics/article_f941353c-3e7f-5814-aa86-6b7c92d76be4.html.

32 As recent as May 22, 2016, multiple gunmen targeted a gay nightclub, La Madame, in the city of Veracruz, killing seven people and injuring twelve. Public officials attempted to blame narco-traffickers' "territorial fights" for the attack, but local advocates and witnesses underscored the homophobia of the violence. "The Massacre at a Mexican Gay Bar That No One Talked About," teleSUR, June 14, 2016, www.telesurtv.net/english/news/The-Massacre-at-a-Mexican-Gay-Bar-That-No-One-Talked-About-20160614-0035.html.

33 Pelot-Hobbs, *Prison Capital*, 209–22.

34 Pelot-Hobbs, *Prison Capital*, 247–48; BreakOUT! and El Congreso, *From Vice to ICE Toolkit*, 4, accessed February 21, 2024, www.wesleycarverware.com/_files/ugd/c1b234_60d6e205a80346b684f0271006808d2.pdf.

35 "ID Documents Center: Louisiana," National Center for Transgender Equality, accessed April 14, 2023, https://transequality.org/documents/state/louisiana#:~:text=In%20order%20to%20update%20the,a%20successful%20gender%20change%2Freassignment.

36 BreakOUT! and El Congreso, *From Vice to ICE Toolkit*.

37 Algiers neighborhood is technically in Orleans Parish, but it sits just 500 feet from the Jefferson Parish line.

Conclusion

1 Katy Reckdahl, "Immigrant Halts Deportation after Challenging Border Patrol Arrest," *Times-Picayune* (New Orleans), August 11, 2012.

2 Gonzalez and Rosenbaum, "Making Justice Real," 4. Prosecutorial discretion refers to the power of a prosecutor to decide whether or not to charge a person for a crime. See "Doyle Memorandum: Frequently Asked Questions and Additional Instructions ICE," May 15, 2024, www.ice.gov/about-ice/opla/prosecutorial-discretion; and US congressional letter of support for the

Southern 32, September 24, 2012, posted on National Immigration Law Center website, www.nilc.org/wp-content/uploads/2015/11/Southern32-prosecutorial-discretion-ltr-2012-09-24.pdf.

3 Jennifer Larino, "Who Is Buying the Historic Holy Angels Campus in Bywater?," *Times-Picayune* (New Orleans), February 26, 2016.

4 In 2014, the *Times-Picayune* reported there were just 155 Marianites in the world, 15 of whom lived in Holy Angels. Their median age at the time was eighty. Tyler Bridges, "Holy Angels Campus in Bywater Up for Sale after Being Home to Marianites for 165 Years," *Times-Picayune* (New Orleans), November 18, 2014, www.nola.com/news/holy-angels-campus-in-bywater-up-for-sale-after-being-home-to-marianites-for-165/article_8526c11f-d221-540b-9a61-99d23fcd7701.html.

5 See *Navarro Hernandez v. U.S. Customs and Border Patrol*, accessed September 30, 2024, www.govinfo.gov/app/details/USCOURTS-laed-2_10-cv-04602. Brought by Joaquin Navarro Hernandez, a reconstruction worker in New Orleans, following his arrest by Border Patrol at the Franklin day-laborer corner, this litigation sought documents about his arrest and about Customs and Border Patrol's surveillance of day laborers in New Orleans generally. The court ordered Customs and Border Patrol to disclose documents and awarded attorneys' fees, recognizing that "plaintiff has used the records disclosed as a result of this case . . . to facilitate public oversight of CBP's enforcement of federal immigration law in the New Orleans area, both as it relates to his own case and in general," Co-Counsel: New Orleans Workers' Center for Racial Justice.

6 Reckdahl, "Immigrant Halts Deportation."

7 The Border Patrol's jurisdiction is the 100-mile radius zone around the entire perimeter of US territory, which means officers can operate immigrant checkpoints within this area. The ACLU notes that territory range entails "almost 2 out 3 people in the United States." The ACLU argues, "Border Patrol, nevertheless, cannot pull anyone over without 'reasonable suspicion' of an immigration violation or crime (reasonable suspicion is more than just a 'hunch'). Similarly, Border Patrol cannot search vehicles in the 100-mile zone without a warrant or 'probable cause' (a reasonable belief, based on the circumstances, that an immigration violation or crime has likely occurred)." See "Know Your Rights: 100 Mile Border Zone," American Civil Liberties Union, accessed September 30, 2024, www.aclu.org/know-your-rights/border-zone.

8 Florida, *Rise of the Creative Class*. I am certainly aware of my involvement in this transplant community and its contribution to the city's gentrification. I am deeply entangled in these complex and uneven power dynamics while doing my best to address and, when possible, mitigate my impact. My field research unfolded in neighborhoods where I've resided, notably the Seventh Ward and

Upper Ninth Ward, both areas experiencing significant gentrification. In the course of my time in each place, I've indulged in an abundance of offerings from the upscale establishments central to the discussions in this chapter (and the broader book) and attempted to be transparent about it throughout. I am often grappling with my role in these gentrification processes while aiming to contribute positively to the ongoing conversation and efforts to address gentrification's impact.

9 For more on visibility, historian Alecia Long's work on post-Katrina redevelopment with historical framing on the eradication of the vice districts is useful. This article helped me with framing on visibility and linking that with class and poverty: Long, "Poverty Is the New Prostitution."

10 "Galaxie Tacos," Colectivo, accessed February 22, 2024, https://colectivonola.com/Galaxie-Tacos.

11 In 2024 they hired another chef.

12 At the time of this writing, the only Michelin cities in the United States are New York, Los Angeles, and Washington DC.

13 "Bywater Statistical Data," Data Research Center, August 24, 2022, www.datacenterresearch.org/data-resources/neighborhood-data/district-7/bywater.

14 Katherine Sayre, "On a Gentrifying Corner of New Orleans, Celebrity vs. Neighborhood Fight Emerges," NOLA.com, July 28, 2015, www.nola.com/news/business/on-a-gentrifying-corner-of-new-orleans-celebrity-vs-neighborhood-fight-emerges/article_546684b9-ef15-5cc7-a978-9776bdcce36c.html.

15 DeDecker, Nichols, and Griffin, *Short Term Rentals*.

16 Mostly because it wasn't sustainable with just fifteen Marianite nuns on the campus premises.

17 Bridges, "Holy Angels Campus in Bywater Up for Sale after Being Home to Marianites for 165 Years."

18 Tyler Bridges, "Developer Pres Kabacoff's Plan for Downtown," WWNO, September 25, 2013, www.wwno.org/2013-09-25/developer-pres-kabacoffs-plan-for-downtown.

19 "Former Iberville Housing Complex Reimagined as New Community: 'It Changed for the Better,'" HRI Properties, accessed February 22, 2024, www.hriproperties.com/2019/11/14/former-iberville-housing-complex-reimagined-as-new-community-it-changed-for-the-better. This statement attempts to justify the demolition of the public housing because of crimes in the complex. The organization C3/Hands Off Iberville sought the refurbishing of the existing public housing complexes, including the 821 units in Iberville, rather than the demolition of them and sent a letter to this effect to the president of the United States and other federal, state, and local stakeholders.

20 Roberta Brandes Gratz, "Who Killed Public Housing in New Orleans?," *The Nation*, June 2, 2015, www.thenation.com/article/archive/requiem-bricks.

21 Monica Novotny, "A Voodoo Revival in New Orleans," NBC News, December 18, 2003, www.nbcnews.com/id/wbna3748834.

22 Karen Gadbois, "Three Years after St. Roch Property Sold to Favored Buyer, It Lies Fallow," *The Lens* (blog), December 12, 2013, https://thelensnola.org/2013/12/12/three-years-after-st-claude-avenue-property-sold-to-favored-buyer-it-lies-fallow.

23 Gadbois, "Three Years after St. Roch Property Sold to Favored Buyer, It Lies Fallow."

24 The New Orleans Food Cooperative offered more sustainable sourcing, better labor practices, and more community buy-in, which resulted in higher product costs.

25 Fullilove, Peterson, and Bassett, *Root Shock*.

26 Mimi Read, "Where the Walls Do Talk," *New York Times*, June 6, 2012, www.nytimes.com/2012/06/07/greathomesanddestinations/in-new-orleans-a-building-where-the-graffiti-takes-center-stage.html.

27 Meg Farris, "Dr. Donates Statue in Honor of Latin American Workers Who Helped Rebuild N.O.," WWLTV, November 9, 2018, www.wwltv.com/article/news/local/orleans/dr-donates-statue-in-honor-of-latin-american-workers-who-helped-rebuild-no/289-613141249.

28 Interview conducted by Abigail Cramer for a Tulane course LAST 4960: Food, Immigration and Culture, in which we exhibited clips from oral histories at the Southern Food and Beverage Museum in May 2017.

Bibliography

PRIMARY SOURCES

Selected Interviews by Author

Alfredo, April 2013, July 2019, February 2021
Melissa Araujo, September 2018
Santos Canales, January 2020
Carlos, March 2023
Daniel Castellanos, July 2019
Tri Cung, April 2023
Angela Dix, October 2017
Maria G., November 2014
Gloria, June 2015, April 2017
Jacinta Gonzalez, April 2013
Imelda, July 2017
Iris, September 2022
Ivan, March 2012, July 2017, March 2023
Juan José, July 2017
Junior, July 2015
Toya Ex Lewis, January 2020
Alfred Marshall, January 2020
Mateo, November 2016
Curtis Muhammad, July 2019
Olivia, June 2015
Ted Quant, February 2020
Sara, July 2017
Sofia, June 2015
Denis Soriano, November 2011, July 2022
Colette Tippy, August 2019
Officer V., May 2018
Venecia, July 2017, July 2022
Victorine, October 2017
Williana, July 2022
Xiomara, July 2017
Sllim Ydur, January and July 2022

Archival and Manuscript Collections

Antonio de Sedella Collection. Howard-Tilton Memorial Library, Tulane University, New Orleans.

Louisiana Research Collection. Howard-Tilton Memorial Library, Tulane University, New Orleans.

Government Publications

"City Council July 25, 2013 Regular Meeting Summary." New Orleans City Council. July 25, 2013. www.nolacitycouncil.com/news/meetingsummary.asp?id=%7B7D937B57-15BA-466C-96CA-6F1AFC0749F1%7D.

Dale, Charles V. "Katrina Relief: U.S. Labor Department Exemption of Contractors from Written Affirmative Action Requirements." Report. UNT Digital Library. Library of Congress, Congressional Research Service, September 27, 2005. https://digital.library.unt.edu/ark:/67531/metacrs7654.

Federal Writers' Project. *New Orleans City Guide*. 1938. Cambridge, MA: Riverside Press, 1952.

"Formaldehyde Exposure in Homes: A Reference for State Officials to Use in Decision-Making." Centers for Disease Control and Prevention. Accessed September 30, 2024. https://stacks.cdc.gov/view/cdc/40715.

"Hurricane Costs." NOAA Office for Coastal Management. Accessed September 30, 2024. https://coast.noaa.gov/states/fast-facts/hurricane-costs.html.

Murphy, Brett. "Broken Promises: An Examination of Ongoing and Developing Crises in the New Orleans Region." Congressional Hunger Center, February 14, 2006. www.hungercenter.org/wp-content/uploads/2011/07/Broken-Promises-Crises-in-New-Orleans-Murphy.pdf.

"NOPD Consent Decree Monitor, New Orleans, Louisiana." NOLA.gov, September 22, 2016. www.nola.gov/getattachment/NOPD/NOPD-Consent-Decree/Chapter-41-6-1-Immigration-Status-approval.pdf.

"Table 39. Aliens Removed or Returned: Fiscal Years 1892 to 2018." Office of Homeland Security Statistics. Accessed February 24, 2024. www.dhs.gov/ohss/topics/immigration/yearbook/2018/table39.

US Department of Housing and Urban Development. "Section 3 of the Housing and Development Act of 1968." HUD.gov. Accessed February 24, 2024. www.hud.gov/section3.

US Department of the Interior, Bureau of Indian Affairs. Memorandum regarding Tunica-Biloxi Indian Tribe, 1980. BIA.gov. www.bia.gov/sites/default/files/dup/assets/as-ia/ofa/petition/001_tunbil_LA/001_pf.pdf.

"World Directory of Minorities: Afro-Hondurans." Minority Rights Group International. Last modified January 4, 2017. www.justice.gov/sites/default/files/eoir/legacy/2014/02/19/Afro-Hondurans.pdf.

Newspapers, Periodicals, News Channels, and Websites

The Advocate (Baton Rouge, LA)
Antigravity (magazine)
Biz New Orleans
Bloomberg.com
Books and Ideas
CBS News
CNN
C-SPAN
Eater New Orleans
El Misisipi (New Orleans)
Fox8 Live
Fox News
The Gambit (New Orleans)
Gayot
Grist
The Guardian
Harper's New Monthly Magazine
Heated
HuffPost
Hyphen
In These Times
KLFY.com
La Nación (Buenos Aires, Argentina)
La Prensa (San Pedro Sula, Honduras)
Latino USA
La Voz Latina (New Orleans)
The Lens (blog)
Los Angeles Times
The Lumberjack (Alexandria, LA)
The Nation
NBC News
New Orleans Advocate
New Orleans City Business
New Orleans Magazine
New York Times
Next City
NOLA.com
Nolavie
NPR
People's Tribune
ProPublica
Salon
64 Parishes
Statista
teleSUR
Time
Times-Picayune (New Orleans)
Tripod
Upside Down World
USA Today
Verite News
Very Local
Vice
Vox
Washington Post
World's Top Exports
World Vision
WWLTV
WWNO

Nongovernmental Reports and Publications

Brogan, Katherine, Elizabeth McGuinness, and Erwin Alvarez. *Field Report No. 19: Assessment of Remittances in Honduras*. USAID, ACDI VOCA, and FHI 360, October 2013. www.marketlinks.org/sites/default/files/resource/files/FIELD%20Report%20No%2019%20Honduras%20Remittances%20Assessment.pdf.

Browne-Dianis, J., J. Lai, M. Hincapie, and S. Soni. "And Injustice for All: Workers' Lives in the Reconstruction of New Orleans." Advancement

Project, 2006. https://workercenterlibrary.org/product/and-injustice-for-all-workers-lives-in-the-reconstruction-of-new-orleans.

Burgi-Palomino, Daniella. *Nowhere to Call Home: Internally Displaced in Honduras and El Salvador*. Latin America Working Group. Accessed September 30, 2024. www.lawg.org/nowhere-to-call-home-internally-displaced-in-honduras-and-el-salvador.

"Cedar Point Nursery v. Hassid." SCOTUSblog. Accessed February 24, 2024. www.scotusblog.com/case-files/cases/cedar-point-nursery-v-hassid.

"Closed Cases." NDLON. Accessed February 24, 2024. https://ndlon.org/our-work/litigation/closed-cases.

DeDecker, Breonne, Lydia Y. Nichols, and Shana M. Griffin. *Short-Term Rentals, Long-Term Impacts: The Corrosion of Housing Access and Affordability in New Orleans*. Jane Place Neighborhood Sustainability Initiative. Accessed September 30, 2024. https://jpnsi.org/advocacy/short-term-rentals.html.

Fletcher, Laurel E., Phuong Pham, Eric Stover, and Patrick Vinck. *Rebuilding after Katrina: A Population-Based Study of Labor and Human Rights in New Orleans*. Human Rights Center, University of California at Berkeley, June 1, 2006. https://escholarship.org/uc/item/5jc0909m.

Gonzalez, Jacinta, and J. J. Rosenbaum. "Making Justice Real: The Importance of the Civil, Labor, and Human Rights Provisions of ICE's Prosecutorial Discretion Policy." Report. New Orleans: New Orleans Workers' Center for Racial Justice, June 2012.

Gonzalez-Barrera, Ana, and Jens Manuel Krogstad. "U.S. Deportations of Immigrants Reach Record High in 2013." Pew Research Center, October 2, 2014. www.pewresearch.org/fact-tank/2014/10/02/u-s-deportations-of-immigrants-reach-record-high-in-2013.

"Immigration and Customs Enforcement Removals." TRAC: Immigration. Accessed February 20, 2024. https://trac.syr.edu/phptools/immigration/remove.

Laisne, Mathilde, Jon Wool, and Christian Henrichson. *Past Due: Examining the Costs and Consequences of Charging for Justice in New Orleans*. Vera Institute of Justice, January 2017. www.vera.org/downloads/publications/past-due-costs-consequences-charging-for-justice-new-orleans.pdf.

Lesage, Colombine, and Laurene Feintrenie. *Are Sustainable Pathways Possible for Oil Palm Development in Latin America?* World Bank Conference on Land and Poverty, March 2018. https://agritrop.cirad.fr/587928/1/LESAGE_2018_Oil%20palm%20in%20Latin%20America%20literature%20review.pdf.

"Mid-City Statistical Area." The Data Center, last updated January 29, 2024. www.datacenterresearch.org/data-resources/neighborhood-data/district-4/mid-city.

"New Orleans: Prisoners Abandoned to Floodwaters." Human Rights Watch, September 21, 2005. www.hrw.org/news/2005/09/21/new-orleans-prisoners-abandoned-floodwaters.

"New Report: The Criminal Alien Removal Initiative in New Orleans." Not One More Deportation, December 2013. www.notonemoredeportation.com/2013/12/20/ice-raids-new-orleans (site discontinued).

"NOWCRJ Mission." NOWCRJ. Accessed February 24, 2024. https://www.nowcrj.org/about-nowcrj.

"Peoples Hurricane Relief Fund and Oversight Coalition." Katrina Reader. Accessed September 30, 2024. http://katrinareader.cwsworkshop.org/peoples-hurricane-relief-fund-and-oversight-coalition.html.

"Planning District 4." The Data Center. Accessed February 24, 2024. www.datacenterresearch.org/data-resources/neighborhood-data/district-4.

Plyer, Allison. "Facts for Features: Katrina Impact." The Data Center, August 26, 2016. www.datacenterresearch.org/data-resources/katrina/facts-for-impact.

Quigley, Bill, and Sara H. Godchaux. "Locked Out and Torn Down: Public Housing Post Katrina." *Bill Quigley: Social Justice Advocacy* (blog), June 8, 2015. https://billquigley.wordpress.com/2015/06/08/locked-out-and-torn-down-public-housing-post-katrina-by-bill-quigley-and-sara-h-godchaux.

"Read Our Report." NOLA Shakedown. Accessed March 11, 2023. www.nolashakedown.org/report (site discontinued).

Ritchie, Hannah. *Palm Oil*. Our World in Data, February 4, 2021. https://ourworldindata.org/palm-oil.

"Statement of the OAS General Secretariat on the Conclusion of the MACCIH." OAS, January 17, 2020. www.oas.org/en/media_center/press_release.asp?sCodigo=E-003/20.

"A Thriving Lagoon." Coral Reef Alliance, December 7, 2015. https://coral.org/en/blog/a-thriving-lagoon.

"Who Lives in New Orleans and Metro Parishes Now?" The Data Center. Accessed September 30, 2024. www.datacenterresearch.org/data-resources/who-lives-in-new-orleans-now.

Films, Documentaries, and Podcasts

Freeston, Jesse, dir. *Resistencia: The Fight for the Agúan Valley*. Written by Diego Briceño-Orduz and Jesse Freeston, 2015. http://resistenciathefilm.com.

Keber, Lily, dir. *Buckjumping*. Documentary. Mairzy Doats Productions, 2018.

López, Fernando, dir. *Project Neutral Grounds*. Documentary. Produced by Sarah Fouts, Toya Ex Lewis, and Fernando López, 2023, 20 min.

Newkirk, Vann R., II, host. *Floodlines: The Story of an Unnatural Disaster* (podcast), 2020. www.theatlantic.com/podcasts/floodlines.

SECONDARY SOURCES

Adams, Thomas J., and Steve Striffler. *Working in the Big Easy: The History and Politics of Labor in New Orleans*. Lafayette: University of Louisiana at Lafayette Press, 2014.

Alkon, Alison Hope, Yuki Kato, and Joshua Sbicca. *A Recipe for Gentrification: Food, Power, and Resistance in the City*. New York: New York University Press, 2020.

Aslakson, Kenneth. "Immigrant Lawyers and Slavery in Territorial New Orleans." *Tulane European and Civil Law Forum* 31, no. 31–32 (2017): 33–77.

Barrios, Roberto E. *Governing Affect: Neoliberalism and Disaster Reconstruction*. Lincoln: University of Nebraska Press, 2017.

Beriss, David. "Red Beans and Rebuilding: An Iconic Dish, Memory, and Culture in New Orleans." In *Rice and Beans: A Unique Dish in a Hundred Places*, edited by Richard Wilk, Livia Barbosa, and Sidney Mintz, 241–63. London: Berg, 2012.

Bloxom, Jennifer Michelle. "Fueling the Appetite for Water: The Palm Oil Biofuel Industry in San Pedro Sula Honduras." Master's thesis, University of Arizona, 2009.

Bourgois, Philippe I. *Ethnicity at Work: Divided Labor on a Central American Banana Plantation*. Baltimore: Johns Hopkins University Press, 1989.

Brenner, Neil, and Peter Marcuse. *Cities for People, Not for Profit: Critical Urban Theory and the Right to the City*. New York: Routledge, 2012.

Cacho, Lisa Marie. *Social Death: Racialized Rightlessness and the Criminalization of the Unprotected*. New York: New York University Press, 2012.

Campanella, Richard. *Geographies of New Orleans: Urban Fabrics before the Storm*. Lafayette: Center for Louisiana Studies, 2006.

Canak, William, and Berkeley Miller. "Gumbo Politics: Unions, Business, and Louisiana Right-to-Work Legislation." *Industrial and Labor Relations Review* 3, no. 2 (1990): 258–71.

Centeno, Miguel Angel, and Alejandro Portes. "The Informal Economy in the Shadow of the State." In *Out of the Shadows: Political Action and the Informal Economy in Latin America*, edited by Patricia Fernández-Kelly and John Shefner, 227–48. University Park: Penn State Press, 2006.

Chaney, James. "Malleable Identities: Placing the Garínagu in New Orleans." *Journal of Latin American Geography* 11, no. 2 (2012): 121–44.

Chapman, Peter. *Bananas: How the United Fruit Company Shaped the World*. First Trade Paper ed. Edinburgh: Canongate US, 2009.

Chatterjee, Ipsita. *Displacement, Revolution, and the New Urban Condition: Theories and Case Studies*. New Delhi: SAGE Publications India, 2014.

Chomsky, Aviva. "Afro-Jamaican Traditions and Labor Organizing on United Fruit Company Plantations in Costa Rica, 1910." *Journal of Social History* 28, no. 4 (1995): 837–55.

———. *West Indian Workers and the United Fruit Company in Costa Rica, 1870–1940.* Baton Rouge: Louisiana State University Press, 1996.

Cohen, Rich. *The Fish That Ate the Whale: The Life and Times of America's Banana King.* New York: Picador, 2013.

Croegaert, Ana. "Architectures of Pain: Racism and Monuments Removal Activism in the 'New' New Orleans." *City and Society* 32, no. 3 (December 2020): 579–602.

Cuervo, Isabel, Les Leopold, and Sherry Baron. "Promoting Community Preparedness and Resilience: A Latino Immigrant Community-Driven Project Following Hurricane Sandy." *American Journal of Public Health* 107, no. S2 (September 2017): 161–64.

Darensbourg, Jeffery U., and Carmen Price. "Hunting Memories of the Grass Things: An Indigenous Reflection on Bison in Louisiana." *Southern Cultures* 27, no. 1 (2021): 14–24.

Daser, Deniz. "Citizens of the City: Undocumented Latinx Migrants Organising Politically in Post-Katrina New Orleans." *Public Anthropologist* 3, no. 1 (January 2021): 148–76.

Daser, Deniz, and Sarah Fouts. "The Great Unbuilding: Land, Labor, and Dispossession in New Orleans and Honduras." *Southern Cultures* 27, no. 2 (July 2021): 110–25.

Dávila, Arlene. *Culture Works: Space, Value, and Mobility across the Neoliberal Americas.* New York: NYU Press, 2012.

Davis, Mike. "Who Killed New Orleans? Questions for an Autopsy." *International Socialist Review* 44 (November–December 2005). https://isreview.org/issues/44/whokilledNO.

Donato, Katharine, Nicole Trujillo-Pagán, Carl L. Bankston III, and Audrey Singer. "Immigration, Reconstruction, and Settlement: Hurricane Katrina and the Emergence of Immigrant Communities." In *The Sociology of Katrina: Perspectives on a Modern Catastrophe*, edited by David Brunsma, David Overfelt, Steve Picou, Carl L. Bankston III, John Barnshaw, Christine Bevc, George E. Capowich, et al., 267–97. Lanham, MD: Rowman and Littlefield, 2007.

Ehrenfeucht, Renia, and Ana Croegaert. "Learning from New Orleans: Will Revising or Relaxing Public Space Ordinances Create a Just Environment for Street Commerce?" In *Food Trucks, Cultural Identity, and Social Justice: From Loncheras to Lobsta Love*, edited by Julian Agyeman, Caitlin Matthews, and Hannah Sobel, 109–27. Cambridge, MA: MIT Press, 2017.

Ehrenfeucht, Renia, and Marla Nelson. "Young Professionals as Ambivalent Change Agents in New Orleans after the 2005 Hurricanes." *Urban Studies* 50, no. 4 (March 2013): 825–41.

Euraque, Samantha. "'Honduran Memories': Identity, Race, Place and Memory in New Orleans, Louisiana." PhD diss., Louisiana State University, 2004.

Fine, Janice. *Worker Centers: Organizing Communities at the Edge of the Dream*. Ithaca: ILR Press/Cornell University Press, 2006.

Fink, Leon. *The Maya of Morganton: Work and Community in the Nuevo New South*. New ed. Chapel Hill: University of North Carolina Press, 2003.

Firth, Jeanne K. *Feeding New Orleans: Celebrity Chefs and Reimagining Food Justice*. Chapel Hill: University of North Carolina Press, 2023.

Flaherty, Jordan. *Floodlines: Community and Resistance from Katrina to the Jena Six*. Chicago: Haymarket Books, 2010.

Fletcher, Laurel E., Phuong Pham, Eric Stover, and Patrick Vinck. "Latino Workers and Human Rights in the Aftermath of Hurricane Katrina." *Berkeley Journal of Employment and Labor Law* 28, no. 1 (2997): 107–62.

Fletcher, Laurel E., Patrick Vinck, Phuong Pham, and Eric Stover. "Rebuilding after Katrina: A Population-Based Study of Labor and Human Rights in New Orleans." *SSRN Electronic Journal*, June 2006. http://dx.doi.org/10.2139/ssrn.1448373.

Florida, Richard. *The Rise of the Creative Class—Revisited*. Revised ed. New York: Basic Books, 2014.

Fouts, Sarah. "Re-regulating Loncheras, Food Trucks, and Their Clientele: Navigating Bureaucracy and Enforcement in New Orleans." *Gastronomica: The Journal of Critical Food Studies* 18, no. 3 (August 2018): 1–13.

———. "Who Will Rebuild Houston?" NACLA, September 11, 2017. https://nacla.org/news/2017/09/12/who-will-rebuild-houston.

Frank, Dana. *Bananeras: Women Transforming the Banana Unions of Latin America*. New York: South End Press, 2005.

Fullilove, Mindy Thompson, Carlos F. Peterson, and Mary Travis Bassett. *Root Shock: How Tearing Up City Neighborhoods Hurts America, and What We Can Do about It*. 2nd ed. New York: New Village Press, 2016.

Fussell, Elizabeth. "Constructing New Orleans, Constructing Race: A Population History of New Orleans." *Journal of American History* 94 (December 2007): 846–55. http://archive.oah.org/special-issues/katrina/Fussell.html.

———. "Hurricane Chasers in New Orleans: Latino Immigrants as a Source of a Rapid Response Labor Force." *Hispanic Journal of Behavioral Sciences* 31, no. 3 (August 2009): 375–94.

———. "Welcoming the Newcomers: Civic Engagement among Pre-Katrina Latinos." In *Civic Engagement in the Wake of Katrina*, edited by Amy Koritz and George J. Sanchez, 132–46. The New Public Scholarship. Ann Arbor: University of Michigan Press, 2009.

Fussell, Madeline. "'Airbnb Go Home': Tourism Frictions and Short-Term Rentals in New Orleans." Master's thesis, Louisiana State University, May 2021. ProQuest.

Gálvez, Alyshia. *Eating NAFTA: Trade, Food Policies, and the Destruction of Mexico.* Oakland: University of California Press, 2018.

Garth, Hanna, and Ashanté M. Reese, eds. *Black Food Matters: Racial Justice in the Wake of Food Justice.* Minneapolis: University of Minnesota Press, 2020.

Geglia, Beth. "Honduras: Reinventing the Enclave." *NACLA Report on the Americas* 48, no. 4 (October 2016): 353–60.

Gibson, Annie McNeill. *Post-Katrina Brazucas: Brazilian Immigrants in New Orleans.* New Orleans Uno Press, 2012.

Gorman, Leo B. "Latino Migrant Labor Strife and Solidarity in Post-Katrina New Orleans, 2005–2007." *Latin Americanist* 54, no. 1 (2010): 1–33.

Gotham, Kevin. "Marketing Mardi Gras: Commodification, Spectacle and the Political Economy of Tourism in New Orleans." *Urban Studies* 39, no. 10 (2002): 1735–56.

Graeber, David. *The Utopia of Rules: On Technology, Stupidity, and the Secret Joys of Bureaucracy.* Brooklyn: Melville House, 2015.

Green, Rodney D., Marie Kouassi, and Belinda Mambo. "Housing, Race, and Recovery from Hurricane Katrina." *Review of Black Political Economy* 40, no. 2 (January 2013): 145–63.

Gruesz, Kirsten Silva. *Ambassadors of Culture: The Transamerican Origins of Latino Writing.* Princeton: Princeton University Press, 2002.

———. "The Gulf of Mexico System and the 'Latinness' of New Orleans." *American Literary History* 18, no. 3 (August 2006): 468–95.

Hamnett, Brian R. *Juarez.* London: Longman, 1994.

Harpelle, Ronald. "White Zones: American Enclave Communities of Central America." In *Blacks and Blackness in Central America: Between Race and Place,* edited by Lowell Gudmundson and Justin Wolfe, 307–33. Durham, NC: Duke University Press, 2010.

Harvey, David. "The Right to the City." *New Left Review*, no. 53 (October 2008): 23–40.

Hayden, Tiana Bakić. "Street Food as Infrastructure: Consumer Mobility, Vendor Removability and Food Security in Mexico City." *Food, Culture and Society* 24, no. 1 (January 2021): 98–111.

Hondagneu-Sotelo, Pierrette. *Doméstica: Immigrant Workers Cleaning and Caring in the Shadows of Affluence.* 2nd ed. Berkeley: University of California Press, 2007.

Horowitz, Andy. *Katrina: A History, 1915–2015.* Cambridge, MA: Harvard University Press, 2020.

Jabareen, Yosef. "The Right to Space Production and the Right to Necessity: Insurgent versus Legal Rights of Palestinians in Jerusalem." *Planning Theory* 16, no. 1 (2017): 6–31.

Johnson, Jessica Marie. *Wicked Flesh: Black Women, Intimacy, and Freedom in the Atlantic World*. Illustrated ed. Philadelphia: University of Pennsylvania Press, 2020.

Johnson, Kevin R. "The Beginning of the End: The Immigration Act of 1965 and the Emergence of the Modern U.S. Mexico Border State." In *The Immigration and Nationality Act of 1965: Legislating a New America*, edited by Gabriel J. Chin and Rose Cuison Villazor, 116–70. Cambridge: Cambridge University Press, 2015.

Kerssen, Tanya M. *Grabbing Power: The New Struggles for Land, Food and Democracy in Northern Honduras*. Oakland, CA: Food First Books, 2013.

Klein, Naomi. *The Shock Doctrine: The Rise of Disaster Capitalism*. 1st Picador ed. New York: Picador, 2008.

Koeppel, Dan. *Banana: The Fate of the Fruit That Changed the World*. New York: Plume, 2008.

Koritz, Amy, and George J. Sanchez, eds. *Civic Engagement in the Wake of Katrina*. The New Public Scholarship. Ann Arbor: University of Michigan Press, 2009.

Lipsitz, George. *How Racism Takes Place*. Philadelphia: Temple University Press, 2011.

———. *The Possessive Investment in Whiteness: How White People Profit from Identity Politics*. Revised and expanded ed. Philadelphia: Temple University Press, 2006.

Long, Alecia P. "Poverty Is the New Prostitution: Race, Poverty, and Public Housing in Post-Katrina New Orleans." *Journal of American History* 94, no. 3 (December 2007): 795–803.

Loperena, Christopher A. "Honduras Is Open for Business: Extractivist Tourism as Sustainable Development in the Wake of Disaster?" *Journal of Sustainable Tourism* 25, no. 5 (May 2017): 618–33.

———. "Settler Violence? Race and Emergent Frontiers of Progress in Honduras." *American Quarterly* 69, no. 4 (December 2017): 801–7.

MacCameron, Robert. *Bananas, Labor, and Politics in Honduras, 1954–1963*. Syracuse: Maxwell School of Citizenship and Public Affairs, Syracuse University, 1983.

Martin, Nina. "Food Fight! Immigrant Street Vendors, Gourmet Food Trucks and the Differential Valuation of Creative Producers in Chicago." *International Journal of Urban and Regional Research* 38, no. 5 (September 2014): 1867–83.

Mayer, Vicki. *Almost Hollywood, Nearly New Orleans: The Lure of the Local Film Economy*. Oakland: University of California Press, 2017.

McKittrick, Katherine. *Demonic Grounds: Black Women and the Cartographies of Struggle*. Minneapolis: University of Minnesota Press, 2006.

Méndez, María José. "The Silent Violence of Climate Change in Honduras." *NACLA Report on the Americas* 52, no. 4 (October 2020): 436–41.

Miller, Marilyn G. "'Allá En Tierras Del Sur': Horror and Recoil in José Martí's New Orleans." *Global South* 13, no. 1 (2019): 12–32.

Mukhija, Vinit, and Anastasia Loukaitou-Sideris, eds. *The Informal American City: Beyond Taco Trucks and Day Labor*. Cambridge, MA: MIT Press, 2014.

Muñoz Bravo, Pablo. "'Largo y sinuoso camino': La incorporación a la Revolución de Ayutla de los liberales exiliados en Estados Unidos." *Signos históricos* 16, no. 31 (June 2014): 161–89.

Murga, Lorena Aurelia. "Organizing and Rebuilding a Nuevo Orleans: Day Labor Organizing in the Big Easy." In *Working in the Big Easy: The History and Politics of Labor in New Orleans*, edited by Thomas J. Adams and Steve Striffler, 211–27. Lafayette: University of Louisiana at Lafayette, 2014.

———. "The Racialization of Day Labor Work in the U.S. Labor Market: Examining the Exploitation of Immigrant Labor." PhD diss., Texas A&M University, 2012.

Nijman, Jan. *The Life of North American Suburbs*. Toronto: University of Toronto Press, 2020.

O'Neal, John. "Guidelines for Story Circles." In *Acting Together II: Performance and the Creative Transformation of Conflict: Building Just and Inclusive Communities*, edited by Cynthia E. Cohen, Roberto Gutiérrez Varea, and Polly O. Walker, 214–20. New York: New Village Press, 2011.

Ott, Kenneth. "The Closure of New Orleans' Charity Hospital after Hurricane Katrina: A Case of Disaster Capitalism." Master's thesis, University of New Orleans, 2012. https://scholarworks.uno.edu/td/1472.

Palmer, Zella. "Belle New Orleans: The History of Creole Cusineres." *Africology: The Journal of Pan African Studies* 11, no. 6 (April 2018): 186–91.

Pelot-Hobbs, Lydia. *Prison Capital: Mass Incarceration and Struggles for Abolition Democracy in Louisiana*. Chapel Hill: University of North Carolina Press, 2023.

Purcell, Mark. "Possible Worlds: Henri Lefebvre and the Right to the City." *Journal of Urban Affairs* 36, no. 1 (February 2014): 141–54.

Reed, Merl E. "Lumberjacks and Longshoremen: The I.W.W. in Louisiana." *Labor History* 13, no. 1 (Winter 1972): 41–59.

Reese, Ashanté M. *Black Food Geographies: Race, Self-Reliance, and Food Access in Washington, D.C.* Chapel Hill: University of North Carolina Press, 2019.

Regis, Helen A. "Blackness and the Politics of Memory in the New Orleans Second Line." *American Ethnologist* 28, no. 4 (2001): 752–77.

Rodriguez, James. "Garifuna Resistance against Mega-Tourism in Tela Bay." NACLA, August 5, 2008. https://nacla.org/news/garifuna-resistance-against-mega-tourism-tela-bay.

Rosales, Rocío. *Fruteros: Street Vending, Illegality, and Ethnic Community in Los Angeles*. Oakland: University of California Press, 2020.

Ruiz, Vicki. "Citizen Restaurant: American Imaginaries, American Communities." *American Quarterly* 60, no. 1 (2008): 1–21.

Sakakeeny, Matt. *Roll with It: Brass Bands in the Streets of New Orleans*. Refiguring American Music. Durham, NC: Duke University Press, 2013.

Shapiro, Nicholas. "Attuning to the Chemosphere: Domestic Formaldehyde, Bodily Reasoning, and the Chemical Sublime." *Cultural Anthropology* 30, no. 3 (August 2015): 368–93.

Sinha, Anita, and Judith Browne-Dianis. "Exiling the Poor: The Clash of Redevelopment and Fair Housing in Post-Katrina New Orleans." *Howard Law Journal* 51, no. 3 (January 2008): 481–508. https://digitalcommons.wcl.american.edu/facsch_lawrev/1775.

Sluyter, Andrew. "(Post-)K New Orleans and the Hispanic Atlantic: Geographic Method and Meaning." In *New Orleans in the Atlantic World: Between Land and Sea*, edited by William Q. Boelhower, 383–98. London: Routledge, 2013.

Sluyter, Andrew, Case Watkins, James P. Chaney, and Annie M. Gibson. *Hispanic and Latino New Orleans: Immigration and Identity since the Eighteenth Century*. Baton Rouge: Louisiana State University Press, 2015.

Smart, Charles Allen. *Viva Juárez! A Biography*. 1963. Westport, CT: Greenwood Press, 1975.

Solnit, Rebecca, and Rebecca Snedeker. *Unfathomable City: A New Orleans Atlas*. Berkeley: University of California Press, 2013.

Spring, Karen. "The Marriage of Drug Money and Neoliberal Development in Honduras." *NACLA Report on the Americas* 52, no. 4 (October 2020): 397–403.

Stefano, Michelle L. *Practical Considerations for Safeguarding Intangible Cultural Heritage*. London: Routledge/Taylor and Francis Group, 2022.

Stone, Jeremy Thomas. "The New Louisiana Purchase: Gentrification and Disaster in the Heart of New Orleans." PhD diss., University of British Columbia, 2021.

Striffler, Steve. *Chicken: The Dangerous Transformation of America's Favorite Food*. New Haven: Yale University Press, 2005.

Stuesse, Angela. *Scratching Out a Living: Latinos, Race, and Work in the Deep South*. Oakland: University of California Press, 2016.

Taylor, Keeanga-Yamahtta. "New Orleans since the Storm: An American Travesty." *International Socialist Review*, no. 51 (January 2007). https://isreview.org/issues/51/neworleans.

Thomas, Lynnell L. *Desire and Disaster in New Orleans: Tourism, Race, and Historical Memory*. Durham, NC: Duke University Press, 2014.

Tiano, Susan, Moira Murphy-Aguilar, and Brianne Bigej, eds. *Borderline Slavery: Mexico, United States, and the Human Trade.* 1st paperback ed. New York: Routledge, 2016.

Tierney, Kathleen, Christine Bevc, and Erica Kuligowski. "Metaphors Matter: Disaster Myths, Media Frames, and Their Consequences in Hurricane Katrina." *Annals of the American Academy of Political and Social Science* 604 (2006): 57–81.

Trujillo-Pagán, Nicole. "Neoliberal Disasters and Racialisation: The Case of Post-Katrina Latino Labour." *Race and Class* 53, no. 4 (April 2012): 54–66.

———. "Recovering Latinos' Place in New Orleans." *Louisiana History: The Journal of the Louisiana Historical Association* 55, no. 2 (2014): 177–97.

Usner, Daniel H. "From African Captivity to American Slavery: The Introduction of Black Laborers to Colonial Louisiana." *Louisiana History: The Journal of the Louisiana Historical Association* 20, no. 1 (Winter 1979): 25–48.

———. *Indians, Settlers, and Slaves in a Frontier Exchange Economy: The Lower Mississippi Valley before 1783.* Chapel Hill: University of North Carolina Press, 1992.

Verea, Mónica. "Immigration Trends after 20 Years of NAFTA." *Norteamérica: Revista Académica del CISAN-UNAM* 9, no. 2 (July 2014): 109–43.

Vidal, Cécile. *Caribbean New Orleans: Empire, Race, and the Making of a Slave Society.* Illustrated ed. Williamsburg, VA, and Chapel Hill: Omohundro Institute of Early American History and Culture and University of North Carolina Press, 2019.

Waren, W. Wage Theft Among Latino Day Laborers in Post-Katrina New Orleans: Comparing Contractors with Other Employers. *Journal of International Migration and Integration* 15 (2014): 737–51.

Weise, Julie M. *Corazón de Dixie: Mexicanos in the U.S. South since 1910.* Chapel Hill: University of North Carolina Press, 2015.

Woods, Clyde A. *Development Arrested: The Blues and Plantation Power in the Mississippi Delta.* With an introduction by Ruth Wilson Gilmore. 2nd ed. New York: Verso, 2017.

———. *Development Drowned and Reborn: The Blues and Bourbon Restorations in Post-Katrina New Orleans.* Edited by Jordan T. Camp and Laura Pulido. Athens: University of Georgia Press, 2017.

———. "Les Misérables of New Orleans: Trap Economics and the Asset Stripping Blues, Part 1." *American Quarterly* 61, no. 3 (2009): 769–96.

Yúdice, George. *The Expediency of Culture: Uses of Culture in the Global Era.* Durham, NC: Duke University Press, 2003.

Zlolniski, Christian. *Janitors, Street Vendors, and Activists: The Lives of Mexican Immigrants in Silicon Valley.* Berkeley: University of California Press, 2006.

Index

Page numbers in italics refer to illustrations.